ROUTLEDGE LIBRARY EDITIONS: BUSINESS AND ECONOMICS IN ASIA

Volume 5

BUSINESS TRANSFORMATION IN CHINA

BUSINESS TRANSFORMATION
IN CHINA

Edited by
HENRI-CLAUDE DE BETTIGNIES

LONDON AND NEW YORK

First published in 1996 by International Thomson Business Press

This edition first published in 2019
by Routledge
2 Park Square, Milton Park, Abingdon, Oxon OX14 4RN

and by Routledge
52 Vanderbilt Avenue, New York, NY 10017

Routledge is an imprint of the Taylor & Francis Group, an informa business

British Library Cataloguing in Publication Data
A catalogue record for this book is available from the British Library

ISBN: 978-1-138-48274-6 (Set)
ISBN: 978-0-429-42825-8 (Set) (ebk)
ISBN: 978-1-138-36683-1 (Volume 5) (hbk)
ISBN: 978-0-429-42996-5 (Volume 5) (ebk)

Publisher's Note
The publisher has gone to great lengths to ensure the quality of this reprint but
points out that some imperfections in the original copies may be apparent.

Disclaimer
The publisher has made every effort to trace copyright holders and would welcome
correspondence from those they have been unable to trace.

Business transformation in China

Edited by
Henri-Claude de Bettignies

INTERNATIONAL THOMSON BUSINESS PRESS
I ⓣ P An International Thomson Publishing Company

London • Bonn • Boston • Johannesburg • Madrid • Melbourne • Mexico City • New York • Paris
Singapore • Tokyo • Toronto • Albany, NY • Belmont, CA • Cincinnati, OH • Detroit, MI

Business Transformation in China

First published 1996 by International Thomson Business Press

I T P A division of International Thomson Publishing Inc.
The ITP logo is a trademark under licence

British Library Cataloguing-in-Publication Data
A catalogue record for this book is available from the British Library

First edition 1996

Phototypeset by Intype London Ltd
Printed in the UK by St Edmundsbury Press, Bury St Edmunds, Suffolk

ISBN 0–415–12322–4

International Thomson Business
Press
Berkshire House
168–173 High Holborn
London WC1V 7AA
UK

International Thomson Business
Press
20 Park Plaza
13th Floor
Boston MA 02116
USA

Contents

Part I The political evolution

Part II The economic dynamics

Henri-Claude de Bettignies

List of figures

List of tables

Abbreviations

ACFTU	All China Federation of Trade Unions
AFTA	Asian Free Trade Area
APEC	Asia-Pacific Economic Cooperation forum
ASEAN	Association of South-east Asian Nations
BERI	Business Environment Risk Index
CAST	China Association for Science and Technology
CCP	Chinese Communist Party
CEA	Chinese Economist Area
CGA	Customs General Administration (China)
COCOM	Coordinating Committee for Unilateral Export Control
CQCA	China Quality Control Association
CSBTS	China State Bureau of Technical Supervision
EAEC	East Asian Economic Caucus
EC	European Community
EU	European Union
FAE	Foreign-affiliated enterprise
FDI	Foreign direct investment
FEC	Foreign exchange certificate
FIE	Foreign-invested enterprises
FLPSE	First-level purchasing and supply enterprise
FTE	Foreign trade enterprise
GATT	General Agreement on Tariffs and Trade
GDP	Gross domestic product
GNP	Gross national product
GSP	Generalized system of preferences
HS	Harmonized Description and Coding System
IMF	International Monetary Fund
IPR	Intellectual property rights
ITC	International Trade Centre
MFN	Most favoured nation

MOFERT	Ministry of Foreign Economic Relations and Trade
MOFTEC	Ministry of Foreign Trade and Economic Cooperation
MOU	Memorandum of understanding
MW	Megawatt
NAFTA	North American Free Trade Area
NTB	Non-tariff barriers
OECD	Organization for Economic Cooperation and Development
PRC	People's Republic of China
PSSI	Political System Stability Index
SEZ	Special Economic Zone
SITC	Standard International Trade Classification
SLPSE	Second-level purchasing and supply enterprise
SOE	State-owned enterprise
TAM	Trade assessment mechanism
TLW	Third-level wholesaler
TQM	Total quality management
UNCTAD	United Nations Conference on Trade and Development
USTR	United States Trade Representative
WPRF	World Political Risk Forecast
WTO	World Trade Organization

Preface

Scholarship on the Asia-Pacific region is growing throughout the world, yet it remains relatively modest in extent given the area's tremendous strategic importance. Within Europe, in particular, research on Asia is still far from meeting our need for a better understanding of the region's dynamics. We are still inadequately equipped to anticipate Asia's evolution and the consequences of this for the rest of the world.

In founding the Euro-Asia Centre at INSEAD in 1980, I enjoyed the support of a group of enlightened corporate leaders who shared my concern over Europe's lack of insight into Japan and the Asia-Pacific region. The Centre represents an effort to create and disseminate knowledge likely to be of use to decision-makers, helping to build competencies through which Western and Asia Pacific businesses can move towards a better handling of their interdependence. It also seeks to promote networks of personal and institutional relationships, fostering an on-going, mutually rewarding climate of cooperation.

It is in this context that the present series of books has been developed, to present the work of the Euro-Asia Centre's faculty, and the proceedings of conferences, symposia, and public forums organized by the Centre both in Asia and the West.

Initially, the series will present the proceedings of the annual LVMH (*Louis Vuitton Moët Hennessy*) Conference on Asia Pacific in Management Education in Europe, held at the Euro-Asia Centre each year in early spring.

This Conference has been made possible thanks to the support of the highly successful international group LVMH, a world leader in luxury goods, for which sector the Asia Pacific region is becoming the world's largest market. The LVMH Group is of course keenly aware of the need to promote research on the dynamics of the Asia

Pacific region, and has supported the present conference annually since it was first held in 1985.

The initial purpose of the Conference was to bring together Asia specialists and other scholars interested in aspects of Asian studies, to discuss their findings and share their research interests, thus developing closer ties and promoting cooperation between scholars and the many research centres with an interest in Asia. The Conference aimed to encourage the sharing of teaching materials, and to foster academic exchange between professors engaged in developing an understanding of Asia and its future, and in developing the particular skills needed to do business in Asia. Over the years, the LVMH Conference has grown in size and now brings together about a hundred scholars from some fifteen countries for two days of lively exchange on a chosen theme. Recently, the Conference has also invited executives from Asian and Western corporations, eager to exchange views and ideas with the academic community. Their presence has enhanced the gathering and the debate it elicits.

The present series will, initially, present an edited selection of papers from the most recent LVMH Conferences (since 1993).

I would like to express my thanks to the LVMH Group for their support. This series will, I hope, make a modest but useful contribution to our understanding of the Asia-Pacific region – the world's fastest-growing economic pole, and one whose future impact we can ill afford to ignore.

Henri-Claude de Bettignies

Introduction

Future generations will almost certainly regard the opening-up of China during the last two decades of the twentieth century as one of the major world events of recent history. The changes in China since the early 1980s have already had important consequences far beyond the domestic environment of China or, indeed, of the Pacific Basin as a whole. Interest in China has grown considerably throughout the world, and is now much in evidence both in Europe and the USA, as well as in Japan and the rest of Asia.

This phenomenon is, I feel, more than simple curiosity in one country's remarkable development; more, even, than concern for the global consequences of a potential economic giant's awakening. Thanks to its huge size, its vast resources, its geopolitical power, the opportunities it affords, and the unique character of its path through the twentieth century, China has come to symbolize the hopes and fears of nations and individuals, and to represent the power of progress and destiny to change innumerable lives. The very name China evokes a wealth of associations from the distant (often turbulent) and less distant past, from Marco Polo to Mao Tsetung, from the grim catalogue of social innovations that constituted the Cultural Revolution to the 'one country two systems' experiment with Hong Kong. China now presents the most attractive opportunity for business in the Far East, and is fast becoming something of a new 'Far West' for American business pioneers eager to stake their claims. At a time when the consequences of the collapse of the 'bubble' in Japan are still unclear, and when access to Japanese markets is still perceived as difficult despite recent reforms, many Western corporations (particularly in the USA) have turned their attention to China. At Stanford University Business School in California, to cite one small example, graduate students taking my course on Japan's globalization and transformation decreased by a third between 1990 and 1996, almost exactly corresponding to the increase in those taking my course on Management and culture in the Chinese world. It is, of course, imperative that we continue to monitor and understand the dynamics of the situation in Japan. However, it seems that it is now China's turn to be perceived as exotic and fashionable, as Japan was in the mid-1980s. The important difference is that while Japan's development was revered as a model from which we could learn – and one which drew innumerable business pilgrims from the West, eager to receive the gospel of quality and tools for improved competitiveness – China is seen as virgin territory, rich in opportunity.

As the demand for research on China continues to grow, we felt that the LVMH Conference could provide a timely and precious opportunity to share the results of several studies just completed or still in progress. In February 1995 the conference took as its theme the changes taking place in China, with a view to assessing what the future (in the short term) might hold.

The meeting attracted 110 participants, and the present volume brings together twelve of the presentations made, by economists, political scientists and management specialists from institutions in both Europe and in Asia.

Looking initially at the political scene, we have three views of the current changes in Chinese government policy, in China's democratic process, and in her relations with the rest of the Asia-Pacific region. Part II explores China's economic dynamics from a macro viewpoint, considering in particular the needs of foreign corporations trying to make sense of the changes observable in the development of distribution systems in China. In Part III three contributions discuss micro-economic issues related to the changing situation in labour management and human resources in the Chinese firm, and the concern for quality (or indeed, the lack of it). A current research project in Hong Kong reports on the trade-offs of alternative entry strategies, and this section also includes a paper by Wolfgang Klenner of Bochum University, which provides a useful overview of China's economic and political landscape for the benefit of the foreign firm. Section IV presents two rather different papers – one by Gilbert Etienne of Geneva University, a well-known specialist on India, who compares China with Asia's other potential, though still largely dormant, economic giant, and assesses the latter's capacity for future growth together with the two countries' respective areas of competitive advantage. We conclude the volume with a paper by Gian Paolo Casadio of Bologna University reflecting on European attitudes to China in the context of the GATT.

Current scenarios for China present a huge range of possibilities. The most optimistic base their assessment on China's success so far and on the differences between China and the former Soviet Union, while gloomier predictions anticipate China's implosion, triggered by the growing gap between global economic regions. In the first paper in this volume Shaun Breslin of Newcastle University explores the change in China's 'centre/provinces' paradigm. He discusses the conflict between Beijing and the provinces, and the resulting lack of nationwide policy coordination, illustrating how reforms currently in progress fail to pull in one common direction. The transition from a planned to a market economy remains incomplete and Breslin makes clear that 'China has done a better job in opening up to the outside world than in opening its domestic market'. Beijing will, he feels, lose power as market forces play an increased role, but the centrifugal trend will not make the country disintegrate as it moves towards the 'Greater China' concept.

Maria Weber of Bocconi University explores this horizontal authoritarianism and the conflict between reformists and conservatives, which will become still more vivid at the time of Deng Xiaoping's succession. While she sees a return to the past as virtually impossible, she identifies three scenarios ranging from the consolidation of horizontal authoritarianism to a return to vertical authoritarianism (controlled by the conservatives, and which would limit the expansion of the market economy to some sectors, but not stop the liberalization process currently under way), plus a possible, though unlikely, return to the Lords of War regime, or regional conflicts. Maria Weber's message is explicit: a return to the past is not possible, but 'economic liberalization and democracy are not necessarily good bedfellows. . .'

From Sheffield University Robert Taylor takes us, in a very comprehensive and well-documented paper, through the evolution of China's relations with her neighbours, paying particular attention to defence policy which will, in future, have a more specifically Asia-Pacific focus. China maintains that its military forces are exclusively for defence purposes, but this message is not always perceived as credible. Taylor sees economic prosperity and diplomatic outreach as the keys to China's national security, and is convincing when he suggests that China's diplomacy will endeavour to create a peaceful Asian environment conducive to economic growth. Through APEC, and through local sub-regions (north-east Asia, 'Greater China' and south-east Asia), economic complementarity will be explored and developed. Potential tensions and conflicts exist due to the lack of complementarity, and the role of Japan – viewed by its regional neighbours with great suspicion – makes a degree of ambiguity inevitable. Will Japan and China eventually become rivals or partners? This remains unclear and Taylor's conclusion remains open: China's influence from Asia to the Pacific will intensify, but 'whether such influence will be for the good of the region as a whole remains to be seen'.

In Part II we turn to the economic situation, beginning with a data-based analysis of Chinese trade prepared by researchers at the data-rich International Trade Centre in Geneva. Friedrich von Kirchbach and Johanna Aguado illustrate the process by which China has become the world's largest exporting developing country. They show how monitoring China's foreign trade can be instructive for the international community, since it gives 'real-time' information on both the qualitative and quantitative development processes. Trade values have grown by double digits since the opening of China's economy, fuelled by the development of Guangdong province as both a model and locomotive of trade dynamism. Friedrich von Kirchbach makes it clear that barter trade now has limited importance in China, while joint ventures remain the leading vehicle for exports into China. I would add that this will probably remain so for a long time to come, as the pace of China's integration into world trade continues to accelerate.

In his three papers Tseng Choosin, a prolific writer from Hong Kong City Polytechnic, explores a dimension not yet sufficiently analysed, but of growing importance, namely China's outward investment. In his comprehensive paper he traces the evolution of Chinese external investments, and their destinations over time, while suggesting some consequences. Again, Guangdong province is the leader in export capital, followed by Fujian and Shanghai provinces. The role of the Overseas Chinese as privileged partners is described. Though the growth of external investment is higher from China than from other developing countries, it remains small in investment value (the average annual investment in overseas production enterprises is US$2.87 million, of which PRC average equity participation is US$1.23 million). Most of the investment is in the form of joint ventures, mostly (and somewhat surprisingly) of a 'greenfield' type.

In his second paper, with associates Paula Kwan and Fanny Cheung, Professor Tseng describes the changes in the distribution system in China since 1979. Sharing the results of an empirical study, the team of researchers demonstrates the dramatic changes following the lifting of restrictions in retailing, particularly since 1993. The study makes clear the impact of foreign investors in the retail sector, and then gives an insight into the differences in consumer behaviour in Guangzhou, Shanghai and Beijing. Before concluding with some essential advice to foreign firms seeking long-term success in China, the paper gives a concise overview of new forms of distribution of interest to Western market groups, many of them very keen to enter into the potentially huge Chinese market.

Professor Malcolm Warner of Cambridge University gives us a rare insight into current changes in labour relations in China. In the context of the economic reforms since the early 1980s Professor Warner explains how the Chinese labour market functions, before describing how it has changed following labour-management reforms. Outlining the directions signalled by recent changes, the paper also provides data on unionization, the number of unions and their membership. Most importantly, he provides us with a qualitative description of the role and functioning of the unions, which can spring some disagreeable surprises on the unprepared foreign investor. Taylor draws distinctions between state enterprises and collectively and privately-owned enterprises. The implications for joint venture partners are many. Realistically, he makes clear that over time the role of trade unions and workers' congress will decrease as enterprise directors are granted more discretionary powers.

Wong Yuk-Lan of Lingman College, Hong Kong and Wan Wai-Chai of the Hong Kong City Polytechnic share in their paper the results of a 1993 survey of eighty-three Chinese firms. They conclude that quality is not yet an 'innate' feature of firms in China. It is not seen as a built-in part of operations, but rather as a post-manufacturing task without real strategic perspective. The paper gives details of the data collected.

Professor Wolfgang Klenner of Bochum University explores China's economic reforms and questions their success. His analysis rightly differentiates between the rural, private, collective and state sectors. In rural areas farmers soon lose responsibility for the maintenance of the collective infrastructure, when collective duties are removed. Other half-heartedly applied reforms have failed to produce results, and Professor Klenner finds – in common with other speakers at the Conference – that the imperatives of economic growth and social stability are often, if not contradictory, at least pulling in two different directions.

Professor Tseng's third paper, in collaboration with Paula Kwan and Fanny Cheung of the Hong Kong City Polytechnic, explores further the issue of entry strategies for consumer goods into China. The licensing route is shown to be expensive in transaction costs, and risky due to the lack of enforcement of legislation protecting foreign firms' technology and expertise. The authors give examples of successful joint ventures, in which both partners were satisfied, as well as reporting cases of foreign firms which preferred to 'go it alone'. The secret of success in China, say the authors, is long-term commitment through direct investment, an approach most likely to be rewarded with 'favoured' status on the part of the host.

The last two papers address broader issues, looking at China in comparison with India, and offering advice to European firms on how to treat China as a trade partner. Professor Gilbert Etienne of Geneva University measures his observations in China against his inside knowledge of India, and draws some interesting comparisons. He acknowledges that China has made far greater progress than India in a short time, and sees many positive factors in the Chinese model. However, he also cites many examples of India's potential competitive advantage over China, given the linguistic and administrative legacy of its long period of British rule. Professor Etienne presents a wealth of argument and insight regarding the potential of these two 'sleeping giants' to develop peacefully into effective modern nations.

The final paper in this volume discusses China's new role in world trade, and advises European firms on handling China as a trading partner – a timely and valuable exercise given that European firms' competence in managing relations with China will have to keep pace with the latter's increasing strategic importance as a participant in global business.

We are, at present, only just beginning to work towards a more mature handling of business with China. Whether this volume provides a fully comprehensive view of the challenges faced by China and her partners in their future cooperations, only time will tell. The purpose of the Conference from which this book is drawn was first and foremost to invite discussion among a group of 'concerned' scholars, committed to preparing the way for improved partnership with China. Western firms are now setting out on their own 'long road' into China. They need inputs along the way – data-based reports, thorough analysis and models, together with informed discussion and reassessment of earlier work, plentiful debate and the willingness to challenge their own understanding in light of new evidence, new insights. This book – and the series of which it is a part – should provide a step in that direction.

Henri-Claude de Bettignies
INSEAD Euro-Asia Centre
Visiting Professor, Stanford University
May 1996

Part I
The political evolution

1 The changing centre/provinces paradigm and the policy-making process in post-Mao China

Shaun Breslin

ECONOMIC TRANSFORMATION AND POLITICAL CHANGE

When the post-Mao leadership initiated reform of the economic system in 1978, they also set in motion a process of political reform. The term 'political reform' here is not used to refer to the introduction of a multiparty political system. Nor does it refer to the end of Communist party rule as witnessed in eastern Europe and the Soviet Union, although this cannot be totally discounted as a long-term consequence of economic reform in China. Rather, it refers to the massive changes in both the processes and functioning of political power within the existing framework of CCP rule.

The instigation of political reform was partly a matter of deliberate choice. The post-Hua leadership recognized that a degree of political reform was essential in order to maintain the leading role of the CCP. The Cultural Revolution having resulted in a loss of faith in Communist party rule, it was deemed necessary gradually to transform a politically mobilized society into a primarily economically mobilized society (Wang Huning 1988a). This change in emphasis represented an important political reform in itself, gradually altering the underlying precepts of decision-making within the PRC. But in the process of facilitating the economic growth to which China's people and key leaders aspired, this transformation has itself generated further unanticipated and often dysfunctional political reform.

The complex interaction between economic and political reform can be demonstrated by an analysis of centre/provinces relationships in the post-Mao era.[1] As Wang Huning (1988b) commented in 1988:

> Even if the change now being made in the relationship between China's central government and local government mainly orig-

inated in the economic realm, it possesses a political significance that cannot be underestimated, and has led to a major conflict within the political system.

The purpose of this chapter is to identify the determinants of the changing centre/provinces paradigm, and to assess their significance for the emerging political and economic system in China. It will attempt to show that the growth in both centre/provinces and inter-provincial conflict was partly an inevitable consequence of the reformulation of China's development strategy. However, these 'inevitable' consequences of reform have been exacerbated and compounded by a lack of coordination between reforms in key areas – a lack of coordination which owes much to the decision-making processes that have characterized the era of reform.

THE POLICY-MAKING PROCESS

The relationship between the central authorities and the provinces[2] is a complex one determined by the interaction of a number of variables. Assessing the impact of the changes in almost all of these variables is therefore an inherently difficult process, and the CCP leadership can hardly be blamed for failing to predict the cumulative impact of economic reform on their relations with the provinces. Nevertheless, the style of policy-making employed in post-Mao China did not increase their chances of success. This is not to say that there was no coordination, or that major economic and political changes were not subject to intense discussion and investigation, but, too often, the direction of national policy was shaped by the culmination and interaction of a fragmented policy-making process.[3]

A quantum leap to a totally new political and economic system was out of the question, and change has thus proceeded in several small steps. Two key elements should be emphasized here: first, the impact of a lack of elite consensus on the scope and direction of reforms, and second, the fragmentation of decision-making responsibilities in the reform era.

Intra-elite conflict

Although the post-Mao leadership shared a conviction that the Maoist political-economic system had to be reformed, disagreement existed over the pace, scope and ultimate direction of the reform process. This lack of elite consensus at the centre meant that an incremental approach to change became an attractive option for those leaders who favoured fairly radical reform. A full package of reform proposals would leave the radicals open to a full-scale challenge from the conservatives, while smaller changes at the margins made it easier to defend each reform in turn, and also drove a wedge between different groups of conservative leaders (Bachman 1988). Furthermore, if conservative opposition were to hold out against a particular reform, then it was relatively easy to make partial retreat and address specific grievances without jeopardizing the overall direction of the reform process.

However, this largely reactive style of policy-making also had its costs. Naughton argues that: 'Unable to dominate events, the government has had to scramble repeatedly to "put out fires" and prevent disastrous outcomes' (Naughton 1985: 224)[4]. As a result of this preoccupation with short-term problems and solutions, the CCP elites were unable to 'formulate a consistent programme of economic changes' (Naughton 1985: 224). Notions of intra-elite conflict had other implications for centre/provinces relations. Opponents to market reforms were relatively strongly represented within the central planning and finance agencies – not least because the wider extension of market reforms threatened their authority and in some cases their very existence. As such, decentralizing decision-making powers away from the centre to the provincial authorities can be seen as an attempt to undercut the authority of more conservative central planners, and simultaneously build a reform coalition with provincial leaders (World Bank 1990: 3; You Ji 1991). Thus, it can be hypothesized that the administrative decentralization undertaken in the post-Mao era (and, in particular, the 1984 decentralization movement) was not so much an end in itself, as a means to achieving other ends, namely the facilitation of the expansion of market decentralization.

Fragmented decision-making processes

The problems associated with this lack of elite consensus were compounded by the second important feature, concerning the way in which policy changes in individual areas were concluded. Given the sheer number of reforms undertaken in recent times, it has not been possible for a single central agency to formulate specific reform packages. Individual ministries and agencies have thus been granted a significant degree of autonomy to oversee policy changes in their fields.[5] This has resulted in what Kenneth Lieberthal has termed 'fragmented authoritarianism' (Lieberthal 1992), which further exacerbated the problems of coordination.

The resulting restructuring of the economic system meant that the traditional winners and losers under the old system could no longer be certain of their position. In order to placate the fears of existing 'winners' and subsequently prevent strong opposition to reform emerging, an ethos of fairness came to dominate policy-making which Shirk calls an ideology of 'balancism' (Shirk 1992: 77). In practice, this meant that policy options were chosen so as to ensure that no unit or actor lost too much, rather than on the basis of what was best for the country as a whole. In short, rather than choosing the best policy, decision-makers chose the most 'satisficing' policy – that which did just enough to satisfy and suffice.[6]

Incremental decision-making and centre/provinces relations

The wider implication of this style of policy-making on the trajectory of China's political evolution will be dealt with in detail in the conclusion to this chapter. In this section, I will assess the relevance of an uncoordinated reform process to the specific question of centre/provinces relations.

The first point to be made is that insufficient time and expertise were expended on thinking through the consequences of reform. Where such prior planning did exist, the hoped for consequences were often distorted by the impact of later reforms. For example, Li Xianguo argues that strategic planning ahead of policy implementation is crucial for successful regional development policy (Li Xianguo 1988). The local environment (both physical and economic) has to be fully researched and recognized before the impact of policy changes on that area can be fully understood. But Li argues that the need to push ahead with reform quickly meant that effective prior planning did not occur, and problems became apparent only after they had already become problems.

Second, for both political leaders and enterprise managers in the provinces, the inherent problems of coming to terms with the demands and rigours of the new system were further complicated. Of course, experience is most often gained just after it is most needed. Decision-making powers were decentralized to economic decision-makers who lacked the experience to utilize them effectively. Part of this problem arises simply from ignorance of the demands and rigours of the new system. For example, after decades of being told what to do by superiors in the planning administrative machinery, enterprise managers were suddenly faced with difficult decisions themselves. It is not surprising that many acted without adequately assessing input costs, raw material supplies and potential markets. They had neither the experience nor the entrepreneurial spirit to use effectively the new powers they had been granted.

It is difficult to see how this problem could have been avoided given the modernizing priorities of the state. Nevertheless, the process of assimilation was further complicated by inconsistencies in the reform programme. Reforms in different areas were frequently not compatible, and pulled in different directions. For example, Ferdinand has demonstrated how the reform of the system of remitting profits to the centre was at odds with earlier changes in centre/province revenue sharing arrangements (Ferdinand 1987). This problem was recognized by the Chinese economist Chen Zhao, who noted that 'contradictions often arise between China's monetary policy and other economic policies' (Chen Zhao 1987), and with different policy changes pulling in different directions, 'the central bank is often at a loss as to what to do'.[7]

In addition, the central authorities have responded to their own financial crises by deploying emergency methods to gain finances from the provinces. At various stages, the provinces were forced to lend money to the centre, buy central government bonds, and renegotiate financial arrangements to the centre's benefit. These *ad hoc* interventions in the economic system contributed to the financial uncertainty caused by the lack of coordination in reforms, and undermined the certainty in planning that the original revenue-sharing reforms were supposed to have brought. It is difficult enough to adapt to a rapidly changing environment at the best of times, but much more so when a multiplicity of changes frequently conflict with each other.

Third, and related to the second point, the CCP's reluctance to expose economic decision-makers to the penalties as well as the benefits of the market economy further complicated this learning process. Fearful of the political consequences of rising unemployment and the economic consequences of wasting investment capital, party and government officials proved reluctant to allow loss-making enterprises to go bankrupt. As a result, managers at different levels were not exposed to the range of experiences (both positive and negative) needed for them to become effective decision-makers in a more fully functioning market economy. According to Zhuang Qidong and Wang Di (1987), such administrative interference gave decision-makers the benefits of both the planned and market systems, and the penalties of neither:

> Under the current double structure, enterprises can continue 'eating from the same big pot' of the old structure and enjoy the benefits of commodity producers, thus gaining advantages from both sides.

This brings us to the fourth issue. The transition from a planned to a market economy was (and still remains) incomplete. Whilst the instruments of state planning were dismantled, their replacement with effective and functioning market macro-control mechanisms was slow. With the national economy uncoordinated either by plan or market, provincial planners were allowed (almost forced) to make decisions on largely local considerations.

Fifth, this tendency was reinforced by both the style and structure of economic planning at a local level. The intention of market decentralization reforms was to distance (or remove) the hand of the state from economic decision-making. But the only partial introduction of market reforms combined with administrative decentralization to prevent market decentralization reforms from reaching their intended target. This is a particularly important point for the study of centre/province relations in China in the 1980s.

The partial nature of reform meant that although the price and allocation of many goods were increasingly set by the market, key industrial inputs (most notably energy inputs) remained under state control. This ability to influence local economic activity was compounded by an attitude to local planning that remained largely rooted in the past. What is wrong with allocating scarce energy resources to local enterprises, leaning on banks to provide loans, or erecting trade barriers against 'imports' from other provinces? For the Chinese economist Chen Yizi, this factor was the fundamental obstacle to sustainable economic progress.[8] He argues that these attitudes to economic interference (and even direct management at times) are reinforced by the structure of the political system (Chen Yizi 1987). The structures of provincial bureaucracies from the old days of economic planning remain fundamentally unreformed. Where changes in the economy demanded administrative changes, new structures were simply added to existing ones, rather than replacing the outmoded organizations. With the instrumentalities of the old system still in place, they inevitably continued to be used to control economic activity. Furthermore, this pattern of behaviour was replicated at lower levels, where administrative control over local economic activity was, if anything, more of a problem given the more intimate relationship between party, state and enterprise (He Ganghui 1987).

Perhaps the central element here is the crucial failure to formalize the independence of enterprises from the state. Lee (1992) argues that rather than granting autonomy to enterprises, the reforms have merely redistributed power between bureaucratic agencies – central administrative control was swapped for local administrative control. As a result, Walder (1992: 331–2) believes that businesses in China should not be considered to be independent economic entities, but should instead be categorized as 'quasi-autonomous divisions within a corporate structure'. This failure fully to separate enterprises from the state is usually cited by Chinese authors as the key failing of the reform process in the 1980s.[9]

Impact on centre/provinces relations

Specific decentralization policies and the move towards the market have combined to diffuse decision-making power to a much greater extent than at any time since 1949. Indeed, at the Fifth Plenum of the Thirteenth Central Committee in November 1989, the official communique argued that power had been diffused to too great an extent. As a consequence, local economic activity had not always coincided with the needs and requirements of the national economy as a whole. The plenum's communique maintained that one of the major problems facing the economy at the time was 'over-decentralization of power and the weakened macrocontrol of the state' (*Renmin Ribao* 17 January 1990)

This statement was just one of countless central attacks on provincial autonomy in the recent era. Although the interpretation of events that it presents might appear reasonable at first sight, it represents a failure to look below the surface to identify the fundamental causes of the problems. The diffusion of power and the loss of macro-economic control are not in themselves problematic. For example, the loss of the type of control associated with the pre-reform era is only problematic if it is not replaced by other control mechanisms. The issues identified at the Fifth Plenum are merely the symptoms of a disease rather than the disease in itself. The underlying problem in 1989 was the uneasy coexistence in the Chinese economy of both administrative controls and market mechanisms. With these two control mechanisms sitting uncomfortably side-by-side, economic activity had to try and serve two masters.

Thus, the real source of centre/province tensions lay in the partial nature of reform. The system was no longer controlled by administrative mechanisms, but neither were market forces being allowed to operate in an effective manner. This brings us back to one of the issues identified above, namely that market decentralization measures failed to reach their intended target. Instead, too much of the devolved power became lodged in lower-level administrative units.[10]

The issue of attitudinal hangovers from the old system may in part explain administrative intervention in the affairs of local enterprises. The status and power enjoyed by cadres would have been undermined by the move towards market decentralization. Faced with such a loss of power, some cadres moved to transform their political power into economic power by adopting a hands-on approach to local enterprises (Yu Zunyao 1989).

More importantly, changes in revenue-sharing arrangements between the centre and the provinces obstructed the move towards an efficient economic system built around regional comparative advantage. With local authorities at all levels under severe financial strains, many strove to expand their local revenue base, irrespective of national economic needs and goals (Wong 1991). This feature has not only exacerbated centre/provinces tensions, but also contributed to the growth of inter-provincial tensions.

This brings us to another crucial component of the new centre/provinces paradigm. The development strategy of the post-Mao leadership marked a rejection of the regional self-sufficiency policy of the cultural revolution, and a move towards exploiting regional comparative advantage and economies of scale. However, although inter-provincial trade and other economic contacts have increased, formidable barriers to trade remain to be overcome. By interfering to allocate raw materials to local producers and erecting barriers to prevent imports from other provinces, the more efficient and competitive Chinese economy that the introduction of market forces was expected to bring has been at least partially impeded. Indeed, in many respects, China has made a better job of opening up to the outside world than it has of opening up its own domestic market. As such, we have to ask if the impressive growth figures that China has recorded in the post-Mao era are sustainable? And what proportion of this growth has been achieved by the continuation (and even expansion) of inefficient, outdated and, from a national viewpoint, unnecessary productive capacity?

Local leaders are not only motivated by their own immediate financial concerns, but are also driven by notions of inequity and inter-provincial competition. Rather than allow scarce resources to leave their territory to contribute to the wealth of other areas, local authorities have frequently stepped in to keep as much local wealth as possible within their province. It is not unknown for raw materials supposedly targeted for transportation to other provinces to be diverted for use by local producers. Provincial authorities have also resorted to imposing tariffs and quotas on imports from other provinces to enhance artificially the profitability of local enterprises. As a result, producers in the coastal region (often much more efficient than their counterparts in the interior) were starved of the supplies that the logic of market forces dictated that they should receive. In a now notorious case, trucks sent from Guangdong to buy silk-worm cocoons direct from their cultivators in Sichuan were prevented from leaving again by armed blockades set up by the Sichuan authorities (Xia Yang and Wang Zhigang 1988a). Similar inter-province tensions also emerged over access to rice and wool supplies (Findlay 1992)

Inter-provincial competition over the portioning out of the national economic cake is nothing new. But this conflict certainly seems to have been heightened (or at least become more open) thanks to the post-Mao reforms. There are perhaps two key factors here. First, the reformulation of the Chinese economic system led to the creation of new provincial winners and losers. For example, the concentration of heavy industrial complexes in the north-eastern provinces of Jilin and Heilongjiang, once the source of these province's relative wealth, has now became a millstone around their necks. Provinces that were the major beneficiaries of central planning, state ownership and centrally controlled investment funds perceive that they are the main losers of a strategy that favours small, non-state sector light industrial enterprises.

Second, there is resistance in the interior and west to the preferential treatment granted to provinces in the south and east. There were three main thrusts to this argument. The first is that the retention of low state-set prices for raw materials and semi-finished products while the price of finished produce is increasingly market set (and therefore much higher than the equivalent state-set price) irks many in the raw material centres in the interior. For example, Gansu Governor Ji Zhijie has called for raw material-producing areas to receive a share of the profits that their cheap raw materials helps to generate (He Yiwen 1988). Ji's comments are typical of the complaints made by interior provincial leaders (although few were quite so explicit) in the post-Mao era.[11]

The second thrust is that many leaders in the interior are also disturbed by the special policies implemented in coastal provinces. Guangdong and Fujian have been the main targets for such criticism. Of all China's provinces, Guangdong and Fujian have the greatest freedom to retain income generated in their territory.[12] They are also the site of three of China's four Special Economic Zones (SEZs). In the long run, the development of the coast should aid growth in the interior. Even in the short run, Crane argues convincingly that the SEZs 'helped energise the country as a whole' (Crane 1990: 139). Nevertheless, the development of the SEZs to date has clearly aided development and growth in Guangdong and Fujian much more clearly and concretely than in Gansu or other interior provinces in the 1980s.

These feelings have been heightened because although the SEZs were not intended to fall under the control of their provincial hosts, Shenzhen in particular has become an integral component of Guangdong's provincial economic strategy. Guangdong Governor Ye Xuanping's assertion that 'Shenzhen is a special zone of Guangdong' (Crane 1990: 139) gives a clear indication of how theory had departed from practice, and explains why Zhao Ziyang proposed that Shenzhen be placed under the direct authority of the State Council after visiting the region in early 1988 – an aspiration that Zhao was unable to attain. Although Ye Xuanping was removed from power in 1989, his attitude towards Shenzhen (and indeed the province's economic orientation in general) appears to have outlived his political career in Guangdong.[13]

The third thrust is that leaders in the interior appear sceptical (to say the least) that the much-promised trickle-down of wealth from the coast will in fact occur, and fear that an extension of market forces will instead lead to polarization of wealth. These fears have reinforced the inclination to erect barriers to keep local resources within their own provinces. As this policy obstructs the expansion of inter-provincial trade, the suspicion that trickle-down will not occur may thus become a self-fulfilling prophecy.[14]

Feelings of mistreatment are not, however, simply confined to the interior's antipathy to the development of the coast. Indeed, leaders in coastal provinces counter the complaints from the interior by complaining that too much of their income is used by the state for investment in the interior. They argue that if they are allowed to exploit their economic strengths fully, then this will actually aid the interior through a trickle-down process. Furthermore, even within the coastal region itself, there is considerable inter-provincial conflict, particularly over the extent of Guangdong's privilege. Concern in Shanghai about its role in the new order led to it successfully challenging Beijing over its financial obligations. A draft report was submitted to the State Council in January 1987, and after visits by Zhao Ziyang and Yao Yilin to the municipality, new arrangements for Shanghai were finalized in February 1988 (Wang Huning 1988b and Zhang Zhongli 1988).

This readjustment of Shanghai's financial arrangements highlights two important elements in the nature of contemporary centre/province relations in China. First, as Wang Huning notes, it demonstrates a new provincial confidence in dealing with the central authorities:

> [Shanghai's] action in taking the initiative to ask for a new system to be put in practice differed from the old model for reform in which the central government took the initiative in these matters.
> (Wang Huning 1988b)

Second, it generated a wave of lobbying from other provinces with grievances about current policy. Immediately following Shanghai's successful approach to the centre, Inner Mongolia and Jilin formally asked (without success) to be allowed to move to the Shanghai system. Hunan and Jiangsu officials similarly asked to be granted some of the preferential treatment afforded to Guangdong, and we can only guess at the extent of the informal lobbying that also occurred.[15]

Competition between regions for preferential treatment from the centre has always occurred in China – indeed lobbying skills were well honed by provincial leaders used to fighting for their share of resources under the old planning system. But the higher potential gains made possible by the post-Mao economic reforms have enhanced this competition, and also represent a heightened perception of provincial interest generated by the uneven central treatment of different provinces.

The central authorities are thus faced with the almost impossible process of balancing the varied and often conflicting provincial demands for action. If Beijing listens to Shanghai and allows the latter to retain more of its locally generated income, then Beijing either has to take more money from other provinces, or reduce its investment commitments and grants to less well-off areas. To make matters worse, although all of China's provinces are now better off than they were in 1976, the desire for a bigger provincial share of the national cake appears to be insatiable. As many other reformers have found to their cost, once a reform process is set in motion, expectations can all too easily run ahead of what the state can provide.

CONSEQUENCES AND PROSPECTS

Perhaps the clearest lesson that we can learn from this chapter is that no clear or final pattern of centre/province relationships has yet emerged. What we have seen in the post-Mao era is a political and economic system in the process of transformation. New relationships were formed, but then often reformed as the impact of other reforms became clear. Indeed, the fact that provincial leaders were forced almost continuously to adapt to new situations must have been a key determinant of centre/province relations in itself. China remains very much a system in flux, and there is no certainty that unexpected and radical changes in policy will not occur.

Centre/province relations in China in the 1980s were shaped by the complex interaction of a number of variables. Predicting what will happen to any one of those variables presents sufficient problems to be able to make any predictions with certainty. Predicting what will happen to all, and how they will interact, is all but impossible. Nevertheless, based on the evidence of the 1980s, it is possible to make some tentative observations about the future of China.

From political centre to economic core?

Although a major industrial, commercial and business centre in its own right, the notion of Beijing as 'the centre' of the Chinese economy stemmed from its position as the political centre. Under a centrally planned economic system, the concentration of political power in Beijing naturally entailed a concentration of economic power. Indeed, as noted above, the economic control that Beijing exerted over the provinces was one of its main tools of ensuring political control.

With the changes that occurred in the 1980s, the position of Beijing as the economic centre was much weakened. In general, the lesser the scope for central planning and guidance in the Chinese economy, the weaker Beijing's claim to be its central force. As market forces play an increasingly important role within the Chinese economy, then power will continue to seep from Beijing to economic decision-makers at various levels in various other places.

Throughout the post-Mao period, Beijing has continued to play a very important role in shaping developments, but local decision-makers increasingly looked to other factors to inform their decisions. The requirements of the local economy – or more correctly, the perceived short-term requirements of the local economy – became a crucial consideration for many decision-makers. In addition, for the southern and coastal provinces in particular, external factors played increasingly important roles. The common cultural and linguistic connections between Hong Kong and the Cantonese speaking mainland made the Pearl River Delta region an attractive prospect for the colony's businessmen. Cheap industrial inputs (labour, land, raw materials), fiscal incentives, and improved communications between Hong Kong and the mainland all also enhanced the region's foreign investment environment. Taiwanese businessmen also see this region and neighbouring Fujian as an attractive prospect. The fortunes of the Hang Seng index and all of the variables that combine to influence business confidence in Hong Kong and elsewhere play an increasingly important role in economic decision-making in parts of China.

Beijing will clearly continue to be an important economic centre in China, not least because of the strength of its own local economy. Furthermore, as the financial functions associated with macro-control of a market economy are fully developed, its position as the administrative centre of the Chinese economy should actually be strengthened. However, there is no guarantee that Beijing will host all of the new economic entities. It should be noted that China's first two stock exchanges were both located away from Beijing, in Shanghai and Shenzhen. The latter's opening was not without considerable opposition from Beijing, which wanted the Shanghai market to be China's first and finest. The fact that Shenzhen still managed to jump the gun without the central financial and technical aid granted to Shanghai says a lot about the economic dynamism of both the Shenzhen zone and Guangdong Province.

However, given the increased scope and role of market mechanisms in the Chinese economy, it is difficult to see how the spatial imperatives of market economies can fail to gain strength. We should perhaps turn our attention away from centre/province relationships in China, and study economic core/periphery relations instead. The potential for such a shift in the spatial nature of Chinese economics was identified by Donnithorne in 1972, who argued that:

> The economies of scale in modern industry are so great that those local units (eg: Shanghai) that can afford to establish large factories will be at an enormous advantage over poorer areas. They

will thus be in a position to supply their rural hinterlands with manufactures in return for agricultural foodstuffs and raw materials at a rate of exchange that makes it overwhelmingly worthwhile for the country area to specialise in agriculture and to buy most of their manufactured goods from the larger industrial centres.

(Donnithorne 1972)

As a result, there would be a 'spread of the economic influence of the major industrial centres as they seek to widen their markets and provide themselves with raw materials'.

Donnithorne's argument was that the system of self-sufficiency would enhance comparative advantage and lead to trade between the regional centre and its hinterland, which would then break down the cellular nature of the economy.

With the reforms of the 1980s, the first element of this process should have been removed, while the emphasis on regional division of labour coupled with the great advantages presented to the coastal region should have meant that the dominant regions – in Donnithorne's example, Shanghai – would be in an even stronger position to exploit their comparative advantage. However, the partial nature of post-Maoist reform meant that administrative barriers to trade did not disappear, and, partly as a consequence, developed areas were not always able to exploit comparative advantage or economies of scale in dealing with other areas.

The situation was further complicated by the government's uneven handling of different regions. In particular, Shanghai was not allowed to *fully* exploit its advantage over other areas simply because it was so dominant and so important for national development. So although Shanghai remained the core of economic activity in China, Fujian and Guangdong increased their relative economic power in the 1980s thanks to the uneven nature of reform.

China is so large and complex – both physically and in terms of economic activity – that the existence of more than one economic core can be sustained. Indeed, given the size of China and the infrastructural defects that dogged developments in the 1980s, building a nationally integrated economic market would be fraught with difficulties. In addition, obstacles to inter-provincial trade were not smashed in the 1980s, but remained an important impediment to the evolution of a truly national market. As such, the existence of a number of regional economic centres dominating their surrounding hinterlands, predicted by Donnithorne in the early 1970s, is not only still possible, but perhaps represents the most realistic approach to breaking down administrative barriers and opening the entire economy more fully to market mechanisms.

The current problems of satisfying competing and conflicting provincial demands can be solved only by ironing out the existing irrationalities in the economy, and allowing all provinces to play by the same rules. But even then, provincial tensions and problems will not simply disappear. What we, and the CCP leadership, have to recognize is that transforming the Chinese political-economic system is an inherently difficult process. In the long run, the CCP leadership may conclude that generating growth is much much easier than managing the contradictions and instabilities that growth entails. In short, rapid economic development may prove to be as destabilizing as economic stagnation.

The crisis of the Chinese state

The Chinese state is facing (or will soon be facing) a crisis. By 'crisis', I do not mean an immediate threat to the existence of the CCP, but rather a problematic but solvable identity crisis on the part of the state system. In Maoist terminology, the crisis represents a non-antagonistic contradiction. But if it is not successfully resolved, then it could become an antagonistic contradiction that will threaten the continued existence of both the CCP and PRC, and possibly of the unitary Chinese state as we know it today. This identity crisis revolves around two issues: the state's desire to reformulate its functions, and its ability to make these changes.

The evidence of the centre's attempts to control the provinces in recent years suggests that the central state machinery in China has yet to define its new role in the emerging (and still evolving) political-economic system. Rather than developing new paradigms that correspond with the new system, the central elites have instead relied on tried (but not particularly trusted) methods of controlling the provinces.

This failing was replicated even when important structural reforms had been implemented. For example, writing in 1987, Chen Zhao admitted that the focus of monetary policy in the three years following the People's Bank's designation as a central bank had been, in his words, 'incorrect' (Chen Zhao 1987). Despite important changes, China's economic policy was still dominated by old notions and strategies. Under the old system, demand was largely regulated by management of the supply side in economic planning. Coming to terms with demand management had been a slow and incomplete process, with supply-side control dominating macro-economic policy. Thus, the People's Bank had concentrated on checking the growth of investment spending by controlling the money supply and had neglected policies such as interest-rate management which influenced the demand for capital.[16]

The centre's ability to change its functions was also influenced by conflicting desires and impulses. On the one hand, there is a real desire to turn China into an efficient economic producer able to compete on international markets. But on the other hand, the party leadership fears that the price of a more efficient industrial economy would be increased urban unemployment, and a decrease in the standards of living for the urban working classes. In an attempt to find a middle way, the purchasing power of losers (particularly of permanent state employees) was kept relatively high through the payment of subsidies and bonuses unrelated to productivity.[17] This has combined with the policy of keeping loss-making enterprises operating to maintain employment, to put considerable strains on national finances. According to official Chinese sources, over one-third of the national state budget is now spent on subsidies of one kind or another aimed at offsetting the detrimental impact of the market. Given that the centre's share of revenue is falling relative to that retained by the provinces, it is difficult to see how this policy can continue for long without increased fiscal burdens or financial responsibilities being placed on the provinces.

This brings us to the centre's ability to make changes. Increasing the financial responsibilities of the provinces would generate considerable discontent. The reform process has created powerful vested interests across the country that may prove very difficult to break down.[18] Too many people are doing too well from the present system to countenance further reform that would threaten their position. For example, opening up internal trade is, I believe, a prerequisite of sustainable economic development in the country as a whole. But there is some reluctance in the coast to open up inwards, and even greater fear in the interior of the polarization and economic colonialism that this move is perceived as bringing. As such, what is economically logical, and what is politically feasible, may prove to be two contradicting factors.

Towards disintegration?

Any discussion of the future prospects for centre/provinces relations in China would be lacking if it did not at least address the potential of an end to the unitary Chinese state in its present form. The relative growth of provincial autonomy at the expense of central control in the 1980s (and in particular the growth of Guangdong's economy) has prompted the suggestion by some Western academics that China may be in the process of disintegration.[19] As the centre proves less and less able to control affairs, centrifugal tendencies will begin to take hold and the integrity of the Chinese state will be threatened. This concept of the future is not without its advocates in China itself. Although officially unavailable in China, the Hong Kong-published novel *Huanghou ('Yellow Peril')* has found a wide audience amongst Chinese students. The story is set in the not-so-distant future, and tells of civil war between a prosperous southern China, and a depressed northern region dominated by old industrial complexes and habits.

The experience of the collapse of central control in the Soviet Union, Yugoslavia and, to an extent, Czechoslovakia, have all brought this question of disintegration more firmly into focus. But these were all federal states where unity under Communist party rule hid considerable ethnic divergence. In China, the Tibetan people have a long-held dream of independence. With the establishment of Moslem states on China's north-west borders, the situation in Xinjiang is also far from stable, as this quotation from Wang Enmao, Chairman of the Xinjiang Communist Party, demonstrates: 'National separatists are asserting independence in an attempt to split the integration of our motherland and damage national unity' (Mok 1992). But although these aspirations may become a reality if the central Chinese state weakens, ethnic tensions do not represent a fundamental problem for the future of 'Chinese China'.

According to Delfs, a key force acting against disintegration is the way in which 'the cities have been bought off'. For example, urban wages across the country have been kept in parity, and urban purchasing power maintained through vast spending on subsidies. Thus, 'since urban residents do not experience significant region-based relative deprivation, they are unlikely to take the lead in expressing regional dissatisfaction through political means' (Delfs 1991). Whilst this is true, the relative wealth of the urban population was maintained at a price. The long-term strains on the national budget identified above may prove to be intolerable. In addition, there have been growing signs that the rural population in some areas are demanding a bigger share of growth for themselves.[20]

Perhaps the biggest argument for the survival of the Chinese state is provided by asking what would anybody have to gain from secession? The development of the southern coastal provinces in the 1980s was at least partly built around the supply of subsidized raw materials from the Chinese interior. Although the removal of price controls on basic raw materials will remove this hidden subsidy for the south's development, the best long-term prospects for the south will probably be through exploiting the economic complementarity of its light industrial bases with the raw material bases of the interior. It would be far better for China's coastal region to become the key link in China's regional economic integration, thus taking its place in the super-national division of labour that has become a focus of east Asian developmental nations.

Indeed, rather than presaging the disintegration of China, the culmination of the reforms may result in an enlarged Chinese economic entity (if not a formal Chinese state). The reintegration of Hong Kong into China in 1997 will now be a question of the hand-over of formal political power and sovereignty. The economies of southern China and Hong Kong are already so intertwined that economic integration will be completed before 1997. With economic convergence between southern China and Taiwan accelerating, the economic unification of the two sides of the Taiwan Straits may soon become a formality.[21]

An economic belt encompassing southern China (including Hainan), Hong Kong, Taiwan and possibly Singapore would be a dynamic force in regional (if not world) economics in the twenty-first century. Utilizing the natural resources of the Chinese interior may not be an attractive prospect for hard-line leaders in Beijing, but would provide the motor for economic development in the so-called 'Pacific Century'.

If the reforms of the 1980s presage disintegration, then the unity of the CCP is more under threat than the integrity of the Chinese state. Under the pre-reform system, the Party was the main (with the army, only) vehicle for personal advancement. Not only was economic power inextricably linked with political power, but economic privilege was also closely associated with political power. The changes of the 1980s led to an important shift in this situation. Although the Communist party remains the dominant organization in China, the dependence of individuals on the Party has been weakened. New channels for personal advancement have begun to emerge with the separation of economic activity from state control.

However, the separation of functions is not complete. Local authorities retain (both legally and illicitly) powers to allocate key goods and resources to enterprises. Not surprisingly, the 'allocators' have become important agents within the emerging economic system. This trend concerns us in terms of its implications for the regional pattern of development. But there is also a more long-term potential consequence to be considered. Cadres at various levels have been 'persuaded' to become board members of enterprises to which they allocate goods. In some cases, they have even established their own private companies and enterprises, and then allocated goods to themselves. The process of transferring political power to economic power in Communist party states is still at a very early stage. But with the expansion of the market, the time may come when former (and present) cadres no longer depend on the Party for their position. If they are no longer dependent on the party for their position, then the potential for the Party to wither away from within cannot be ignored.

NOTES

1 I refer to provinces in the plural, since the singular may imply (incorrectly) that there is a single, universal relationship between the centre and all provinces.
2 For the sake of convenience, the term 'province' is used here to refer to all provincial-level authorities. As such, it includes provincial-level municipalities and autonomous regions as well as provinces.
3 For example, the level of development of a province's infrastructural base is shaped by the legacy of pre-1949 policies, regional development priorities, national defence considerations, the location of raw material supplies, and so on.
4 Although he was specifically analysing the 1978-83 period, these comments can be applied to the entire post-Mao period.
5 A feature that Kenneth Lieberthal (1992) has termed 'fragmented authoritarianism'.
6 A term used by Lindblom in his incremental model of policy-making.
7 Chen Zhao was chairman of the Finance Department of the Central Finance Research Institute.
8 Chen Yizi was director of the China Economic Structural Reform Research Institute.
9 For example, see Wang Huning 1988b, He Ganghui 1987, Zhang Youyu 1987 and the views of doctoral students at the Chinese Academy of Social Sciences outlined in *Jingji Ribao* 31 October 1987.
10 Not just in provincial-level authorities, but also in county and township administrations.

11 The annual sessions of the National People's Congress became an increasingly open forum for pleading provincial grievances in the 1980s, which were only partially and temporarily dampened by the conservative backlash in 1989.

12 For more detail on revenue-sharing arrangements in China, see Tong 1989.

13 Ye was to become one of the more notable provincial casualties of the post-Mao era. Despite being officially promoted to vice-chair of the Chinese People's Political Consultative Conference, this represented a clear case of trying to cut a powerful provincial leader off from his local power-base.

14 It should be noted that even proponents of the trickle-down process argue that the 'tunnel effect' means that polarization has to occur in the medium term to allow wealth to trickle down in the long term.

15 For further details of provincial lobbying in post-Mao China, see the analysis of the decision to expand the number of open cities in February 1984 in Hamrin 1990: 83.

16 See, for example, Li Guixian 1988.

17 Which contributed to a budget deficit of 30 billion yuan in 1993, a 26 per cent increase on 1992, and 50 per cent higher than the revised deficit target set in March 1993 by the Ministry of Finance.

18 Note that the central government was forced to back down on the introduction of a new tax on capital gains from land sales in February 1994 in the face of opposition from Guangdong and Shanghai.

19 For example, see the arguments for disintegration repeated in Chang 1992.

20 Indeed, it may perhaps be more pertinent to analyse the impact of polarization within individual provinces, rather than across regions.

21 Trade between Taiwan and the mainland reached US$13.65 billion in the first 11 months of 1993. Over 16 per cent of Taiwan's exports now go to China (either directly or through Hong Kong).

BIBLIOGRAPHY

Bachman, D. (1988) 'Varieties of Chinese Conservatism and the Fall of Hu Yaobang' in *The Journal of Northeast Asian Studies* Spring, pp. 22–46.

Chang, M. (1992) 'China's Future: Regionalism, Federation or Disunity', *Studies in Comparative Communism*, 25, 3.

Chen Yizi (1987) 'Zhengzhi Tizhi Gaige Shi Jingji Tizhi Gaige De Baozhen (Reform of the Political Structure is a Guarantee of Reform of the Economic Structure)', *Shijie Jingji Daobao (World Economic Herald)*, 13 July.

Chen Zhao (1987) 'Shift the Focus of our Money Supply', *Shijie Jingji Daobao (World Economic Herald)*, 11 May.

Crane, G. (1990) *The Political Economy of China's Special Economic Zones*, Armonk, NY: M.E. Sharpe: 165.

Delfs, R. (1991) 'Lop-Sided Growth', *Far Eastern Economic Review*, 4 April: 24.

Donnithorne, A. (1972) 'China's Cellular Economy: Some Economic Trends Since the Cultural Revolution', *The China Quarterly* 52: 619.

Ferdinand, P. (1987) *Centre/province Relations in the PRC Since the Death of Mao: Financial Dimensions*, Warwick: University of Warwick Working Paper 47: 7–9.

Findlay, D. (ed.) (1992) *Challenges of Economic Reform and Industrial Growth: China's Wool War*, North Sydney: Allen and Unwin.

Hamrin, C. (1990) *China and the Challenge of the Future*, Westview: Boulder.

He Guanghui (1987) 'Zhenyang Zai Zhongdeng Chengshi Zuo Zhuzhi Gaige (How to Tackle Organizational Reform in Middle Ranking Cities)', *Zhongguo Jingji Tizhi Gaige (China Economic System Reform)*, 23 June: 4–8 and 14.

He Yiwen (1988) 'Western Provinces Face New Challenges and New Opportunities', *Ching-chi Tao-pao (Economic Herald)* 15.

Lee, K. (1992) *Chinese Firms and the State in Transition: Property Rights and Agency Problems in the Reform Era*, Armonk, NY: M.E. Sharpe.

Li Guixian (1988) 'Jixu Guanche Zhixing Congjin Fangzhen, Cuji Jingji Wending Fazhan (Implement the Tight Money Policy, Promote the Stable Development of the Economy)', *Zhongguo Jinrong (China Finance)* 7: 4–7

Li Xianguo (1988) 'Quyu Fazhan Zhanlue De Neiyong Ji Zhiding Fangfa (The Contents and Formulation Methods for a Regional Development Strategy)', *Keyan Guanli (Science Research)* 2, April: 14–19.

Lieberthal, K. (1992) 'Introduction: The "Fragmented Authoritarianism" Model and Its Implications', in Lieberthal, K. and Lampton, D. (eds) *Bureaucracy, Politics and Decision-making in Post-Mao China*, Berkeley: University of California Press.

Lindblom, C. (1979) 'Still Muddling, Not Yet Through', *Public Administration*, 39: 517–26.

Mok, C. (1992) 'Xinjiang Official Slams Separatism and "Western Enemy Forces"', *China News Digest*, 18 May.

Naughton, B. (1985) 'False Starts and Second Wind: Financial Reforms in China's Industrial System' in Perry, E. and Wong, C. (eds) *The Political Economy of Reform in Post-Mao China*, Cambridge, Ma.: Harvard University Press.

Shirk, S. (1992) 'The Chinese Political System and the Political Strategy of Economic Reform' in Lieberthal, K. and Lampton, D. (eds) *Bureaucracy, Politics and Decision-making in Post-Mao China*, Berkeley: University of California Press.

Tong, J. 1989 'Fiscal Reform, Elite Turnover and Central Provincial Relations in Post Mao China', *The Australian Journal of Chinese Affairs* 22: 1–28.

Walder, A. (1992) 'Local Bargaining Relationships and Urban Industrial Finance' in Lieberthal, K. and Lampton, D (eds) *Bureaucracy, Politics, and Decision-making in Post-Mao China*, Berkeley: University of California Press: 331–2.

Wang Huning (1988a) '*Zhongguo Zhengzhi-Xingzheng Tizhi Gaige De Jingji Fenxi* (An Economic Analysis of the Reform of China's Political-

Administrative System) in *Shehui Kexue Zhanxian (Social Sciences Front)* No 2, p. 107–115.

Wang Huning (1988b) 'Zhongguo Bianhuazhong De Zhongyang He Difang Zhengfu De Guanxi: Zhengzhi De Hanyi (Ramifications of Changing Relationships between Central and Local Government in China)', *Fudan Xuebao (Fudan University Journal)* 5: 1–8 and 30.

Wong, C. (1991) 'Central-Local Relations in an Era of Fiscal Decline: The Paradox of Fiscal Decentralization in Post-Mao China', *The China Quarterly* 28: 693.

World Bank (1990) *China: Macroeconomic Instability and Industrial Growth Under Decentralized Socialism*, Washington D.C.: World Bank.

Xia Yang and Wang Zhigang (1988a) 'Difang Fencha Yu Hongguan Kong (Local Independence and Macroscopic Control)', *Liaowang (Outlook)* 39, 26 September.

—— (1988b) ' "Biantong" Yu Shi Heng ("Flexibility" and Lack of Balance)' *Liaowang (Outlook)* 40, 3 October.

You Ji (1991) 'Zhao Ziyang and the Politics of Inflation', *The Australian Journal of Chinese Affairs* 25: 69–91.

Yu Zunyao (1989) 'Du Shenhua Gaige de Zhanlue Xuanze de Zaisikao (Rethinking the Choices of Strategy for Deepening Reform)', *Jingji Yanjiu (Economic Research)* 5: 22–31.

Zhang Youyu (1987) 'Dangzhen Fenli Shi Zhengzhi Zhidu Gaige Guanjian (Separation of Party and Government is the Key to the Political System)', *Shijie Jingji Daobao (World Economic Herald)*, 31 October.

Zhang Zhongli (1988) 'Shanghai He Shanghai Jingjiqu Zai Zhongguo Jingji Xiandaihua Zhong De Diwei He Zuoyong (The Position and Role of Shanghai and its Economic Zones in the Modernization of China's Economy)', *Shehui Kexue (Social Sciences)* 1: 18–22.

Zhuang Qidong and Wang Di (1987) 'Probing the Reform of the Distribution System in China', *Renmin Ribao*, 5 June: 3.

2 China

From a quasi-free market economy to a more democratic system?

Maria Weber

WILL A LIBERALIZED ECONOMY BRING LIBERALIZED POLICIES?

Observers agree that the People's Republic of China will continue its economic reform policy in the 2000s (Howel 1993a; Weber 1993a) while preserving the features typical of authoritative systems at a political level. Some authors claim, however, that the Chinese system is now developing from a typically 'vertical' authoritarianism, towards a new concept of 'horizontal' or 'disjointed authoritarianism' (Zhao Quansheng 1992). Vertical authoritarianism is characterized by a policy-making process featuring one leader at the head of a 'cascade' decision-making system, and who gives binding and vertical orders. Mao Tsetung's China, Stalin's Soviet Union and Kim Il Sung's Korea are classical examples of vertical authoritarianism. On the other hand, horizontal or disjointed authoritarianism is characterized by decision-making processes that are basically authoritative and centralized, but at the same time show a degree of structural differentiation, i.e. those processes that have more than one power centre coordinating different interests and opinions. Horizontal authoritarianism is, then, an authoritative system, but less customized, more institutional, and better able to react to the challenges of the social environment in a country pursuing rapid economic development. Some authors maintain that horizontal authoritarianism is fairly likely to develop, in turn, into a potentially more democratic system.

The factors that contributed to change the decision-making process in China from vertical to horizontal, or disjointed, authoritarianism emerge both from the effects of the economic reform process, i.e. the gradual decentralization of the decision-making process, and from the planned reorganization of the political and management system, implemented from 1982 onwards (Lieberthal and Lampton 1992; Weber 1993a). Deng Xiaoping has always supported greater administrative efficiency. To this end, he considerably simplified the systems of government, in an attempt to attribute greater decision-making powers to some institutions, such as the National Assembly, thus initiating the actual reorganization of government 'in the name of efficiency and of the specific skills of the managing staff'. The Government Reorganization Plan, approved in March 1982, launched a number of operations that greatly altered China's bureaucratic system. After the abolition of the concept of appointment for life for political officials, a system was set up to assign roles according to professional and managing skills. The top-heavy system was improved by measures encouraging senior cadres to resign and make way for younger and better-educated workers.

Along with the progressive improvement of professional skills in the bureaucratic system came a generally less 'Big Brotherly' approach, with less use of ideological mass propaganda campaigns, and less monitoring and constriction of the populace. Indeed, reforms contributed to a new distribution of information flows within the political system, and greatly reduced the role of ideology as a policy-implementing tool. However, the implementation of any political decision is still enormously influenced by the system's bureaucratic frame, albeit now professionally trained, younger and considerably reduced in size.

Set on this 'new course' after centuries of Confucian tradition, China also began to transform itself into a constitutional state (Shapiro *et al.* 1991; Crespi Reghizzi and Cavalieri 1991). Imperial China was not governed by written laws; societal behaviour was regulated by Confucian ethics and received tradition. The Empire's management was centralized and bureaucratic and had no notion of the separation of powers: the Emperor was the supreme chief and law-maker, enforcing such rules and taxes as he pleased upon his subjects. In the last decades, the opening of frontiers and the development of foreign trade contributed to the implementation of a legal system in China. The Office for Legislation, a government-controlled institution, is working very hard on new bills. In the first six months of 1993, it drew up 80 new acts to be submitted to the National Assembly for approval. These projects include a competition act, a new economic-monitoring act, a package of acts on the increasingly prevalent share-system and a new foreign trade act.

China's efforts to fill a centuries-old legislative vacuum are even more important in the light of the experience of other countries: as soon as a political system starts changing into a constitutional state, a demand for greater political involvement usually arises, and the political system is forced to respond, either by supporting or repressing the growing demand for democracy and the protection of individual rights. This process in China certainly does not promise to be either painless or quick, but some factors already hint at a possible, very gradual, development towards economic liberalization and political competition. It seems that China is progressively yielding to demands for a more active participation of its citizens in its political life, while at the same time remaining an essentially authoritarian country. Some recent political reforms may be interpreted in this light. Legislation stipulating that the number of electoral candidates should exceed the number of seats available, for example, was introduced in 1988; the margin was raised to 50 per cent in 1992, for elections to the National Assembly. Greater participation does not necessarily involve greater freedom, even though the Beijing government is doing its best to improve its image internationally in the field of civil rights. At the end of the summer of 1993, Xu Wenli, China's leading dissident, serving a 13-year prison sentence, was released. The Chinese government thus kept its promise to perform a 'deed of goodwill' aimed at improving its credibility abroad.

The reform policy is not supported by the whole of the Communist leadership today, however. Within the Chinese Communist Party, the struggle between reformists and conservatives, inclined towards a more limited economic development, will probably break out again after Deng's death. Since 1978 Deng Xiaoping's path to economic reforms has zig-zagged between slow-downs, even reversals, and great leaps forward. But this fluctuation may also be seen as part and parcel of the search for harmony peculiar to the culture of this great country. 'The devil moves in straight lines', as the Chinese say, 'to be safe along the way, better follow a zig-zag'. Chinese gardens feature only zigzag pathways. And the Communist leadership could be said to have zig-zagged its way through the last 40 years, with successive minor changes characterized by a phase of transition following each phase of development.

Similarly, reforms stalled after an initial burst of activity: at the end of the 1980s, for instance, conservatives and reformists were constantly at loggerheads. In 1988 a new 'moderate reform policy' was instigated, due to the predominance of the Party's conservative line. The never-ending struggle between reformists and conservatives intensified further after the student protest of May 1989, ruthlessly put down by the army during the night of June 4. The Tiananmen Square slaughter was seen world-wide as a ruthless put-down of calls for democracy, putting China back into international isolation, paralysing the domestic political situation and strengthening the power of the Party's conservative wing. However, in the years 1990-1, despite the prevailing policy of 'moderate reform' line, the SEZs went on achieving amazing results, and China made its first attempts to move out of international isolation. At the CCP Congress in October 1992, Deng once again enforced his line, heralding a new period of 'reform consolidation'.

In March 1993 the People's National Assembly (i.e. China's Parliament) approved decisions taken during the October Congress. Reform consolidation was institutionalized with the introduction of important changes to the Constitution and the amendment of eight of its 138 articles. The 'socialist market economy' was officially introduced into the Constitution, marking a move away from the centrally planned economy; 'Government-controlled companies' have now become 'State-owned companies', and the 'responsibility system', linking individual income to production (already in place for some time in the agricultural sector), was officially introduced in industry, making a company's management responsible for its economic results.

The new political organization chart, approved in March 1993 by the National Assembly, reveals Deng's concern to ensure the continuity of his reform policy. Several political roles were concentrated in the person of one previously undistinguished figure, namely Jiang Zemin, who had built up his fortune under the protection of Deng Xiaoping. This may be interpreted as an attempt to consolidate the reform policy, while putting off the struggle between conservative and reformist factions for a few years. This concern is also evident in the uncertain balance of the government organization chart. Li Peng, a conservative, is still the head of government, but following his bout of illness, whether real or political, his role is essentially supervisory, while the reformist Deputy Prime Minister Zhu Rongji, also known as the 'Red Capitalist' for his commitment to the support of the implementation of the 'free market in a Socialist economy', acts as prime minister, especially as far as economic issues and development strategies are concerned. According to a Hong Kong source, Zou Jiahua now coordinates the activity of 17 economic ministries, while the following ministers' responsibilities were unchanged: i.e. Qian Qichen for foreign policy, Li Tieying for culture, Song Jian for science and technology, Chi Haotian for defence, Li Guixian for financial institutions, Chen Junshen for agriculture,

Ismail Amat for ethnic minorities, Peng Peiyun for family planning and health, and Luo Gan for public security.

WHAT WILL HAPPEN AFTER DENG'S DEATH?

Deng Xiaoping is very old, and observers are inevitably asking what will happen after his death. This is a central question for international business, since prior to deciding whether or not to invest in another country, political factors such as a rapid regime change, the possibility of revolution or a coup need to be considered. Economic and financial risk analysis has received much attention during the past 30 years, and many techniques have been developed, but the same cannot be said for political risk. Political risk has been variously defined as the risk of political change or instability, or the probability of the occurrence of political upheaval and its potential to affect investment profitability. Political risk is also sometimes considered as one aspect of the more general 'country risk', or as the 'probability that a political event can intervene to modify the economic situation' (which more correctly means an evaluation of an index of political stability), and it may also be considered simply in terms of 'possible trends in the international credit market'. Obviously, as the definition of political risk changes, so, too, do the variables considered in its analysis.

The close links between economic conditions and political events first became apparent as late as the mid-1970s, thanks also to the oil crisis. Since then, intellectual attention has been focused on the evaluation of political risk with the aim of creating general guidelines and systematic theories on the subject. Major international banks, pushed by the growing indebtedness of developing countries, have promoted a great deal of research into the analysis of 'country risk' with the aim of forecasting the risk of non-payment by countries asking for loans. Many indices used in the evaluation of country risk from a political point of view have since been created. Some of these indices emphasize social rifts, such as ethnic or linguistic divisions, tribal wars and religious tensions, intended as variables of social fragmentation that are potentially conflictual in nature and that can give rise to guerrilla warfare, revolts, etc. Other indices tried to focus on the potential impact on investments of non-economic factors such as government politics and the attitude of governments towards foreign investors. This would help in evaluating the risk of expropriation or of nationalization, in addition to the risk of civil war and political instability. Moreover, these indices are based on explicit causal relationships and are supported by econometric analysis, with the obvious advantage of allowing comparison between different countries, even if the rigidity of the indicators often prevents their adaptation to the individual countries in question.

Two indices stand out in particular: the BERI and the WPRF. The BERI (Business Environment Risk Index), one of the first of its kind, allows an analysis based on the classification of variables into four basic categories: political, management, financial and national. The index is created on the basis of expert opinion worldwide which is then evaluated by other experts. Another system of evaluation is the Frost and Sullivan WPRF (World Political Risk Forecast), which is very similar to the previous index but allows a different weighting to be given to certain variables depending on the needs of the users, or in order to include new information when this is considered an improvement.

In 1979, the PSSI (Political System Stability Index), dedicated to the analysis of political risk, was added to these two general indices. Developed by Haendel in 1979, it measured the stability of a political system starting from 15 socio-economic and political indicators that allow the construction of conflict and stability indices. The concept of political stability merits some thought: the instability of a political system does not, in itself, coincide with the political risk. Moreover, it is only one of the factors to check when trying to make an analysis of political risk. The measure of political instability on the basis of empirical indicators, such as *coups d'état*, does not necessarily contribute to the evaluation of the risk. As highlighted well by Gori (1985),

> there can be political risk both when there is a stable situation and when there is an instable situation, just as political risk can be absent in situations which, from our point of view, we would define as far too instable. In any case, what destabilises one political structure may not have the same effect on another.

For example, if *coups d'état* are only one manifestation of political instability, it is certainly not to be assumed that they represent a political risk. In fact, in some contexts, the recourse to authoritarianism has helped the emergence and strengthening of modernizing leadership, opening up the way to the economic development of the country.

Hence, political risk is evaluated differently from different viewpoints. Political risk in the eyes of a foreign investor differs from that seen by an international concern or bank. For this reason, political risk analysis must be as rich in information as possible and always with a view to allowing comparison. Supplying a lot of information is one way of facilitating the interpretation of data. For example, if social disorder in a country has brought about a radical change in the regime, that country is registered as seriously politically unstable, even though the instability may not necessarily continue in the future, or involve any degree of political risk. We can, therefore, define 'political risk' as the product of the negative effects of political events on economic and financial decisions. Political risk is a sort of 'uncertain strategy' which can be defined quantitatively as 'the product of the probability of the verification of a political event whose intensity is determined over a precise period of time for the damage connected with such an event'.

Considering this literature on political risk, three possible 'post-Deng' scenarios may be outlined. The first, and most likely, is the consolidation of the horizontal authoritarianism model, which will gradually open the 'control room' to the emerging social forces. The need for a greater involvement of citizens in the decision-making process clearly emerged in March 1993, in actions of the National Assembly. For the first time, National Assembly delegates put forward a number of amendments, mostly aiming at an increase in the power of the Assembly itself. Another novelty is the foreword of the new Constitution, which states that 'a system of cooperation among parties and a system of consultation, headed by the Communist party, will exist and develop in time'. This may be merely a formal nod to the growing demand for participation, but it might also mark the beginning of a slow and gradual shift towards democracy. In this respect, the spreading of decision-making power may be expected to reach political groups that are prepared to cooperate with the leading party. Remember that China acknowledges the legal status of a dozen minor political groups besides the CCP, called 'small parties' or, in the Western literature, 'democratic parties' grouped together into the United Democratic Front. Such political groups existed before the CCP took power, and accepted the 'leadership of the Communist Party'. In 1949, the CCP invited 121 representatives of these small parties to Beijing, to take part in the Political-Advisory Conference in charge of the drawing up of the first Constitution. Since then, these small parties have had their own representatives in the National Assembly and in the Political-Advisory Conference (a non-institutional advisory organization). Their influence is very likely to increase in the near future.

Table 2.1 Possible medium-term political scenarios

1 CONSOLIDATION OF THE HORIZONTAL AUTHORITARIANISM MODEL (= *virtually non-existent political risk*) Structural differentiation and gradual functional specialization Continuing economic reform policy in the whole country Gradual extension of political participation
2 RETURN TO A VERTICAL AUTHORITARIANISM MODEL (= *slight political risk*) Absolute power to the party Economic reform policy limited to the Special Economic Zones Gradual separation of southern regions
3 RETURN TO THE 'LORDS OF THE WAR' REGIME (= *high political risk*) Military state control Separationist demand by southern regions Reform policy block

Source: Weber 1993a

Besides the consolidation of the current horizontal authoritative model, however, two more scenarios are possible:

- the restoration of absolute power to the Party along with a revival of the vertical authoritative model, and some form of restriction or limitation to economic reforms; and
- the revival of a new form of the 'lords of the war' regime.

Both hypotheses are founded on the crucial role played by the army in the outcome of the political crisis of June 1989 (Bergère 1991). The armed forces' involvement in the repression of the student revolt at Tiananmen Square brought them back into the political spotlight, and their influence is proved by the growing importance of the Commission for Military Affairs in political matters. Should the succession to Deng Xiaoping bring a new crisis, the army's role would be decisive. The economic development process triggered by the reform policy makes a return to the past virtually impossible. The return to vertical authoritarianism (the second of the three scenarios), controlled by the conservatives, could limit the expansion of the market economy to a few areas or sectors, but Chinese pragmatism would see to it that no political leadership would try to stop the economic liberalization process currently underway. The main conservative leader, old Chen Yun, never suggested the halting of economic liberalization in the countryside or in small industries, but simply struggled to keep some strategically important industrial sectors under state control. A victory of the conservative line, if any, would therefore never really threaten foreign investors.

Let us finally consider the third scenario, in my opinion not very likely, of a revival of the 'lords of the war' regime, founded on a possible increase in regional rivalries, quite frequent in China, linked to economic imbalance, and leading to a separationist trend in the southern regions. Regional pressures within the military and civil system could lead the country back to the regional conflicts that characterized the 'lords of the war' period. China's history shows that the military has often played a crucial role in political balance, but the 'lords of the war' period was characterized by an essentially feudal system, hardly associated with widespread welfare. Indeed, the reform policy has triggered a process of change, with social and political effects that are more revolutionary for the Chinese society than any other previous revolution.

As to the military, its presence on the political scene may hamper the gradual development towards democracy, but will hardly stop economic liberalization. If the armed forces support the more conservative wing of the Party after Deng's death, they will prevent the spreading of political participation and stifle the growing demand for democracy expressed by society. But the tragic experience of Tiananmen Square shows that economic liberalization and democracy are not necessarily good bedfellows: the SEZs achieved their best results in the years 1990-2. To be sure, the army should look for a new identity. If it is willing to play a major role in the 'new world order', it should update its equipment and resort to computer science for defence systems. But the military machine is also involved in economic development, and is moving towards denationalization: some joint ventures (such as the Palace Hotel in Beijing) represent investments made by the military as a business operator, and many independent business activities are already headed by members of the army.

Economic liberalization certainly altered China's centuries-old 'bureaucratic feudal model', while political reforms, even though partly implemented, supported the demand for greater participation on the part of the populace and gave life to some expectations for greater political pluralism. This complex process can hardly be stopped, the rapid economic development which China is undergoing is altering people's life-styles and cultural references, and makes a return to the past virtually impossible.

BIBLIOGRAPHY

Banerjee, D. (1991) 'China's Policies in the 1990s', *Strategic Analysis* 14, 1: 3–16.

Baum, R. (1992) 'Political Stability in Post-Deng China: Problems and Prospects', *Asian Survey* 32, 6: 491–505.

Bell, M.W., Khor, H.E. and Kockhar, K. (1993) 'China at the Threshold of a Market Economy', *International Monetary Fund*, occasional paper 107.

Bergère, M.C. (1991) 'La Crisi di Tiananmen: Un Bilancio Distaccato', in Dassù, M. and Saich, T. (eds) *La Cina di Deng Xiaoping: il decennio delle riforme dalle speranze del dopo Mao alla crisi di Tienanmen*, Rome: CESPI: 137–55.

Boddewyn, J. and Cracco, E.F. (1972) 'The Political Game in World Business', *Columbia Journal of World Business*, January.

Bunn, D.W. and Mustafaglu, M.M. (1978) 'Forecasting Political Risk', *Management Science* 24.

Crespi Reghizzi, G. and Cavalieri, R. (eds) (1991) *Diritto Commerciale e Arbitrato in Cina*, Milan: EGEA.

Garnaut, R. and Guoguang, L. (eds) (1992) *Economic Reform and Internationalisation: China and the Pacific Region*, Sydney: Allen and Unwin.

Gibelli, M.C. and Weber, M. (eds) (1983) *Una Modernizzazione Difficile: Economia e Società in Cina dopo Mao*, Milan: Angeli.

Gori, U. (1985) 'Analisi Critica dei Metodi di Valutazione del Rischio Politico', *Guida All'esportazione dei Beni Industriali*, Rome: Efibanca.

—— (1986) 'Rischio Politico e Politica Estera', *Affari Esteri* 71.

Green, R.T. (1974) 'Political Structures as a Predictor of Radical Political Change', *Columbia Journal of World Business*, Spring.

Howell, J. (1993) *China Opens Its Doors, The Politics of Economic Transition*, Harvester Wheatsheaf: Lynne Rienner Publ.

Lieberthal, K.G. and Lampton, D.M. (eds) (1992) *Bureaucracy, Politics, and Decision Making in Post-Mao China*, Berkeley: University of California Press.

Schurmann, F. (1991) *Ideologia, Organizzazione e Società in Cina dalla Liberazione alla Rivoluzione Culturale*, Milan: Il saggiatore.

Segal, G. (1992) 'Opening and Dividing China', *The World Today*, May: 77–80.

Shapiro, J.A., Behrman, J.N., Fischer, W.G. and Powell, S.G. (1991) *Direct Investment and Joint Ventures in China*, New York: Quoram Books.

Simon, J.D. (1982) 'Political Risk Assessment: Past Trends and Future Prospects', *Columbia Journal of World Business*, Fall.

Solomon, R.H. (1971) *Mao's Revolution and the Chinese Political Culture*, Berkeley: University of California Press.

Stobaugh, B.B. (1969) 'How to Analyze Foreign Investments Climates', *Harvard Business Review*, September.

Studies in Comparative Communism (1989), special number on China, 2–3.

The Annals of American Academy (1992), special number on China, 519.

Tisdell, C. (1993) *Economic Development in the Context of China*, New York: St Martin's Press.

Van Agtmael, A.W. (1976) 'How Business had dealt with Political Risk', *Financial Executive*, January.

Weber, M. (1990) 'La Valutazione del Rischio Politico', in Peviani, L. and Weber, M. (eds) *Le Economie Emergenti del Sud Est Asiatico*, Torino: Fondazione Agnelli: 3–33.

—— (1993a) 'Cina 1993: Una Valutazione del Rischio Politico', *Quaderni ISESAO* 1, Bocconi University.

—— (1993b) 'Cina: La Politica della Porta Aperta', *Relazioni Internazionali* 4.

Xiao Zhi Yue (1993) *The EC and China, Current EC Legal Developments*, London: Butterworths.

Zhao Quansheng (1992) 'Domestic Factors of Chinese Foreign Policy: From Vertical to Horizontal Authoritarianism', *The Annals of the American Academy*, 519.

3 Chinese policy towards the Asia-Pacific region

Contemporary perspectives

Robert Taylor

INTRODUCTION

In the post-Cold War context, Chinese foreign policy perspectives are increasingly being structured by the demands of economic development and the shifting balance of power in the Asia-Pacific region. Although in implementation often more flexible than the public rhetoric of Chinese leaders seemed to suggest, the foreign relations of the Chinese People's Republic were, until the early 1970s, informed by the ideological certainties of Marxism/Leninism and frequently expressed in terms of commitment to world revolution, including support for armed insurgency in south-east Asia. Since the institution of the economic open-door policy in 1978, however, and especially since the beginning of the 1990s, Chinese foreign policy has been omnidirectional and issue-orientated, with the stress on multilateral diplomacy designed to establish and improve relations with both developed and developing countries, and on practicality rather than dogma. The Five Principles of Peaceful Coexistence – first enunciated by the Chinese in the wake of the 1955 Bandung Conference of non-aligned countries – have been given renewed emphasis, and are now seen by China's leaders as key guidelines in the conduct of diplomacy with countries of different political persuasions. China claims to envisage a new international order built on those five principles:

1 Mutual respect for sovereignty and territorial integrity
2 Mutual non-aggression
3 Non-interference in each other's internal affairs
4 Equality and mutual benefit
5 Peaceful coexistence

In the past, and particularly in the days of an ostensibly monolithic international Communist movement, the Chinese Communist Party (CCP) placed as much, if not more, emphasis on relations between itself and other Marxist/Leninist parties as it did on state-to-state relations; but now that the open-door policy demands increased interaction between Chinese economic organizations and individuals and their foreign counterparts, the Chinese leaders are putting renewed stress on the CCP's contacts with other political parties of varying views. Such party relationships are ostensibly economically rather than ideologically orientated, and supplement inter-governmental relations and trade cooperation as well as educational and cultural exchanges. Similarly, China's state-to-state relations, whether with the developed nations of the West or the fast-developing countries of the Asia-Pacific, are now increasingly governed by an economic imperative: the need to acquire expertise and experience in such areas as technology transfer, vocational training and the reform of industrial management. Officially, of course, such relations are still stated in Chinese official sources to be similarly governed by the Five Principles.[1] In summary, China's foreign policy in the 1990s and beyond will be largely, though not exclusively, determined by the country's economic development needs.

FROM EAST–WEST CONFRONTATION TO NORTH–SOUTH DIVIDE: CHINA'S WORLD VIEW

Despite disagreements in the Chinese leadership concerning foreign policy during the years since 1949, support for the aspirations of developing countries has been a constant factor. In the 1990s, Chinese official speakers have, in common with other commentators world-wide, moved away from outmoded definitions of the 'Third World', with its inevitable connotations of exploitation and disadvantage, and have recognized the reality of multipolarity and the need for more flexible categories of analysis. According to China's Premier, Li Peng, in a speech to a United Nations Security Council Meeting in January 1992, the emergence of new conflicts has made the post-Cold War world an even more dangerous place, with the North–South divide continuing to widen, as the rich countries become richer and the poor poorer. Other Chinese sources have taken up this theme, arguing that the developed countries, accounting for 23 per cent of the world's population and possessing 85 per cent of the world's wealth, contrast sharply with developing countries, which include 77 per cent of global population but share only 15 per cent of the world's wealth. Chinese official rhetoric continually stresses the need for global peace and development, and the unsatisfactory response of the world's leaders to date.[2]

China's official view of prospects for the Asia-Pacific region glosses over the area's growing economic disparities, and is largely optimistic, contrasting its relative stability with a turbulent Europe. The Asia-Pacific region is, of course, the world's fastest-growing economic pole, and a stable and economically prosperous China is seen as crucial to the maintenance of peace and stability in the region as a whole. Similarly, if China is to attain her goal of 'socialism with Chinese characteristics' – i.e. the full utilization of market forces while retaining the hegemony of the CCP – she will need a long period of peace and stability both at home and abroad; hence China's commitment to equality among states and mutual non-interference in internal affairs. China's leaders seek trade and economic cooperation with all countries, especially in the Asia-Pacific region, regardless of their political complexion; human rights, where China has been especially vulnerable to criticism by Western powers, are seen in terms of national prosperity, rather than the rights of the individual.

Finally, China's leadership remains firmly convinced that a nation's overall strength lies in a sound economy buttressed by advanced technology. Since the end of the Cold War, China has seen scientific competition as a crucial component of international economic rivalry in general. Wealth, in China's view, is the key to national security.

CHINA'S DEFENCE POLICY: AN ASIA-PACIFIC FOCUS

The March 1993 session of the National People's Congress defined China's twin goals as a prosperous economy and a strong military. Chinese sources have, however, been at pains to emphasize the purely defensive role of the latter, as witnessed by the apparently low level of defence expenditure which accounted for about 2.2 per cent and 1.6 per cent of GNP in 1985 and 1992 respectively, and is estimated at 1.5 per cent in 1993. In addition, current per capita military spending is said to be only US$6 as compared to US$1,100 in the United States and US$300 in Japan. Such comparisons, of course, often tend to be invidious, given the marked differences in, for example, salary levels in the countries in question. But China is clearly at pains to demonstrate that her defence policy and infrastructure are conceived essentially as a safeguard for the implementation of the open-door policy – as explained in reports on the

Chinese Defence Minister Chi Haotian's visit to Malaysia in May 1993.[3]

In reality, China's defence strategy is, of course, formulated on the basis of perceived threats to China's security, which are in turn attendant upon the emergence of a new, multipolar international diplomacy, as noted earlier. Whereas Chinese foreign policy was previously concerned primarily with the confrontation of two hegemonic powers, the United States and the Soviet Union, it is now focused on the various rivals for supremacy in the Asia-Pacific region. In the immediate term, Chinese defence analysts see little likelihood of aggression against China, but in the longer run the threat to the country's borders could increase markedly. Like other national leaders, China's policy-makers operate on two fronts: the diplomatic and the military. The latter will be discussed later in the context of potential national rivals to China's influence in the Asia-Pacific region. Examples of the former include the restoration of diplomatic relations with Indonesia and the establishment of official ties with Singapore, Brunei, the Republic of Korea and the republics of the former Soviet Union. Relations have also been normalized with Vietnam and Laos.

China's international relations journals have latterly been providing ample analysis of the new regional balance of power as viewed by the Chinese leadership. The new strategic balance is seen as pluralist, based on the mutual constraint of a number of Asia-Pacific powers in the region. The United States, wary of involvement in local conflicts, is reducing its military forces stationed abroad and looking to Japan to take greater security responsibilities commensurate with its economic power. Additionally, the Americans seek fuller participation in ASEAN consultations on Asia-Pacific security issues. As for Japan, it is too early to judge the long-term intentions of the Hosokawa government, but the previous Liberal Democrat administration of Kiichi Miyazawa did propose to establish a security guarantee mechanism in the region through negotiation among ASEAN foreign ministers. The other major power in the region, namely Russia, is said to have modified its objectives in seeking a peaceful environment for the economic development of its own Far East and to be seeking further cooperation in north-east Asia as a whole through closer relations with the United States, China and the Republic of Korea. The latter's main concern is reunification of the Korean peninsula, but its leaders reject the Miyazawa proposal for a collective security system in the Asia-Pacific region in the foreseeable future on the grounds of historical, cultural, political and economic diversity. Finally, ASEAN states favour the idea of an Asia-Pacific security mechanism, seeking to extend discussions to include such countries as China, Russia, Laos and Cambodia.

The peripheral reaches of the Asia-Pacific region have only relatively recently entered Chinese diplomatic thinking to any degree. However, Australia, for example, is now becoming economically more closely integrated with Asia and seeks participation in the discussion of security issues, as witnessed by Premier Keating's proposal, after talks with Miyazawa, for an Asia-Pacific regional summit conference to be held.[4]

In summary, the Chinese claim that their military forces are for defence purposes only, although foreign opinion is generally sceptical of this. Economic prosperity and diplomatic outreach are also seen as keys to China's national security. The main thrust of China's diplomacy is thus directed towards creating a peaceful Asian environment conducive to Chinese economic growth.

PERCEIVED THREATS TO CHINA

Having discussed China's perceptions of her own defence needs, as well as the views of the other major Asian and Pacific countries concerning regional security, we are now in a position to examine how the leaders in Beijing view specific threats to their country's sovereignty and territorial integrity. Following their country's experience of Japanese invasion during the Pacific War, China's leaders remain suspicious of Japanese motives, in spite of Japan's extensive trade and investment in China. As Japan takes on erstwhile American security responsibilities in the region, Chinese sources speak of accelerated Japanese conventional weapons development, both quantitatively and qualitatively, allegedly over and above Japan's purely national defence needs. In addition, given Japan's growing economic stake in south-east Asia, the Chinese fear future Japanese hegemony in what was regarded for centuries as China's particular sphere of influence. China also views India as another potential rival, and has been engaged in periodic border disputes with the latter since the late 1950s; this perception is now coloured by greater Indian openness to foreign investment and a considerable nuclear capacity. Moreover, China is also engaged in territorial disputes and contention over maritime rights and interests with Vietnam. And members of ASEAN are accused of attempting, albeit in vain, to encroach on the Spratly Islands, claimed by China.

CHINA'S MILITARY STRATEGY

Chinese military strategists see no immediate danger to China's security, the country's vast territory, huge population and growing defensive strength being considered sufficient deterrents. Should a threat occur, however, analysts envisage a conventional border war. Should an attack come from further afield, a limited conventional war with a major power could pose a tactical nuclear threat, in anticipation of which eventuality China needs to prepare a distinctively mobile nuclear deterrent in conjunction with the conventional one.[5] But as China plays a greater role in international trade and becomes more integrated into the world economy, the country will be increasingly vulnerable to blockade, with sea channels assuming greater significance for national security. Thus the development of naval power, currently considered by Chinese analysts as the weak link in China's defences, is being given greater priority, especially in view of the Spratly Islands, coveted by other south-east Asian nations, allegedly for their natural resources. Accordingly, Chinese naval strategists are concentrating in the short term on the transformation of the navy from a coastal defence force into an offshore fleet capable of defending China's territorial interests. Objectives include the building of a nuclear-powered aircraft carrier, the establishment of a carrier fleet and the development of laser weapons systems.[6] To extend naval capability beyond coastal waters, three large naval bases are to be built along China's eastern seaboard by 1998 in order to provide key logistical support to a new-style Chinese fleet capable of ocean-going operations. The new facilities will be located in Liaoning Province in north-east China, at a second site near Shanghai, and another at Zhanjiang in southern China'a Guangdong Province. These facilities are designed as a logistical support system capable of sustaining aircraft carriers in the future; a strong mobile fleet will act as a deterrent force as naval operations are extended from coastal protection duties to ocean patrols.[7]

In China's view, as we have seen, economic growth enhances national security; in turn, it is hoped that stronger defence parameters will protect future Chinese living standards. Other world powers, however, remain unconvinced of China's peaceful intentions.

THE ASIA-PACIFIC ECONOMIC COMMUNITY

The term 'Pacific century' has become commonplace among Western academic commentators, but Chinese official sources, while generally supportive of this notion, express reservations, particularly concerning the optimum pace and extent of regional economic integration.[8] The first barrier to unity is the North–South divide and the uneven economic development within the area as a whole, both between different regions and different nations. For example, while per capita GNP in Cambodia is only US$110 per annum, the equivalent for Hong Kong is US$14,000 and for Singapore US$13,600. Similarly, in regional terms south Asia lags behind south-east Asia economically. Moreover, there are huge disparities within individual countries, the contrast between China's south-eastern seaboard and the western hinterland being a case in point. Second, Chinese sources have been at pains to point out that for the foreseeable future the Asia-Pacific region will not be able to sustain its development without substantial integration with the world economy as well as trade links with and investment input from countries outside the region. For instance, even allowing for the role of Japan as a market and a source of technology transfer, east and south-east Asia remain dependent on trade surpluses with the United States for their economic growth. In fact, bilateral trade between the United States and the Asia-Pacific region has grown very rapidly and is expected to double by the end of the century. One-fifth of America's total investment abroad is in the region.[9]

Finally, the creation of an Asia-Pacific economic bloc will ultimately depend on the resolution of regional tensions born of different social, political and economic systems. But, in spite of such differences and the continuing importance of the roles to be played by the United States and the European Community (EC) in, for instance, the economic transformation of China, there are powerful arguments, in Chinese and other Asian views, for gradual moves towards the creation of an Asia-Pacific economic community in the long term.

A compelling argument for closer economic ties within the region is the growth of other regional blocs throughout the world, with attendant suspicions of exclusivity and protectionism voiced by outsiders, the EU being but one example. Chinese official writers note this trend towards 'regionalization', arguing that relations between blocs are replacing relations between individual countries in the economic sphere, even though the intensity of interaction varies. More importantly, during the last 30 years, the economic growth rate of the Asia-Pacific region has been impressive by any standards; statistics show an average rate of 6 per cent during the last two decades, twice that of other regions. Contributing factors have been the economic miracle of Japan, which by 1990 had a GNP of 62.8 per cent of the United States and in per capita terms 25 per cent higher than America, and the emergence of the so-called Four Dragons – Singapore, South Korea, Hong Kong and Taiwan – which in many respects have emulated Japan, their export-led growth being derived from production sectors latterly vacated by Japanese manufacturers because of rising domestic costs.[10] China is to a large extent following this path. Recent Chinese sources are replete with discussions of the virtues of such economic strategies as import substitution and export-led development. There is continuing commitment to the open-door policy which the leadership claims will remain unchanged for a hundred years. A decision to follow the export-led strategy, thus emulating the Four Dragons, has been reflected in measures designed to attract foreign investment from Asia and elsewhere as a reduction in foreign exchange controls, greater tax concessions to overseas investors and the establishment of free ports. Given, however, the creation of the European Single Market and the coming of the north American Free Trade Area (NAFTA), the Asia-Pacific countries, including China, will not be able to sustain, let alone substantially increase, their exports to the United States (currently China's third largest trade partner) and western Europe. As with China's foreign trade, for which the Chinese have always diversified their markets and sources of supply so as not to be dependent on any one partner, China's leaders have also encouraged and received investment from a number of countries. While joint ventures financed by European and American companies, in addition to major investors such as Hong Kong, Taiwan and Japan, have become prominent, investment in future could increasingly be diverted to EC countries and the United States. There are strong indications that the further development of the Asia-Pacific will be generated through cross-investment within the region.

Significantly, the foundations for greater Asia-Pacific economic integration are being laid through the establishment of bilateral relations and multilateral political mechanisms. A major example of the latter is the Ministerial Conference on Asia-Pacific Economic Co-operation (APEC), with representation from the region's main powers, including China and Japan; it is clearly destined to play a leading role in coordinating economic relations. Although internal trade among Asian countries has already reached half of their total trade volume, with dependence on EU and north American markets reduced, varying levels of economic development in the

Asia-Pacific region as a whole suggest the need for further cooperation and coordination. In this area much is being achieved. Advanced countries such as Japan, Singapore, the Republic of Korea, Hong Kong and Taiwan are all exporting capital and technology to Asia-Pacific countries to further their industrial renovation and restructuring.

Thus a division of labour is emerging and in the 1990s this will increasingly take place in the context of sub-regional cooperation. There are three main sub-regions, namely the north-east Asia economic cooperation zone, Greater China and the south-east Asian economic zone. We will briefly discuss each in turn before a more detailed analysis is provided.

The north-east zone has not been formally established but Chinese policy-makers regard it as having great potential. It includes the three north-eastern provinces of China, together with Japan, and North Korea, South Korea and the former Soviet Union Far East. Ideally, the finance and technology of Japan and South Korea could be allied to the natural and human resources of China and the other relatively underdeveloped areas. Surveys and feasibility studies are being conducted under a United Nations programmeme. The zone is not yet a reality, and so we will concentrate in detail on the remaining two sub-regions.

The existence of the south China economic zone is suggestive of the concept of Greater China and encompasses the south-eastern coastal provinces of China, Hong Kong, Macau and Taiwan. The existence of the zone has, of course, implications for the position of Hong Kong after its return to Chinese sovereignty in 1997 and the possible political reunification of Taiwan with the mainland. The south China zone undoubtedly has tremendous economic potential, with the mainland's huge market and relatively cheap labour force allied to the marketing skills of Taiwan and the financial and information services of Hong Kong.

The south-east Asian economic zone comprises the countries of ASEAN and Indochina. In January 1992, as a step towards regional economic integration, the leaders of ASEAN announced a plan to establish a free trade area within 15 years, and signed an agreement on common tariffs. Given growing intra-regional trade and investment, closer links may well be forged between the south-east Asia and south China economic zones. The opportunity is there for both China and Japan to promote multilateral regional cooperation, whether as partners or rivals. It must, however, be noted that Chinese official attitudes to Japanese influence in the region are at best ambivalent. Nonetheless, China's economic ties with the area as a whole will undoubtedly intensify, and already 80 per cent of the country's total foreign trade is with the Asia-Pacific region.[11]

GREATER CHINA: ECONOMIC COMPLEMENTARITY

While emphasizing the crucial importance of long-term Asia-Pacific integration for China's future interests, Chinese policy-makers, for reasons of historical and cultural affinity as well as current potential economic complementarity, also stress the establishment and maintenance of closer ties with the east Asian region, composed of the Chinese mainland, Hong Kong, Macau and Taiwan, an area itself enjoying rapid development. While acknowledging the political issues involved in national reunification, Chinese mainland sources are full of references to and quotations from Taiwanese studies chronicling the island's post-1949 economic miracle. In brief, the examples cited stress Taiwan's export-led strategy based on the early institution of relatively low foreign exchange rates, free trade policies, commodity price stability and attractive interest rates for savings depositors. Notably, the 1959 foreign exchange measures in Taiwan find an echo in recent reforms on the Chinese mainland.[12]

Taiwan's early economic take-off depended, however, on exports to the developed countries of the West, an option that may not be as available to China. If entrepôt trade via Hong Kong is included, exports to the United States constituted 30 per cent of China's total exports. A further 11 per cent of exports went to the EC in 1991. Moreover, Hong Kong and Taiwan were even more dependent, 60 per cent of their exports being destined for the United States and 20 per cent for the EC. Any export-led growth model can thus be hampered by regional protectionism. It is precisely in order to counter potential protectionism in the EC and the new NAFTA that the Chinese propose regional economic cooperation between the Chinese mainland, Hong Kong, Macau and Taiwan.[13]

Such co-operation is posited on economic complementarity and division of labour. The mainland can supply natural resources to Hong Kong, Macau and Taiwan; the latter in turn can provide funds as well as advanced technical and marketing expertise to access international markets. The advantages of economic cooperation for the respective parties will now be examined. In the case of the mainland, apart from the obvious trading and investment prospects, cooperation is increasingly considered as an aid to macro-economic reform. Given the Chinese leadership's avowed desire to create a free market economy, overseas investors can bring international information that would be invaluable if Chinese producers are to satisfy foreign market needs. More significantly, overseas investment may facilitate state enterprise reform in the transition from a command to a market economy, with the demands of foreign customers assisting restructuring and promoting competitiveness.

Chinese officialdom is also keen to point out that China offers lucrative opportunities to investors from Taiwan, Hong Kong and Macau. In view of the need for country-of-origin certificates for export goods, investment in the mainland means that China's export quota may be utilized, especially when Sino-foreign joint ventures seek to sell abroad. Land, labour, water and electricity are cheaper on the mainland, thus conferring product price competitiveness on world markets. Additionally, some goods may be sold on the Chinese domestic market where overseas-style manufactures are in increasing demand. Taiwan, for example, is transferring labour-intensive manufacturing offshore in order to compete more effectively with south-east Asian producers while promoting the input of new technology at home to aid industrial restructuring. Finally, the three territories need outlets for their share capital, occasioned in Taiwan's case by massive trade surpluses.[14]

We will now focus in detail on the three territories' trade with and investment in China. Because of Taiwan's small population, lack of natural resources and limited domestic market, foreign trade plays a decisive role in her economy. Taiwan has, however, long depended on the United States, with which it has an unacceptably high trade surplus. Precisely because of the resulting need to diversify export markets, the Chinese mainland has become crucially important to Taiwan. Significantly, the United States accounted for 48 per cent of Taiwan's total exports in 1984 but only 30.4 per cent in 1990; this was because of the expansion of exports to the mainland. Mainland/Taiwan trade, including both official indirect trade, usually channelled through Hong Kong, and illegal direct trade, is estimated at US$15 billion for 1992, representing 10 per cent of Taiwan's world total, overwhelmingly in the island's favour.

In addition, the mainland confers a number of unrivalled advantages for Taiwan's investors, as compared to south-east Asia. Even more important than common linguistic and cultural factors, geographical proximity facilitates the use of Hong Kong's transhipment facilities, and the colony's personnel exchange and information services. Low wages and land prices on the mainland itself are also an attraction; it is estimated that over 12,000 businesses from Taiwan have already set up ventures in China. Chinese reports have stated that total investment by value is about US$9 billion, although sources in Taipei regard this as an understatement.[15]

Like Taiwan, Hong Kong is becoming increasingly dependent on trade with the mainland, which amounted to about HK$400 billion in 1970. Although heavily in China's favour, the figure nevertheless included over HK$110 billion in re-exports from Hong Kong. In a further parallel with Taiwan, Hong Kong is becoming less dependent on trade with the United States, which since 1985 has been supplanted by the mainland as Hong Kong's largest trading partner; exports to the United States declined from 44.5 per cent of the port's total in 1984 to 29.4 per cent in 1990.

In spite of contentious issues relating to the return of Hong Kong to Chinese sovereignty in 1997, the port has become the mainland's largest source of foreign capital, with Hong Kong manufacturers moving many of their plants to southern China. Conversely, more than 1,000 Chinese firms now have investments in the port, exceeding US$20 billion in total; China-funded banks have become the second largest banking group in the territory. Additionally, Hong Kong is also an entrepôt for trade with and investment in China, the vast proportion of economic activity between the mainland and Taiwan being conducted through the port. Given the accelerated development of service industries such as banking, transport and warehousing, Hong Kong is likely to play a major role as an entrepôt and financial centre in the Asia-Pacific region.[16]

The last of the three territories to be discussed is Macau, which is adjacent to Zhuhai, one of the first Special Economic Zones to be created in China. With rapidly growing export industries fuelling its foreign trade, Macau is poised to become a second Hong Kong, playing a major intermediary role in the Asia-Pacific region. While possessing funds and business marketing networks, Macau lacks land and labour resources which Zhuhai has in abundance. Thus the scope for Macau–Zhuhai cooperation is considerable, with Zhuhai benefiting from Macau's ties to international markets and sources of capital. Under the terms of the Joint Declaration, the Chinese and Portuguese governments agreed to a date for Macau's return to Chinese sovereignty while guaranteeing the territory's basic orientation as an unchanged capitalist system for a subsequent 50 years (Cai Musheng 1993).

As an indicator of these trends towards economic integration, it is worth emphasizing that in 1991 over 50 per cent of the outside capital absorbed by the mainland came from Hong Kong, Macau and Taiwan, and of Chinese exports 42 per cent was destined for the three territories (State Statistical Bureau 1992). Nevertheless, the optimism expressed by the Chinese and their partners concerning prospects for economic integration should be regarded with some caution. To date the mainland's trade and economic cooperation has been based on the principle of comparative advantage; differing social systems and levels of development have precluded closer economic integration which would require cooperation across entire industries and in sectors of high technology in order to further greater interdependence. The Chinese have upheld the virtues of cooperation with the three territories but east Asia is still at least partially dependent on the trade and technology of Western countries, the above statistical trends notwithstanding. There are also political ramifications. While a successor to Deng Xiaoping would be unlikely to reverse the economic open-door policy, further Chinese moves to participate in the economic integration of east and south-east Asia could depend on the ability of a new leadership to establish its own legitimacy. Future leaders will need to contain any political dissent born of rising expectations among the populace. Any untoward repercussions arising from political turmoil on the mainland could be reflected in future Communist Chinese attitudes to Hong Kong and Macau. Finally, Taiwan's officialdom could come to fear that intensifying mainland economic involvement by the island's manufacturers could lead to reunification on Communist terms.

THE SOUTH-EAST ASIAN ECONOMIC ZONE

There is a potential conflict between the Chinese desire for economic integration in east Asia and their proclaimed policy of closer ties with south-east Asia. Commercial sectors in a number of south-east Asian countries have long been dominated by Overseas Chinese who are being lured to invest in the mainland, where their cultural knowledge is a distinct advantage. Furthermore, Taiwan, a top investor in Malaysia and Indonesia in 1991, tripled its investments in China in 1992 but simultaneously reduced its stake in the two south-east Asian countries. In fact, it could be argued that China's preoccupation with the three Chinese territories might be at the expense of its investment in south-east Asia as a whole, were it not for the major factor of national security which is itself a motivation for the expansion of economic contacts with, for example, the ASEAN countries. Moreover, it is possible that the Chinese leaders may be able to capitalize on suspicions of Japan in the region, a traditional sphere of Chinese influence. The Chinese desire to establish economic links could be seen in the context of an attempt to counter growing Japanese power. As evidence of unease in the region, we may cite concern expressed in Indonesia and Singapore over the 1992 law allowing the Japanese government to send troops abroad, albeit only for peace-keeping operations. Other Asian countries that suffered under Japanese occupation in the Second World War have similarly voiced fears over the prospect of a resurgence of Japanese militarism (Jiang Yaping 1992).

To reassure regional governments of China's peaceful intentions, Chinese leaders have reiterated the concept of 'development guaranteeing defence': China is still a developing country and can hope to catch up with advanced nations in per capita GNP only after generations of hard work, as emphasized by CCP General Secretary Jiang Zemin in talks with Prime Minister Mahathir Mohamad of Malaysia, in June 1993. Similarly, during a 1992 visit to Singapore, the then Chinese president, Yang Shangkun, stated that China did not wish to see military rivalry interfere with peace and development in the Asia-Pacific region. Accordingly, Chinese leaders have continued to stress the North–South divide in their negotiations with south-east Asian countries, attacking developed countries for trying to impose strictures concerning human rights and democracy as conditions for trade and investment.[17] As far as China and other Asian countries are concerned, such rights are seen in terms of the sovereignty, economic development and political stability of the nation, not the personal liberty of the individual as such. National prosperity is the priority. To this end the Chinese have supported Malaysian suggestions for a united south-east Asian voice in international trade negotiations and responded positively to the programme of the East Asian Economic Caucus (EAEC) proposed by Malaysia. In addition, at a recent meeting, China's foreign minister, Qian Qichen, envisaged ASEAN as a base for his proposed programme of economic and trade cooperation in the region. On the basis of China's trade with ASEAN, which reached US$8 billion in 1991, together with mutual investment of US$1.2 billion for the same year, indicating economic complementarity, Qian called for the establishment of Sino-ASEAN scientific and technological development centres – one in Beijing to train personnel in computer software and other high-tech fields, and the other, within ASEAN, to facilitate the manufacture of products using China's technology.

Chinese officialdom has also commented favourably on the 1992

ASEAN Singapore declaration agreeing to a common effective preferential tariff, ultimately to be set at a rate between 0 and 5 per cent, as well as an ASEAN free trade area (AFTA) to be established over 15 years beginning in 1993. This agreement is considered a prelude to further economic integration in south-east Asia and is justified in terms of the need to overcome international competition, given the world-wide trend towards the creation of trade blocs (Cai Ximei and Qi Deliang 1992).

Nevertheless, in spite of China's ostensible growing involvement in south-east Asian economic integration, Chinese trade and investment relations with the rest of the region are still relatively low, especially when compared to interaction between the Chinese territories of east Asia. For example, current Chinese trade with Malaysia stands at only US$1.5 billion, although the signing of contracts by Malaysian businessmen during Prime Minister Mahathir Mohamad's visit to China in June 1993 offered promise of closer economic ties, including substantial investment. China's rapidly growing economy is proving a powerful magnet for south-east Asian traders and investors.[18] Investment, though in its infancy, is two-way: during the Mahathir visit, China and Malaysia signed 32 economic cooperation agreements, covering petrochemicals, civil aviation, maintenance, building materials and the power industry. Energy contracts were particularly notable; China's petrochemical corporation (SINOPEC) agreed to buy 5,000 to 7,000 barrels of crude oil from Malaysia, while the Malaysian property development group, Metroplex, signed a US$600 million contract for the joint construction of an oil-fuelled power plant in China's Guangdong Province. Already 37 companies have invested in China, and Chinese investors are being sought for Malaysia and other south-east Asian countries. Significantly, Singapore, with its ethnic Chinese majority, has become the fourth largest investor in China. In July 1993 a delegation led by the senior minister, Lee Kuan Yew, visited Shandong Province to assess the possibility of Singapore's participation in township development, one of the city state's areas of expertise.[19]

In conclusion, although China may profit to a degree from suspicion of Japan in the region, it nevertheless presents a potential competitor for the textile and electronic goods produced by south-east Asian countries. But such a threat may be reduced as such countries move into more high-tech areas, following the stages of development taken by Japan. In turn, Japan may take even more of the region's manufactures, even though the United States and the EC will remain important export markets for south-east Asian countries.

Finally, while the Chinese leaders claim to eschew military involvement in the region, their policies are undoubtedly motivated by their perceived need to defend their growing stake in international trade. But a purely military relationship with any south-east Asian country or countries would seem to be precluded by the spirit of the Treaty of Amity and Co-operation, signed in Bali in 1976 by the ASEAN powers, the terms of which forbid defence alliances with states outside the region. In any case, China's leaders undoubtedly regard south-east Asia as their traditional sphere of influence, and major world powers as well as countries in the region are justifiably suspicious of Chinese motives, especially in view of the fact that China's military modernization has been paid for, at least in part, by arms exports.

CHINA'S OUTREACH TO THE PACIFIC

China's foreign policy focus on Pacific countries, notably Australia and New Zealand, has evolved slowly in the post-war period, despite the fact that economic interests have increased markedly since the establishment of diplomatic relations with the two countries just over 20 years ago. Chinese official analyses stress economic complementarity but also convey a defence dimension; Australian governments are praised for actively promoting peace and cooperation in the Asia-Pacific region, and for their belief in Australia's future within the region.[20] Enthusiasm for trade and investment is shared, especially given the emergence of a potentially protectionist single market in the EC – a traditional destination for Australian and New Zealand exports – and as witnessed by the number of prominent Chinese leaders visiting the two countries in the last decade. Hinting at the great potential for further economic cooperation, a recent Chinese source stated that currently seven out of ten Australian export markets are in Asia; in 1992, for instance, 11 per cent of exports went to east Asia, including China but excluding Japan. In addition, exports to that sub-region were growing more rapidly than Australian sales to Europe and north America. Similarly, Asia has become both the main avenue for Australian investment and an important source of foreign funds (Shi Zhongxin 1993).

In recent years, Sino–Australian economic relations have grown rapidly; in 1992 bilateral trade reached US$2.8 billion and was in Australia's favour. Australia is now China's eleventh largest trading partner and China is Australia's ninth largest. China's imports from Australia include wheat, barley, steel, iron ore, coal and wool; exports to Australia range from textile products to food and machinery. Moreover, last year Australian concerns invested US$228 million in China, while Chinese investment in Australia amounted to US$256 million.[21]

During the June 1993 visit of Australian Prime Minister Paul Keating to China, the two countries pledged themselves to increase cooperation in a variety of fields, including manufacturing, animal husbandry, science and technology and the tertiary sector, thus exploiting their respective strengths. Current Australian-funded projects in China are mainly in agriculture, light industry, food processing and electronics; China has invested in iron ore mines, aluminium smelters and small farm projects in Australia.[22]

In summary, economic cooperation benefits both parties, as Australia diversifies her overseas markets and the Chinese reap the benefit of preferential Australian government loans to purchase the technology needed to further China's long-term economic reforms.

On the issue of defence cooperation, however, the Australian side is cautious, and the embargo on military sales in the wake of the 1989 Tiananmen incident is still in force. Australia is sceptical, too, of Chinese support for the Malaysian proposal for a rival economic forum to APEC: the putative East Asian Economic Caucus could effectively reduce the influence of such developed countries as the United States in the affairs of the region.

New Zealand, like Australia, provides China with natural resources. In 1991, New Zealand–China trade amounted to US$235 million, and China is the largest buyer of New Zealand wool, taking 25 per cent of the latter's exports. In 1992, two-way trade increased by 50 per cent over the previous year. Furthermore, the New Zealand government is continually targeting the market in China for forest products, coal and dairy produce. As a small agricultural country, New Zealand is an alternative source of supply for China; the former is also a destination for Chinese investment. In fact, New Zealand is one of the few developed countries that actually receives more in investment from China than it invests in China itself. Undoubtedly, there is further scope for cooperation in sectors such as food processing and marine produce.[23]

In conclusion, while Australia and New Zealand do not yet loom as large as Asian states in China's foreign policy thinking, growing relations nevertheless reflect the priorities of China's economic development and represent a projection of Chinese defence interests in the Asia-Pacific region as whole.

SUMMARY AND CONCLUSIONS

When placed in the post-war context, contemporary Chinese policy towards the Asia-Pacific region displays elements of continuity and change and is informed by China's own economic development priorities, as well as by the shifting balance of power within the region as a whole. The success of the post-1978 open-door policy has itself been seen by its progenitors as the best guarantee of national security; China's former support for armed revolutionary struggle in the developing countries of Asia has now been rejected, and the Five Principles of Peaceful Coexistence, enunciated in the 1950s, are upheld as the basis for China's relations with non-Communist countries. Chinese foreign policy is therefore now more pragmatic and issue-oriented, although support for the economic interests of developing countries has remained a constant theme in the post-war period, most often expressed in terms of the North–South divide.

Certain caveats should, of course, be noted. The Chinese system of government remains totalitarian and the economic freedoms granted to promote market forces have not been followed by liberties in the political domain. Furthermore, China's leaders, in spite of their apparent stress on conventional diplomacy in recent years, have not disavowed the cause of revolution at home and abroad, and their ongoing defence build-up indicates a nationalist, if not revolutionary, desire to extend Chinese influence in the Asia-Pacific region, if necessary at the expense of other regional powers.

The Asia-Pacific region is the main focus of China's defence policy. Perceived threats are more difficult to define, but suspicions of Japanese motives in the region, growing Indian military potential, and territorial disputes – for example over the Spratly Islands, claimed by China and a number of other countries – may be cited. China's increasing dependence on international trade makes her more vulnerable to naval blockade; hence the establishment of coastal bases providing facilities for a fleet capable of ocean-going operations.

Of course, diplomacy is also an instrument of defence, and the Chinese seek to engage in the multilateral and bilateral mechanisms of a burgeoning Asia-Pacific economic community. But barriers to true regional economic integration remain, particularly the continuing dependence on the EU and United States markets. In addition, there are glaring disparities in development among the countries of the region. It remains unclear whether Japan and China will eventually become rivals or partners, particularly in view of the fact that Japan has been entrusted with economic and defence responsibilities in the region by the United States.

Intensified economic interaction between China and Taiwan, Hong Kong and Macau would seem far more likely, harnessing the mainland's manpower and raw material resources to the three territories' capital, technology and marketing expertise. Within certain limits, Taiwan's export-led strategy could be a lesson for China.

China is a magnet for investment in the Asia-Pacific region, and overseas Chinese funds could flow there at the expense of the southeast Asian countries. While Chinese trade and investment relations with the ASEAN countries are growing, China could prove a competitor in manufactures such as textiles. Nevertheless, China will in any case prove a key player in the region in the decades to come.

China's post-war relations with Australia and New Zealand developed relatively late; given economic complementarity, the advantages for China include alternative sources of technological cooperation and raw materials, offering scope for further mutual benefit. The projection of Chinese influence outward from Asia to the Pacific is a reflection of economic priorities and defence interests. That projection seems set to intensify in the twenty-first century, though whether such influence will be for the good of the region as a whole remains to be seen.

NOTES

1 See, for example, references to the major revision of the CCP's constitution at the fourteenth CCP Congress, as reported in *Renmin Ribao*, 8 February 1993.
2 Li Peng's speech to the United Nations appears in the *Beijing Review*, 17–23 February, 1992: 8–10.
3 The GNP and per capita figures were given during a televised news conference by Qian Qichen on China Central Television on 23 March 1993, *Summary of World Broadcasts* (hereafter *SWB*) FE/1645 C2/1.
4 A full discussion of Chinese perceptions of defence issues appears in an article by Yan Xiangjun and Huang Tingwei 1993. Similar issues are raised in Qi Fa 1993.
5 *Ibid.*
6 These references to the further development of the Chinese navy are based on an article published in the February 1993 edition of *Modern Ships*, a monthly journal of the China Naval Ships Research Academy, as quoted in *SWB*, FE/1622i.

7 'Three Large Naval Bases Planned for East Coast', Kyodo News Service, Tokyo, 11 January 1993, *SWB*, FE/1585 B2/10.
8 A major Chinese critique of the Pacific Century notion is provided in Yang Guanqun 1993.
9 GNP figures and references to United States investment are given in Yan Xiangjun 1992.
10 Li Xiao pursues this theme in his 1993 article.
11 A number of Chinese sources focus on Asia-Pacific regional integration. A discussion of a division of labour appears in 'Qian, For Closer Asia-Pacific Economic Cooperation', *Beijing Review*, 10–16 May 1993: 8–9; for the sub-regions, see Chen Jingbiao; the Sino-Japanese perspective is discussed in Liu Jiangyong 1992.
12 These measures are amply outlined in Jiang Shuojie 1992.
13 The relevant percentages are given in 'Cooperation with Hong Kong, Macau and Taiwan Outlined', *Guoji Maoyi Wenti (International Trade Journal)*, 5, 30 May 1993: 10-12, *JPRS*, CAR-93-061.
14 Details are taken from Shih Hua, 1993.
15 Taiwan–United States trade figures appear in Ji Wenxiu, 1992; figures for Taiwan's trade and investment with the mainland vary but those quoted are taken from a report in the *Daily Telegraph*, 8 October 1993. For variations from the latter see 'Cross-Strait Trade Growing', as reported in *SWB*, FE/WO 235 A/9.
16 Relevant statistics are outlined in Ji Wenxiu 1992. Chinese banking in Hong Kong is discussed in a report by Zhongguo Xinwen She on the 2 June 1993, *Foreign Broadcasts Information Service* (hereafter *FBIS*) CHI-93-105.
17 President Yang Shangkun's visit to Singapore was reported in 'China Seeks Close Ties with ASEAN Nations', *Beijing Review* 20–26 January 1992: 4.
18 For the Mahathir visit, see a report by the Xinhua News Agency on 14 June 1993, *SWB*, FE/1715/A2/1.
19 'China Seeks Close Ties with ASEAN Nations', *Beijing Review*, 20–26 January 1992: 4; see also a report by Shandong Broadcasting Station on 9 July 1993.
20 Such views were expressed by China's foreign minister, Qian Qichen, in a speech made during a visit to Australia, as reported in 'Asia, China and Australia', *Beijing Review*, 6–12 July 1992: 10–14.
21 Details revealed during the visit of Paul Keating, the Australian prime minister, to China, as reported by the Xinhua domestic service on 11 June 1993, *FBIS*, CHI-93-120. See also a report from Zhongguo Xinwen She, in *Beijing Review*.
22 'Australia's Paul Keating Arrives in Beijing', Xinhua broadcast, 23 June 1993, *FBIS*, CHI-93-119.
23 Two-way trade statistics appear in details given by the Xinhua News Agency on 12 August 1992, *SWB*, FE/WO 245 A/5, and in another Xinhua report dated 12 May 1993.

BIBLIOGRAPHY

Amsden, A. (1989) Asia's Next Giant, New York: Oxford University Press.

Cai Musheng (1993) 'On the Strategy and Policy Involved in Macau – Zhuhai Economic Cooperation', *Jingji Kexue (Economic Science)* 1, 20 February: 44–9, Joint Publications Research Service, CAZ–93–038.

Cai Ximei and Qi Deliang (1992) 'ASEAN Sets New Targets for Cooperation', *Beijing Review*, 24 February–1 March: 11.

Chen Jingbiao (1993) 'Asia-Pacific Ties Grow Closer', *Beijing Review*, 8–14 February: 8–10.

Cronin, R.P. (1992) *Japan, The United States and Prospects for the Asia-Pacific Century: Three Scenarios for the Future*, New York: St Martin's Press.

Dore, R.P. (1987) *Taking Japan Seriously: a Confucian Perspective on Leading Economic Issues*, London: Athlone.

Ji Wenxiu (1992) 'Strengthen Trade and Economic Cooperation among the Mainland, Hong Kong and Taiwan', *Guoji Maoyi Wenti (International Trade Journal)* 10, 30 October: 16–19, Joint Publications Research Service, CAR–93–010.

Jiang Shuojie (1992) 'Analysing the Myth of Taiwan's Economic Success', *Guomin Jingji Hua Yu Guanli* 8: 169–78.

Jiang Yaping (1992) 'Troops Law Arouses Concern in Asian Countries', *Beijing Review*, 27 June–5 July: 9.

Li Xiao (1993) 'New Characteristics in the Present Phase of Regionalisation in the World Economy', *Guoji Shangbao*, 27 March: 3, Joint Publications Research Service, CAR–93–038.

Liu Jiangyong (1992) 'Sino–Japanese Cooperation in a Changed Situation', *Beijing Review*, 6–12 April: 12–13.

Minami, R. (1994) *The Economic Development of China: a Comparison with Japanese Experience*, London: Macmillan.

Noland, M. (1990) *Pacific Basin Developing Countries*, Washington: Institute of International Economics.

Oshima, H. (1987) *Economic Growth in Modern Asia: a Comparative Survey*, Tokyo: University of Tokyo.

Pearson, M. (1991) *Joint Ventures in the People's Republic of China*, Princeton, NJ: Princeton Unversity Press.

Qi Fa (1993) 'Build a Distinctively Chinese Conventional Deterrent', *Xiandai Bingqi (Modern Weaponry)* 3, 8 March: 6–7, Joint Publications Research Service, CAR–93–036.

Shi Zhongxin (1993) 'Australia Merging into Asia', *Beijing Review*, 18–31 January: 13.

Shih Hua (1993) 'Every Dick and Jane is Going to Invest in the Mainland', *Chiv-Shih Nien-Tai (The Nineties)* 5, May, Joint Publications Research Service, CAR–93–040.

State Statistical Bureau (1992) *Tangji Ziliao Xinxi (China Statistical Digest)*, China Statistics Publishing House.

Thoburn, J. (*et al.*) (1990) *Foreign Investment in China under the Open Door Policy*, Aldershot: Avebury.

Tokunaga, S. (ed.) (1992) *Japan's Foreign Investment and Asian Economic Interdependence*, Tokyo: University of Tokyo Press.

Warner, M. (1987) *Management Reform in China*, London: Routledge and Kegan Paul

Wedley, W.C. (1992) *Changes in the Iron Rice Bowl*, Greenwich: JAI Press Inc.,

Yan Xiangjun (1992) 'Cursory Analysis of the Asia-Pacific Situation during the 1990s', *Xiandai Guoji Guanxi (Contemporary International Relations)* 38, 31 December: 32–6, Joint Publications Research Service, CAR–93–021.

Yan Xiangjun and Huang Tingwei (1993) 'The Security Situation in the Asia-Pacfic Region and the Relevant Parties' Ideas on a Security Mechanism,' *Xiandai Guoji Guanxi* (*Contempory International Relations*) 43, 20 May: 1–5, Joint Publications Research Service, CAR–93–060.

Yang Guanqun (1993) 'Will the Pacific Century Really Arrive?', *Guoji Wenti Yanjui*, 1: 34–8.

Part II

The economic dynamics

4 China's foreign trade expansion

The changing face of Chinese exporters and importers

Friedrich von Kirchbach and Johanna Aguado

INTRODUCTION

China's foreign trade expansion has become a fashionable subject of awe for businessmen and economists alike. No other country has moved up as rapidly in the ranking of the GATT's list of leading exporters (from twenty-first in 1973 to tenth in 1992, or fifth if the EU is counted as one).[1] No other socialist country has come anywhere near matching China's achievement of converting a policy framework unintelligible to most Western economists and full of the starkest distortions, into sustained double-digit growth. And no other country has attracted some 50,000 joint ventures within little more than a decade. Until recently, China held the leading position in international rankings according to socio-economic indicators only with respect to her population, but she is nonetheless top of a large, and growing, number of world leagues.

The performance of China's trade sector – as her bridgehead to the outside world – is of prime interest to the international business community. China holds shares in world trade of over 50 per cent in a considerable and growing number of manufactures;[2] it has become the largest developing exporting country in Asia, and its trade ratio is extremely high by any standards (Figure 4.1), but this is, it would seem, only a beginning. Per capita exports remain quite low, with an estimated US$66 in 1993 (Figure 4.2). In fact, half of all provinces registered per capita exports of less than US$20 per annum, i.e. below the corresponding levels of India, the Russian Federation or North Korea. These provinces are making special efforts to emulate the experience of the more outward-looking regions. In the latter, the mood is highly optimistic: the authorities of the Economic and Technical Development Areas of Tianjin, for instance, expect an annual growth rate of 40 per cent until the end

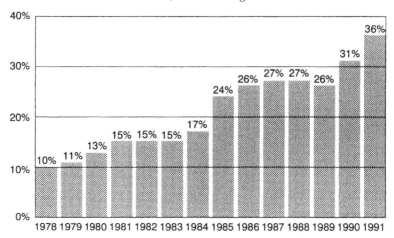

Figure 4.1 China's trade orientation: 1978–91
Source: China Statistical Yearbook, 1992; Asian Development Bank, 1991

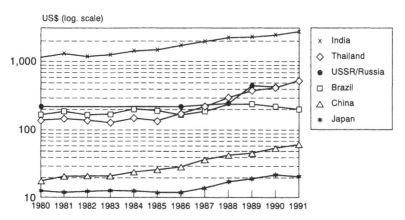

Figure 4.2 Per capita exports of selected countries
*Source:*International Financial Statistical Yearbook, IMF, 1993; Economic
Survey of Europe in 1991–2, UN, ECE, 1992; Demographic Yearbook, 1991,
UN

of the century. These facts are what lies behind the current rapidly-
growing demand for information, understanding and intelligence
on what is happening in China. In response to this demand, the
International Trade Centre UNCTAD/GATT (ITC), in close collaboration with the Customs General Administration of China (CGA),
is making a major effort towards increasing the transparency of
China's foreign trade, and in particular towards finding out more

about the actors. Who are they? How many are there? In what provinces are they operating? What are the respective roles of, and the differences in trade performance between, state-owned enterprises, foreign trade enterprises, joint ventures, collective firms, etc.? And what about the firms involved in processing and assembly trade?

Taken together, these indicators will provide, for the first time, a comprehensive portrait of the actors in China's foreign trade expansion. In addition, the project will generate marketing data in the form of exporters' and importers' directories in which actual traders can be retrieved by product and province (see Appendix 1).

This chapter presents some of the preliminary findings derived from a test phase in which China's trade data was reviewed at the transaction and enterprise level for the first six months of 1993.

METHODOLOGY AND DATA STRUCTURE

The analysis draws on ITC's approach to trade data analysis at the enterprise level.[3] This chapter is based on an analysis of around 3 million declarations for the period January to June 1993.

Since the introduction of enterprise codes in January 1993, the data base of CGA has allowed a detailed and business-oriented assessment of China's foreign trade. It is possible to zoom from the individual transaction or enterprise at the micro-level to aggregated trade flows by countries and commodities at the macro-level. The structure of China's customs data allows the data bases user to address any combination of the following issues:

What products are traded?

Having used the Standard International Trade Classification (SITC) as product nomenclature for foreign trade statistics until 1991, CGA introduced the Harmonized Description and Coding System (HS) as of 1992. The international six-digit code is extended by two additional national digits, and distinguishes some 6,200 products.

Which are the partner countries?

Each declaration has two fields for partner countries. For exports, these are 'country of final destination' and 'country of sale'; and for imports the corresponding fields are the 'country of origin' and the 'country of purchase'. CGA is making a major effort to require traders to indicate the final destination and the country of origin rather than only the country of sale and the country of purchase. These efforts should help in reducing the incidence of Hong Kong being mistakenly indicated as trading partner rather than as an entrepôt/harbour for re-exports.

Who is the Chinese exporter or importer?

Since January 1993, all customs declarations include a company code for the Chinese exporter or importer. Over the first half of 1993, for instance, there were about 50,000 Chinese importers and 30,000 Chinese exporters, for each of which all trade transactions can be retrieved. The company codes contain a variety of additional information on the characteristics of the Chinese enterprises entitled to engage directly in exports and imports, including the following items:

1 Place of registration of the trader in China
2 Type of enterprise, distinguishing between:
   - state-owned enterprises and municipal or provincial foreign-trade enterprises acting as agents for processing and assembling enterprises
   - equity joint ventures
   - contractual (i.e. non-equity) joint ventures, in which rights and obligations of the foreign joint-venture partner are fixed through contractual arrangements rather than through equity participation
   - fully foreign-owned enterprises
   - collective enterprises (including all township and village enterprises that are not joint ventures)
   - private enterprises, and
   - others.

What is the customs regime?

This field distinguishes between different types of trade in terms of customs regimes. The major distinctions are:

   - normal exports and imports
   - imports for inward processing and exports of these processed goods
   - equipment imported for processing and assembly activities

- equipment and materials imported as investment of foreign-affiliated enterprises
- materials or components imported by foreign-affiliated enterprises for products to be sold on the domestic market
- barter trade
- compensation trade
- border trade
- exports of turn-key projects

In addition, data on customs regimes is separated into international aid, leasing, donations from Overseas Chinese, exports and imports on consignment basis, outward processing, entrepôt trade and duty-free articles against payment of foreign currency.

What is the mode of transport?

Data distinguish between the following six modes of transport:

- water (including inland waterways)
- rail
- road
- air
- mail
- other (e.g. pipelines for oil and water, electricity transmission)

Where do the goods enter or leave China?

Some 38 customs districts and over 100 ports and customs offices can be distinguished.

Where do the goods go within China?

Declarations include a field on the location of the domestic producer or consumer. It should be noted that this information does not always appear to be reliable, as goods may be resold again to other locations.

How are the imports financed?

On the import side, declarations provide information on the source of foreign exchange by the following categories:

- central government

- retained foreign exchange of local enterprises and government bodies
- retained foreign exchange of state departments and state enterprises
- imports without payment of foreign exchange
- other sources.

What are the values, quantities and average unit values of exports and imports?

Transaction values (in US$ or rmb) and product-specific quantities
are available at all levels of aggregation. The two can be combined
to calculate average unit values.

NUMBER AND CONCENTRATION OF EXPORTERS AND IMPORTERS

The multiplication of Chinese enterprises directly involved in
exports and imports is one of the most visible signs of China's
foreign trade expansion. The number of direct exporters and
importers has increased even faster than the value of foreign trade.
In the first half of 1993, Chinese exports were handled by 30,232
firms, and imports by 49,029 (excluding those that were newly registered in the course of 1993), compared to a dozen 15 years ago
(Tables 4.1 and 4.2). A lower number of exporters as compared to
importers can be observed in most countries. It reflects primarily
the higher level of concentration in the export product structure as
compared to imports.

Up to the present, collective enterprises were rarely entitled to
export or import directly. Their share in direct trade was accordingly
low – less than 1 per cent both for exports and imports. Yet their
indirect involvement in trade has become very significant: already
in 1991, some 19 million rural industrial firms were estimated to
account for nearly one-quarter of Chinese exports.[4] It is only a
matter of time before many of them become involved directly in
foreign trade transactions. Hence, China's exports and imports may
well continue to expand at close to the triple-digit growth rates
observed in the past.

A ranking of Chinese exporters and importers points to a comparatively low degree of concentration. The largest exporter and the
largest importer each account for less than 4 per cent of China's
total exports and imports respectively; the top ten traders account

Table 4.1 Chinese exporters by location: first half 1993

Province code	Province name	No. of firms	Average export value per firm (US$)	Total exports (US$ million)	Share in national exports (%)	Exports per capita (US$ (annual))
11	Beijing	876	2,883,562	2,526	6.8	233.5
12	Tianjin	748	1,184,492	886	2.4	100.9
13	Hebei	331	2,223,565	736	2.0	12.0
14	Shanxi	100	1,640,000	164	0.4	5.7
15	Inner Mongolia	99	2,252,525	223	0.6	10.4
21	Liaoning	1,108	2,083,935	2,309	6.2	58.5
22	Jilin	223	2,165,919	483	1.3	19.6
23	Heilongjiang	328	2,237,805	734	2.0	20.8
31	Shanghai	1,383	1,697,035	2,347	6.3	175.9
32	Jiangsu	1,713	1,080,560	1,851	5.0	27.6
33	Zhejiang	1,254	1,287,879	1,615	4.3	39.0
34	Anhui	198	1,484,848	294	0.8	5.2
35	Fujian	2,834	740,649	2,099	5.7	69.9
36	Jiangxi	220	1,136,364	250	0.7	6.6
37	Shandong	1,501	1,140,573	1,712	4.6	20.3
41	Henan	181	1,845,304	334	0.9	3.9
42	Hubei	274	1,722,628	472	1.3	8.7
43	Hunan	276	1,663,043	459	1.2	7.6
44	Guangdong	14,243	1,080,180	15,385	41.4	244.9
45	Guangxi	361	1,127,424	407	1.1	9.6
46	Hainan	654	675,841	442	1.2	67.4
51	Sichuan	369	1,197,832	442	1.2	4.1
52	Guizhou	78	1,025,641	80	0.2	0.2
53	Yunnan	409	772,616	316	0.9	8.5
54	Tibet	29	1,103,448	32	0.1	14.6
61	Shaanxi	154	1,733,766	267	0.7	8.1
62	Gansu	79	1,164,557	92	0.2	4.1
63	Qinghai	24	1,041,667	25	0.1	5.6
64	Ningxia	48	562,500	27	0.1	5.8
65	Xinjiang	137	956,204	131	0.4	8.6
Total		30,232	1,228,599	37,143	100.0	32.9

Source: Statistical Department, Customs General Administration, China; ITC

for 13.5 per cent of exports and 16.6 per cent of imports, and the top 20 for 16.4 per cent of exports and 20.3 per cent of imports (Figure 4.3). In many other countries – for instance Brazil – the leading ten traders handle as much as one-quarter of exports and imports.

The same point also emerges from a comparison of average trade turnover per firm over the first half of 1993. The variation in average

Table 4.2 Chinese importers by location: first half 1993

Province code	Province name	No. of firms	Average import value per firm (US$)	Total imports (US$ million)	Share in national imports (%)	Imports per capita (US$ (annual))
11	Beijing	2,479	3,593,384	8,908	21.9	823.4
12	Tianjin	1,460	545,205	796	2.0	90.6
13	Hebei	727	466,300	339	0.8	5.5
14	Shanxi	235	370,213	87	0.2	3.0
15	Inner Mongolia	178	1,320,225	235	0.6	11.0
21	Liaoning	1,637	789,859	1,293	3.2	32.8
22	Jilin	464	1,168,103	542	1.3	22.0
23	Heilongjiang	647	1,046,368	677	1.7	19.2
31	Shanghai	1,613	1,624,303	2,620	6.4	196.4
32	Jiangsu	2,365	730,233	1,727	4.3	25.8
33	Zhejiang	1,607	518,357	833	2.1	20.1
34	Anhui	313	610,224	191	0.5	3.4
35	Fujian	4,034	450,917	1,819	4.5	60.5
36	Jiangxi	568	431,338	245	0.6	6.5
37	Shandong	2,870	441,463	1,267	3.1	15.0
41	Henan	437	453,089	198	0.5	2.3
42	Hubei	717	458,856	329	0.8	6.1
43	Hunan	556	444,245	247	0.6	4.1
44	Guangdong	21,125	763,077	16,120	39.7	256.6
45	Guangxi	1,021	353,575	361	0.9	8.5
46	Hainan	1,737	414,508	720	1.8	109.8
51	Sichuan	870	503,448	438	1.1	4.1
52	Guizhou	146	356,164	52	0.1	1.6
53	Yunnan	422	374,408	158	0.4	4.3
54	Tibet	22	863,636	19	0.0	8.7
61	Shaanxi	348	568,966	198	0.5	6.0
62	Gansu	175	445,714	78	0.2	3.5
63	Qinghai	19	736,842	14	0.0	3.1
64	Ningxia	28	285,714	8	0.0	1.7
65	Xinjiang	209	550,239	115	0.3	7.6
Total		49,029	828,775	40,634	100.0	35.9

Source: As for Table 4.1

export turnover per firm is quite limited between the different provinces: six-monthly averages are between US$1 and US$2 million for 19 provinces and the range is surprisingly narrow: from US$0.6 million per firm for Ningxia to US$2.8 million for Beijing. This variation is, in fact, lower than that of per capita GNP among provinces. The explanation for this result is not clear. Taking into account the marked differences in the export structure of different

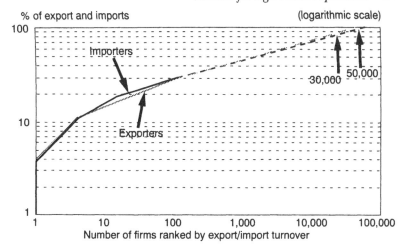

Figure 4.3 Concentration of Chinese exports and imports in terms of number of firms
Source: Statistical Department, General Administration, China: ITC

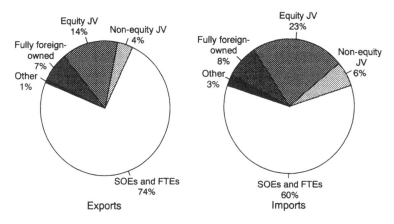

Figure 4.4 Share of different types of enterprises in China's foreign trade
Source: As for Figure 4.3

provinces in terms of product composition, per capita exports, number of traders, etc., one would have expected a much larger variation in average export turnover between provinces.

Due to the larger number of importers, the average import turnover (US$0.8 million) is lower than on the export side and varies more markedly between provinces. Significantly, however, it is not the overall exports and imports of a province that determine average trade turnover at the enterprise level. In Guangdong, for instance, average trade turnover is below the national average both for exports and imports.

The uneven contribution of China's provinces to national trade is well known. As may be gathered from Tables 4.1 and 4.2, Guangdong accounts for about 40 per cent of exports and imports. This confirms the exceptional development of Guangdong, which is quite justifiably regarded as the fifth of the east Asian 'tigers', on a par with the likes of Singapore, Hong Kong and Taiwan. And if Beijing, Liaoning, Shanghai, Jiangsu, Fujian and Shandong are considered togther with Guangdong, we see that the six coastal provinces, plus the capital, handle 76 per cent of national exports and 93 per cent of imports.

Does this represent an excessive geographical concentration? The true differences in outward orientation come out clearly by examining per capita exports and imports (Tables 4.1 and 4.2). These are, indeed, significant. Half of China's provinces have annual per capita exports or imports below US\$20, which is very low when compared internationally, and low in comparison to per capita income. Moreover, discrepancies are more likely to increase in the future than to narrow.

A comparison of the variation of trade-related indicators among provinces with the variation of GNP and GNP per capita confirms that foreign trade tends to accentuate rather than diminish China's economic imbalances in spatial terms. The deviation of the provincial trade performance from national averages was significantly higher, with the above-mentioned exception of average export turnover per firm. This result holds true irrespective of the special role of Guangdong, which is exceptional in terms of total export and import values and the number of exporters and importers, but not as far as per capita exports and imports are concerned, nor with respect to average trade turnover per firm.

ROLE OF DIFFERENT TYPES OF ENTERPRISE

Trade orientation and performance depend to a significant extent on the types of enterprises involved in foreign trade. The extent to which export development hinges primarily on foreign investment (as in Singapore), on comparatively small local firms (as in Taiwan) or on large local trading companies and industrial groupings (as in the Republic of Korea and Japan) constitutes an essential parameter for trade policy and promotion as well as for export and import marketing.

Table 4.3 Foreign trade value by type of enterprise: first half 1993

Type of enterprise	No. of exporters	No. of importers	Exports (US$ million)	Imports (US$ million)	Net exports (US$ million)	Exp/ Imp (%)
SOEs, including FTE	8,771	6,997	27,399	24,335	3,064	112.6
Non-equity JV	4,201	7,577	1,431	2,430	−999	58.9
Equity JV	11,820	22,191	5,342	9,549	−4,207	55.9
Fully foreign-owned firms	4,587	9,186	2,546	3,316	−770	76.8
Collective enterprises	387	363	266	203	63	131.0
Private enterprises	59	52	2	2	0	100.0
Other	407	2,663	158	802	−644	19.7
Sum	30,232	49,029	37,144	40,637	−3,493	91.4

Source: As for Table 4.1

The preliminary results for the first half of 1993 suggest that a dual structure has evolved between state-owned enterprises (SOEs) and foreign trade enterprises (FTEs) on the one hand, and joint ventures on the other.

SOEs and FTEs continue to handle the majority of Chinese exports (74 per cent) and imports (60 per cent). Within this group, the relative importance between direct exports and imports of producing SOEs, FTE transactions on behalf of SOEs, and FTE transactions on behalf of collective producing enterprises is not clear. So far, there is only a limited number of producing SOEs involved directly in foreign trade. The vast majority of the 8,771 exporting and the 6,997 importing companies in this category (Table 4.3) are FTEs, most of them registered at the provincial or municipal level. SOEs and FTEs are the only types of enterprise making a positive contribution to the balance of trade. In the first half of 1993, their exports exceeded their imports by 13 per cent.

Foreign-affiliated enterprises (FAEs) have emerged as the other major player in China's foreign trade. Customs data permit the distinction of three types of FAEs, namely fully foreign-owned firms, joint ventures between Chinese and foreign capital, and non-equity joint ventures. In non-equity joint ventures, the distribution of responsibilities, benefits and risks is done on a contractual basis and does not involve any capital participation by the foreign partner.

In terms of numbers, the 20,000 exporting FAEs, and nearly 40,000 importing FAEs, account for one-third of all enterprises entitled to export and more than 40 per cent of all importers. Their share in the national export value was at 25 per cent, and 38 per cent of imports (Table 4.4). The data clearly show that FAEs have become a major channel for exports into China. The exports of FAEs amounted to less than 60 per cent of their imports, and their combined import surplus over the first half of 1993 was equivalent to 170 per cent of China's total trade deficit.

As may be expected, the number of export and import transactions per firm is much lower for FAEs than for the combined group of SOEs and FTEs (Table 4.5). Whereas there was, on aver-

Table 4.4 Share of different types of enterprise in China's foreign trade: first half 1993

Type of enterprise	Export (%)	Imports (%)	Exports/ imports (%)
SOEs, including FTE	73.8	59.9	87.7
Non-equity JV	3.9	6.0	−28.6
Equity JV	14.4	23.5	−120.4
Fully foreign-owned firms	6.9	8.2	−22.0
Collective enterprises	0.7	0.5	1.8
Private enterprises	0.0	0.0	0.0
Other	0.4	2.0	−18.4
Sum	100.0	100.0	−100.0

Source: As for Table 4.1

Table 4.5 Foreign trade transactions by type of enterprise: first half 1993

Type of enterprise	No. of transactions		Average value of transactions		No. of transactions per firm	
			Exports	Imports		
	Exporters	Importers	(US$)	(US$)	Exporters	Importers
SOEs, including FTE	1,295,265	1,555,997	21,153	15,639	148	222
Non-equity JV	102,907	269,220	13,906	9,026	24	36
Equity JV	225,840	568,279	23,654	16,803	19	26
Fully foreign-owned firms	115,119	344,080	22,116	9,637	25	37
Collective enterprises	47,049	71,527	5,654	2,838	122	197
Private enterprises	110	196	18,182	10,204	2	4
Other	8,200	37,386	19,268	21,452	20	14
Sum/average	1,794,490	2,846,685	20,699	14,275	59	58

Source: As for Table 4.1

age, about one export and one to two import declarations per week for FAEs, FTEs handled roughly six times this volume. Against this background, it will be interesting to assess how China's FTEs can evolve into fully-fledged international trading companies by diversifying their activities in terms of provincial, product and functional coverage.

NORMAL VERSUS PROCESSING TRADE

Normal trade

Chinese customs differentiate between at least 18 different customs regimes, which basically define the applicability and level of tariffs. Normal trade – defined as trade not benefiting from any special customs regimes – does not even account for half of China's trade, but just 47 per cent of exports and 37 per cent of imports. About half of all Chinese direct exporters were declared to be involved in normal trade, and one-fifth of all importers. In terms of the number

Table 4.6 Chinese export values by customs regime: first half 1993

Code		Value (US% million)	Value distrib. (%)	No. of enter-prises	Distrib. (%)	No. of transac-tions	Distrib. (%)
10	Normal exports	17,701	47.7	15,558	51.5	749,906	41.8
11	International aid	6	0.0	38	0.1	195	0.0
13	Compensation trade	116	0.3	398	1.3	4,611	0.3
14	Contractual inward proc.	6,446	17.4	4,108	13.6	500,719	27.9
15	Other inward processing	10,827	29.1	18,221	60.3	487,068	27.1
16	Consignment	0	0.0	9	0.0	25	0.0
19	Border trade	179	0.5	397	1.3	15,788	0.9
22	Turn-key projects etc.	56	0.2	106	0.4	1,485	0.1
27	Outward processing	9	0.0	44	0.1	198	0.0
28	Entrepôt trade	69	0.2	65	0.2	583	0.0
30	Barter trade	1,637	4.4	882	2.9	31,996	1.8
39	Other	96	0.3	273	0.9	1,919	0.1
	Total	37,144	100.0	30,232	100.0	1,794,493	100.0

Source: As for Table 4.1

Table 4.7 Chinese import values by customs regime: first half 1993

Code		Value (US% million)	Value distrib. (%)	No. of enter- prises	Distrib. (%)	No. of transac- tions	Distrib. (%)
10	Normal imports	15,206	37.4	9,488	19.4	265,455	9.7
11	International aid	70	0.2	194	0.4	1,910	0.1
12	Donation by overs. Chin.	358	0.9	1,093	2.2	10,408	0.4
13	Compensation trade	115	0.3	322	0.7	2,051	0.1
14	Contractual inward proc.	5,444	13.4	4,365	8.9	1,109,946	40.5
15	Other inward processing	9,286	22.9	20,898	42.6	897,235	32.8
16	Consignments	55	0.1	72	0.1	2,195	0.1
18	Imports free of charge	85	0.2	2,953	6.0	20.408	0.7
19	Border trade	77	0.2	285	0.6	10,144	0.4
20	Equipment for inw. proc.	571	1.4	933	1.9	180,463	6.6
23	Goods on lease	399	1.0	13	0.0	31	0.0
25	Initial investment of JV	5,771	14.2	26,454	54.0	238,854	8.7
26	Inputs of JV for production for domestic market	992	2.4	1,942	4.0	27,090	1.0
27	Outward processing	12	0.0	49	0.1	266	0.0
28	Entrepôt trade	32	0.1	45	0.1	427	0.0
30	Barter trade	1,545	3.8	797	1.6	30,223	1.1
31	Foreign currency shops	240	0.6	168	0.3	7,433	0.3
39	Other	379	0.9	10,368	21.1	42,156	1.5
	Total	40,637	100.0	49,029	100.0	2,739,100	100.0

Source: As for Table 4.1. Source of discrepancy of no. of transactions with Table 4.5 not clear

of transactions, normal imports represent only 10 per cent of all import transactions (Tables 4.6 and 4.7). On the export side, the average value of normal transactions tends to be slightly above the average and the average number of transactions per firm somewhat below the average. As for imports, normal transactions were significantly below the average both in terms of value and in terms of the number of transactions per firm (Tables 4.8 and 4.9).

Table 4.8 Chinese export transactions by customs regime: first half 1993

Code	Mode of trade	Average value per enterprise (US$)	Average value per transaction (US$)	No. of transactions per firm
10	Normal exports	1,137,743	23,604	48
11	International aid	157,895	30,769	5
13	Compensation trade	291,457	25,157	12
14	Contractual inward processing	1,569,133	12,873	122
15	Other inward processing	594,204	22,229	27
16	Consignment	49,556	17,840	3
19	Border trade	450,882	11,338	40
22	Turn-key projects etc.	528,302	37,710	14
27	Outward processing	204,545	45,455	5
28	Entrepôt trade	1,061,538	118,353	9
30	Barter trade	1,856,009	51,163	36
39	Other	351,648	50,026	7
	Total	1,228,619	20,699	59

Source: As for Table 4.1

The implication is that there is a clear dual structure in China's foreign trade, between normal transactions and special transactions, which relate predominantly to processing trade. For imports, normal transactions have become the exception rather than the rule. The importance of import tariff reductions and exemptions from transactions other than normal trade may be gathered from the fact that import duties collected amounted to only 5.6 per cent of the total import value, although the trade-weighted average import tariff was at 32 per cent in 1992.[5]

The importance of transactions other than normal trade is one of the major reasons for discrepancies between China's foreign trade data and that of her partners, as well as among the various sources of Chinese trade data. It explains MOFTEC's preference for taking into account only the local value-added of processing and assembly trade rather than the contract value, as stipulated by international conventions.

Processing trade

In contrast to normal trade transactions, processing and assembling trade (code 14 in Tables 4.6–4.9) refers to directly related export

Table 4.9 Chinese import transactions by customs regime: first half 1993

Code	Mode of trade	Average value per enterprise (US$)	Average value per transaction (US$)	No. of transactions per firm
10	Normal imports	1,602,318	5,283	28
11	International aid	360,825	36,649	10
12	Donation by overseas Chinese	327,539	34,397	10
13	Compensation trade	357,143	56,070	6
14	Contractual inward processing	1,247,479	4,905	254
15	Other inward processing	444,349	10,350	43
16	Consignments	763,889	25,057	30
18	Imports free of charge	28,784	4,165	7
19	Border trade	270,175	7,591	36
20	Equipment for inward processing	612,004	3,164	193
23	Leasing	30,692,308	12,870,968	2
25	Initial investment of JV	218,152	24,161	9
26	Inputs of JV for production for domestic market	510,551	36,617	14
27	Outward processing	244,898	45,113	5
28	Entrepôt trade	711,111	74,941	9
30	Barter trade	1,937,265	51,094	38
31	Foreign currency shops	1,428,571	32,288	44
39	Other	36,555	8,991	4
	Total average	828,836	14,836	56

Source: As for Table 4.1

and import transactions, in which the imported inputs remain the property of the foreign supplier, benefiting from duty exemption on imported inputs. This type of transaction is primarily handled by FTEs on behalf of smaller manufacturing units in light industries. In economic terms, processing trade differs from normal trade in two major respects. First, local value-added of processing trade in relation to the contract value of the exported goods is quite low, with estimates ranging between 10 and 20 per cent. It follows that processing trade tends to inflate China's foreign trade turnover. Second, processing trade in many ways represents exports of China's production capacity rather than specific products, as the marketing function, including the product design and the selection of inputs, tends to be done by the foreign buyer.

If the Chinese producer or, more commonly, his foreign trade enterprise, source the direct inputs for export processing themselves, the transaction is referred to as 'other inward processing' (code 15 in Tables 4.6–4.9). This customs regime is somewhere in between processing and assembly trade and normal trade. Transactions tend to be handled by the producing companies themselves, or, alternatively, by FTEs.

A perusal of Tables 4.6–4.9 brings out the importance of contractual and other processing trade. On the export side, processing trade included 47 per cent of total exports over the first half of 1993. For imports, the corresponding value was 36 per cent. For other inward processing, the gross retained value (i.e. exports minus imports) amounted to 16 per cent of total export value; in the case of contractual inward processing it amounted to 14 per cent.

If we adopt MOFTEC's method, and consider the value-added rather than the contract value of processing and assembly trade, Chinese export figures would need to be downward-adjusted by 40 per cent and imports by 36 per cent.

The majority of directly exporting enterprises are involved in processing trade: over 22,000 out of a total of 30,232. The same applies to the number of transactions. Processing trade accounts for more than half of all export transactions.

As far as the number of importers and import transactions are concerned, the share of processing trade is equally visible. There are more than twice as many enterprises engaged in imports under processing trade as in normal import transactions, and the number of import transactions under processing trade accounts for nearly three-quarters of the total number (see Tables 4.4 and 4.6).

Export and import transactions under contractual processing are generally handled by foreign trade enterprises. This is why the 4,108 enterprises involved in exports of this type of transaction, and the 4,363 enterprises involved in imports of such transactions, realized above-average trade turnover per enterprise and registered the largest number of transactions per firm over the first half of 1993 (see Tables 4.7 and 4.8). Contractual processing appeared to be typical for the smaller production units, as the average value of these transactions was clearly below that of transactions under other processing.

Initial investment by foreign-affiliated enterprises

Initial investment of foreign-affiliated enterprises is treated as a separate customs regime as it enjoys special import tariffs. This allows us to single out this particular type of import. The results are quite surprising: up to 14 per cent of total imports entered the country under this regime. In fact, more than half of all importing enterprises were involved in this type of transaction. Imports for initial investment apparently account for one-third of total imports of the three types of foreign-affiliated firms (compare Tables 4.3 and 4.7). This confirms the significant importance of foreign-affiliated enterprises in China's foreign trade, as well as their rapid growth. To what extent it reflects overvaluation of initial investment of joint ventures, motivated by reduced import tariffs or other reasons, is impossible to examine with the present data.

Barter trade

After normal trade, processing trade and initial investment of joint ventures, barter trade is the largest customs regime, accounting for 4.4 per cent of exports and 3.8 per cent of imports. The fact that China has a slight trade surplus under this category may be related to the difficulties of partners from the Russian Federation and DPR Korea to deliver goods contracted under barter arrangements.[6] In fact, data on barter trade are very useful for examining the evolution and characteristics of trade with other economies in transition.

Other customs regimes

The classification of customs distinguishes a number of other regimes, none very important in value terms, but many nevertheless of interest. Border trade (primarily trade with Myanmar) is a case in point in the context of China's efforts to develop trade relations with its southern neighbours. Other interesting items include the exports of turn-key projects, compensation trade, goods entering the country under leasing arrangements (e.g. planes), or the foreign currency shops.

LOGISTICS OF CHINA'S FOREIGN TRADE

For many traders, the transport infrastructure represents one of the most critical bottle-necks in China's trade expansion. One may,

Table 4.10 Transit of exports and imports by province: first half 1993

	Share in national exports				Share in national imports			
Provinces/ Municipalities	By location of exporters (%)	By district of customs clearance (%)	Export transit ratio	Export transit overlap	By location of importers (%)	By district of customs clearance (%)	Import transit ratio	Import transit overlap
	1	2	(2/1)	Min of 1.2	3	4	(4/3)	Min of 3,4
Beijing	6.8	0.9	0.1	0.9	21.9	2.3	0.1	2.3
Tianjin	2.4	7.1	3.0	2.4	2.0	6.4	3.2	2.0
Hebei	.2	1.5	0.8	1.5	0.8	0.6	0.8	0.6
Shanxi	0.4	0.0	0.0	0.0	0.2	0.1	0.5	0.1
Inner Mongolia	0.6	1.0	1.7	0.6	0.6	1.1	1.8	0.6
Liaoning	6.2	8.0	1.3	6.2	3.2	4.9	1.5	3.2
Jilin	1.3	0.3	0.2	0.3	1.3	1.1	0.8	1.1
Heilongjiang	.2	1.0	0.5	1.0	1.7	1.1	0.6	1.1
Shanghai	6.3	13.5	2.1	6.3	6.4	14.3	2.2	6.4
Jiangsu	5	4.1	0.8	4.1	4.3	5.3	1.2	4.3
Zhejiang	4.3	1.8	0.4	1.8	2.1	1.8	0.9	1.8
Anhui	0.8	0.2	0.3	0.2	0.5	1.1	2.2	0.5
Fujian	5.7	3.5	0.6	3.5	4.5	4.3	1.0	4.3
Jiangxi	0.7	0.1	0.1	0.1	0.6	0.4	0.7	0.4
Shandong	4.6	4.9	1.1	4.6	3.1	4.9	1.6	3.1
Henan	0.9	0.4	0.4	0.4	0.5	0.4	0.8	0.4
Hubei	1.3	0.5	0.4	0.5	0.8	0.6	0.8	0.6
Hunan	1.2	0.3	0.3	0.3	0.6	0.5	0.8	0.5
Guangdong	41.4	48.3	1.2	41.4	39.7	43.6	1.1	39.7
Guangxi	1.1	0.9	0.8	0.9	0.9	0.9	1.0	0.9
Hainan	1.2	0.3	0.3	0.3	1.8	1.8	1.0	1.8
Sichuan	1.2	0.4	0.3	0.4	1.1	1.0	0.9	1.0
Guizhou	0.2	0.1	0.5	0.1	0.1	0.1	1.0	0.1
Yunnan	0.9	0.7	0.8	0.7	0.4	0.5	1.3	0.4
Tibet	0.1	0.0	0.0	0.0	0.0	0.0	0.0	0.0
Shaanxi	0.7	0.1	0.1	0.1	0.5	0.7	1.4	0.5
Gansu	0.2	0.1	0.5	0.1	0.2	0.1	0.5	0.1
Qinghai	0.1	—	—	0.1	0.0	—	—	0.0
Ningxia	0.1	—	—	0.1	0.0	—	—	0.0
Xinjiang	0.4	0.3	0.8	0.3	0.3	0.4	1.3	0.3
Total	100	100	1	79.2	100	100	1	78.1

Source: Statistical Department, Customs General Administration, China; ITC

indeed, ask whether a unified domestic market has in fact evolved. For the coastal provinces, the lack of efficient inland transport is certainly a factor favouring an export orientation. In this context, it would be very interesting to compare, for each province, trade with other Chinese provinces and foreign trade.

Some insight into the logistics of China's foreign trade may be gleaned from the comparison of the customs district in which trans- actions are cleared and the province where exporters and importers are located. This comparison highlights those provinces that play a role as ports of entry and exit for trade from other provinces (Table 4.10). Overall, there is a close correlation between the two series. The differences between goods cleared and goods exported or imported, at the provincial level, account for only 20 per cent of China's total trade. This points again to the weakness in the domestic transport and distribution system. China's provinces tend to trade directly with their foreign trading partners rather than channelling their exports and imports through other provinces.

Guangdong is the most important exception in this respect. It accounts not only for the largest share in exports in terms of location of exporters and customs clearance, but has also become the largest point of exit for products produced in other provinces: 7 per cent of national exports were channelled through Guangdong without being handled by firms from the province.

As far as modes of transport are concerned, maritime trade – including trade on inland waterways – accounts for half of exports and close to 60 per cent of imports (Table 4.11). Road traffic comes second, with 41 per cent on the export side and 30 per cent on the import side. The large role played by road transport is obviously

Table 4.11 Chinese trade transactions by mode of transport: first half 1993

Mode of transport	No. of exports	No. of imports	No. of total trade	Av. value exports (US$)	Av. value imports (US$)	Av. value total trade (US$)
Water	726,962	648,057	1,375,019	25,498	37,052	30,944
Rail	60,572	65,535	126,107	34,587	24,247	29,213
Road	931,718	2,010,465	2,942,183	16,217	6,094	9,300
Air	72,601	117,255	189,856	16,969	23,402	20,942
Mail	2,528	3,724	6,252	5,538	2,685	3,839
Other	112	1,652	1,764	1,401,786	18,765	106,576
All	1,794,493	2,846,688	4,641,181	20,699	14,275	16,759

Source: Statistical Department, Customs General Administration, China; ITC

Table 4.12 Chinese trade value by mode of transport: first half 1993

Mode of transport	Value exports (US$ million)	Value imports (US$ million)	Total trade (US$ million)	Share in exports (%)	Share in imports (%)	Share in total trade (%)
Water	18,536	24,012	42,548	49.9	59.1	54.7
Rail	2,095	1,589	3,684	5.6	3.9	4.7
Road	15,110	12,251	27,361	40.7	30.1	35.2
Air	1,232	2,744	3,976	3.3	6.8	5.1
Mail	14	10	24	0.0	0.0	0.0
Other	157	31	188	0.4	0.1	0.2
All	37,144	40,637	77,781	100.0	100.0	100.0

Source: As for Table 4.11

related to the role of Hong Kong as China's first trade partner. In fact, more than half of all trade transactions are transported by road, and the average value of export and import transactions is significantly lower for export and import consignments transported by road than for the other modes of transport (excluding mail) (Table 4.12). These data bear witness to the emergence of a closely-knit tissue of business and trade links between Hong Kong and the neighbouring Chinese provinces.

Rail and air each account for about 5 per cent of total trade value. It will be interesting to analyse how the importance of these two modes of transport will evolve, as Chinese producers diversify into higher value-added products depending to a larger extent on air transport, and as rail links with north-east Asian neighbours improve. Other modes of transport include pipelines for water (e.g. Hong Kong) and oil as well as the transmission of electricity.

CONCLUSIONS

The institutional structure of China's foreign trade has come a long way since a dozen foreign trade enterprises monopolized exports and imports in the early 1980s. Trade values have shown double-digit growth rates since the opening-up of the economy, and the number of firms directly involved in exports and imports has recorded triple-digit growth. Moreover, all indicators point to a continuation of this trend. A growing portion of the more than 20 million township and village enterprises, for instance, are likely to join the waiting list for admission to the exclusive club of direct exporters and importers.

The present institutional structure of China's foreign trade is certainly two-faced, if not multifaceted.

On the one hand, the 'normal' trade does not benefit from any special tariff or locational incentives, and shows the traditional division of labour between producers and foreign trade enterprises: the import requirements and export marketing of several millions of locally owned and managed producing firms are handled through the growing number of foreign trade enterprises, of which there were some 8,000 involved in exports and some 6,000 involved in imports (see Tables 4.3, 4.6 and 4.7). In addition, some 7,000 foreign-affiliated companies contribute to normal exports, and some 2,000 foreign-affiliated firms to normal imports. Normal trade accounts for about half of total exports and 37 per cent of imports. Its rapid development since 1978 has been quantitative rather than qualitative.

On the other hand, there is the processing trade, which refers to directly related export and import transactions benefiting from special duty exemptions on imported inputs. This accounts for the other half of China's gross export value and for slightly more than one-third of total imports. Joint ventures account for half of all processing trade, at most, but probably less. Processing trade is mainly done by local producers in collaboration with foreign trade enterprises. A large share of processing trade takes place in Guangdong, the province that alone accounts for about 40 per cent of China's foreign trade. Net exports (i.e. exports minus imports) – as indicator for local value-added or retained value – are estimated at between 15 and 20 per cent of gross exports. If foreign trade were to be calculated on the basis of net rather than gross exports and imports, Chinese export figures would need to be downward-adjusted by 40 per cent and imports by 36 per cent.

The shake-out from the rush on China is some 40,000 joint ventures importing directly into China and some 20,000 on the export side. The discrepancy is, of course, not incidental. Joint ventures have become the leading avenue for exports into China. As much as 38 per cent of all Chinese imports were handled by contractual and equity joint ventures. The number of joint ventures which are basically marketing affiliates is rapidly increasing. Exports of foreign-affiliated enterprises amounted to less than 60 per cent of their imports, and their combined import surplus over the first half of 1993 was equivalent to 170 per cent of China's total trade deficit (see Tables 4.3, 4.4 and 4.5).

Barter, border and compensation trade, typical of old-style socialist countries, has fallen back to marginal importance. In fact, barter trade remains alive only as a second-best way of maintaining trade with neighbouring countries short of foreign exchange, and border trade consists primarily of trade with Burma.

China's foreign trade expansion has clearly exacerbated existing economic imbalances among China's provinces. Total exports and imports, trade per capita and the number of traders all varied significantly more among provinces than GNP and GNP per capita. The large variation is not only the result of the special role of Guangdong in foreign trade. While Guangdong is exceptional in terms of its contribution to exports and imports and the number of exporters and importers, it is less so in terms of per capita trade and quite average in terms of average export and import values per firm (see Tables 4.1, 4.2 and 4.3). In the same line of argument, concentration among exporters and importers is not very pronounced – in keeping with the declining concentration in the product structure of China's foreign trade.

Notwithstanding the watershed between normal and processing trade, there remains a clear egalitarian touch in the portrait of Chinese exporters and importers. Further differentiation and concomitant productivity gains in international trading are bound to come. In sum, the pilot analysis suggests that there is still a long way to go. China's past experience with foreign trade may only be a taste of what is likely to come in the future.

APPENDIX 4.1

PROPOSED OUTPUTS OF CUSTOMS DATA ANALYSIS

Survey of China's Exporters and Importers (annual publication)

This survey will present basic data on Chinese exporters and importers for each province of China, for all Special Economic Zones and for all Economic and Technical Development Areas by major product groups. In addition to quantitative data, each category will include names and addresses of the leading exporters and importers. The basic marketing data of this survey will be particularly useful to foreign enterprises interested in trading with China, and for Chinese exporters and importers. Approximate length: 200 pages. It will appear in an English and a Chinese version. At a later stage, this survey could be prepared in machine-readable form such as diskette, CD-ROMs or on-line database.

Benchmark Survey of China's Foreign Trade

The Benchmark Survey will summarize the results of an in-depth analysis of China's foreign trade on the basis of customs statistics. It will focus on the following areas: concentration of China's foreign trade by enterprises, provinces, products and partner countries/regions; performance profile of new and small traders, joint ventures, state-owned companies, etc.; logistics of China's foreign trade; product and market diversification of different types of enterprises; characteristics of processing trade, barter and compensation trade and other special trade regimes, discrepancies in trade reported by China and its partner countries, etc. This survey will provide analytical support for trade promotion and trade policy as well as for marketing. It should appear in an English and a Chinese version.

NOTES

1 Disregarding Hong Kong's re-exports of US$89 billion in 1992 for the ranking.
2 China's 1992 share in imports of the leading trading nations was 43 per cent for travel goods (SITC 8219), 64 per cent for umbrellas (SITC 8994), 39 per cent for toys (SITC 8942), 45 per cent for portable radio receivers (SITC 7622), 27 per cent for footwear (SITC 8510) and between 20 and 30 per cent for many items of clothing (SITC 84). Source: ITC calculations based on COMTRADE data of the United Nations Statistical Office.
3 See *Trade Data Analysis at Enterprise Level for Trade Promotion*, ITC/007/B1/91-I, Geneva 1991 and *Foreign trade statistics: A guide to their use in market research*, ITC/161/B3/92-IV, Geneva 1992.
4 See 'China Survey', *The Economist*, 28 November 1992: 15.
5 See World Bank (1993), *China, Foreign Trade Reform: Meeting the Challenge of the 1990s*, 18 June: xiv.
6 See, for instance, 'Trade in Continental North-East Asia, Product Patterns and Issues for Trade Promotion', International Trade Centre UNCTAD/GATT Research Paper No. 3, ITC/185/A1/93-VII-TP, Geneva.

5 Foreign direct investment from the People's Republic of China

Tseng Choosin

GENERAL BACKGROUND

Foreign direct investment in the People's Republic of China (PRC) is on the increase following the implementation of the open-door policy in 1978, and the establishment of the four Special Economic Zones (Xiamen, Shantou, Shenzhen and Zuhhai), supplemented in 1984 by the opening of 14 coastal cities, namely Dalian, Qinhuang-dao, Tianjin, Yantai, Qingtao, Lianyungang, Nantong, Shanghai, Ningbo, Wenzhou, Fuzhou, Guangzhou, Zhanjiang and Baihai. (Hainan Island was added to the list in 1988 as the fifth SEZ.) Up to December 1992, the total cumulative contracted investment in China has been estimated at about US$114 billion (*Business China* 13 July 1992: 101; and 28 June 1993: 4).

According to statistics from the Ministry of Foreign Economic Relations and Trade (MOFERT)[1] the leading investment sites in the PRC based on the cumulative contracted investment are as shown in Table 5.1.

But the open-door policy also provides the opportunity for PRC enterprises to expand overseas. According to 1992 MOFERT statistics, by the end of 1992, China had set up 1,363 non-trading enterprises in more than 120 countries other than Hong Kong, including the United States, Australia, Thailand, Indonesia, South America

Table 5.1 Cumulative contracted FDI in China's four leading investment sites

Investment sites	Contracted investment (US$ billion)
Guangdong	20.25
Fujian	4.91
Shanghai	3.46
Beijing	2.24

and the former USSR. The total contracted outward direct investment in non-trading activities was US$3.5 billion, of which China
contributed US$1.58 billion. China has also set up 1,053 trading
firms overseas. China's total investment in trading activities is
US$260 million (*International Economic & Trading News*, Beijing,
9 March 1993)

China's (MOFERT) statistics on overseas outwards investment
are classified into two main types: trading and non-trading. For non-
trading, it is further classified into two types: production and
services. Production comprises both manufacturing and 'extractor'
industries (mining, forestry and fishing), while 'services' covers the
banking, consultancy and restauration industries.

SOURCES OF INVESTMENT FROM DIFFERENT PROVINCES/CITIES

As for sources of investment from different provinces/cities, a survey
carried out by Ye Gang (Ye Gang 1990; Ye Gang and Deng Qinmin
1990) ranks Fujian province first in terms of value of investment.
At the beginning of 1989, there were 190 overseas subsidiaries from
Fujian province. Total investment amounted to US$100 million, of
which PRC enterprises contributed US$60 million. Shanghai ranked
second, with 46 overseas subsidiaries and a total investment of
US$52 million, of which PRC enterprises contributed US$25.32
million.

However, during the course of the study it was discovered that
the top-ranking province in terms of value of overseas investment
was in fact Guangdong. Officials of the Guangdong Commission on
the Foreign Economic Relations and Trade are reluctant to reveal
the actual figures and mentioned only that there were more than
400 overseas enterprises originating from the province. They were
afraid that central government may close down some of the Guang-
don's enterprises overseas if the figure appeared too big. As Professor Ezra F. Vogel of Harvard University, a specialist in Modern
Japan and China has said, Guangdong outwardly appears to be
listening to central government, but in fact does things its own way,
unbeknown to Beijing (Li and Fung Public Lectures: the Reintegration of Hong Kong and the Guangdong Economy, 4 April 1991,
Hong Kong). An unknown number of enterprises from Guangdong
have also set up overseas without going through the proper channels.
The author managed to obtain some figures from three cities in
Guangdong Province, namely Shenzhen and Zhuhai, and the capital

Guangzhou. By the end of November 1991, Shenzhen had set up 85 overseas enterprises with a total contracted investment of US$70 million, of which PRC enterprises contributed US$30 million; Guangzhou had set up 96 overseas enterprises with total contracted investment of US$30 million, of which PRC enterprises contributed US$16 million; and Zhuhai set up more than 70 overseas enterprises with total contracted investment of US$15 million, of which PRC enterprises contributed US$6 million. The total investment from the above three cities was around US$115 million, of which PRC enterprises contributed US$50 million. We understand that enterprises under the control of the Guangdong Provincial Government have invested in some big overseas projects. The other SEZ studied, Shantou in Guangdong Province, also has substantial investment overseas. In addition to the above, there were a number of 'unauthorized' investments overseas. We can deduce that the total contracted overseas outward investment from Guangdong was around US$200 million, with PRC enterprises contributing about US$120 million.

Besides Guangdong, Fujian and Shanghai, who are the top overseas investors, the other coastal provinces (or cities situated in these provinces) account for the majority of the remaining investment (see Figure 5.1).

Zhejiang

Zhejiang Province began setting up overseas non-trade enterprises in 1982. Up to 1991, there were 29 overseas production enterprises approved by the Zhejiang Provincial Government. Total contracted investment is US$92.13 million. The enterprises are spread over Japan, the United Arab Emirates, Thailand, Canada, Australia and New Zealand, and include light industries, arts and crafts, electronics, machinery, chemicals, medicine, agriculture and catering. At the end of 1991, 17 overseas enterprises were in business (China internal references 1992).

Nanjing

By June 1993, 38 overseas enterprises had been set up from Nanjing, ranging from electronics, machinery and agriculture to catering and foodstuffs. In addition to big state enterprises (such as the detergent plant set up by Jinling Petrochemical Corp in Yamer in 1985), small township and district enterprises have also set up plants overseas.

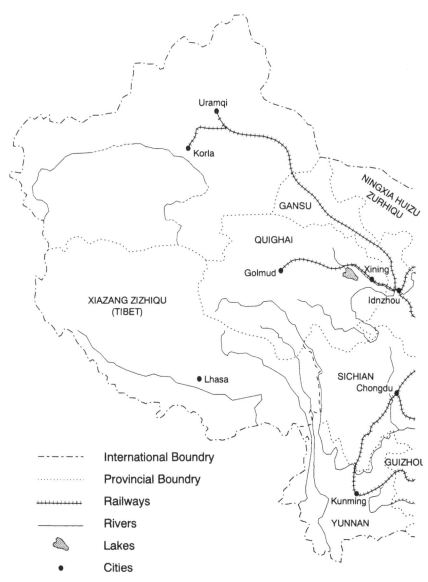

Figure 5.1 People's Republic of China

For example, one district enterprise has set up a bean curd[2] manufacturing plant in Madagascar (*Min Po*, Hong Kong, 10 July 93).

Tianjin

During the first six months of 1992, Tianjin approved 15 overseas enterprises, more than half of which are in the former Soviet Union. By June 1992, Tianjin had set up 116 overseas enterprises. Total contracted investment is US$35.78 million. The enterprises are located in the United States, Japan, England, Australia, Thailand, the former Soviet Union and Hong Kong. Of the 116 enterprises, 98 are now in operation. Most of the enterprises have shown good performance, and six have already repaid their investment (*Wen Wei Po*, Hong Kong, 25 August 1992). The Tianjin Commission for Foreign Economic Relations and Trade also announced plans to encourage enterprises to invest overseas. These include simplifying the approval procedure for enterprises seeking to invest in Laos, eastern Europe, the former Soviet Union and Vietnam. Enterprises can carry out field surveys in these countries without prior registration with the commission. (*Wen Wei Po* 25 August 1992)

Liaoning

By the end of 1991, Liaoning had set up 61 overseas non-trade enterprises, with total investment of US$48.93 million. Before 1987, there were only 17 non-trade enterprises from Liaoning Province. After 1988, overseas investment increased, and by 1994 44 non-trade enterprises were established in the US, Europe and Africa. Of these, 39 were mainly in light industry, textiles, chemicals, electronics, information development and advanced value-added processing. High technology production enterprises are planned for the United States and Japan (*Hong Kong Economic Journal* 11 March 1992).

In addition to the coastal provinces, inner provinces have also set up or plan to set up overseas enterprises. For example: a cotton mill in Xian, capital city of Shanxi, has acquired a garment factory in Mauritius; Hubei Province is also planning to set up overseas enterprises in Europe, America and south-east Asia. The plans include a joint venture motor vehicle spare-parts manufacturing plant in north America, a petroleum cracking plant that involved more than US$100 million, a textile plant (with an investment of rmb25 million) in Cambodia, and chemical plants with investment of more than

US$30 million in Malaysia and Vietnam (*Wen Wei Po* 11 March 1992)

PRC INVESTMENT OVERSEAS

Outward direct investment by PRC enterprises started in 1979 and may be classified into three stages.

Stage I: from 1979 to end 1985

During this period only state-owned import and export cooperations under MOFERT and provincial and municipal international economic and technological cooperation enterprises under the Commission of Foreign Economic Relations and Trade were eligible to invest overseas. The PRC set up 185 non-trading enterprises, mostly in the form of joint ventures, with total contracted investment amounting to US$249 million, of which US$154 million were invested by PRC. These overseas subsidiaries covered 45 countries and/or regions, mostly in the developing world. The businesses were mainly in catering, engineering, finance/insurance and consultancy. Very few overseas enterprises were engaged in manufacturing activities.

Stage II: from 1985 to end 1990

In 1985, MOFERT issued a new directive allowing legal enterprises possessed of sufficient capital as well technical and operational know-how, and with a suitable partner overseas, to be considered for permission to set up a subsidiary or subsidiaries overseas.

During this period, 577 PRC non-trading overseas enterprises were set up – more than three times the number set up during Stage I. Total contracted investment is US$2.3 billion, of which PRC enterprises contributed US$1 billion (respectively 7.9 and 5.9 times more than in Stage I). The overseas enterprises now cover more than 90 countries and/or regions including the United States, Thailand, Australia and the former USSR (many are developed countries). The businesses include metallurgy/minerals, petro-chemicals/chemicals, electronics/light industry, transportation, finance/insurance, medicine and tourism (*Wen Wei Po* 14 December 1990). Because of the new directive issued by MOFERT, parent enterprises have become more numerous and more diverse. In addition to the state-owned import and export corporations and provincial and municipal

'International Economic and Technological Co-operation' enterprises, the parent companies now include manufacturing (many enterprises in China carry out only production functions and have no authority to export their final product or import raw materials) and even a research institute.

One significant characteristic of this period was the emergence of a number of big transnational corporations such as the China National Metals and Minerals Import and Export Corporation, which has established 49 companies, joint ventures and representative offices in 23 countries and regions including Hong Kong, Japan, the United Kingdom, Germany, United States, Brazil and Australia. The current annual business turn-over is US$7 billion, of which US$2.6 billion is from overseas transactions (*China Daily* 17 December 1990). A second example is the China National Chemical Import and Export Corporation (Sinochem), which has 62 overseas subsidiaries in Asia, Europe, the United States and Australia. The annual turn-over in 1989 was US$12.8 billion of which US$4.832 billion was from overseas subsidiaries (*Foreign Economies & Management* December 1990: 45).

Stage III: from 1991 to the present

Since the beginning of the 1990s, PRC investment overseas has seen a drastic increase both in terms of the number of subsidiaries and the amount of investment. For the year 1991, 207 overseas non-trading subsidiaries were set up. Total contracted investment was US$759 million, of which PRC enterprises contributed US$367 million. The overseas enterprises now covered more than 100 countries (MOFERT statistics). For the year of 1992, 305 overseas non-trading subsidiaries were set up. Total contracted investment was US$352 million, of which PRC enterprises contributed US$195 million. The overseas enterprises were now spread over more than 120 countries (*International Economic & Trading News* 9 March 1993). The Chinese government set great store by its multinational corporations, and seminars were organized by MOFERT and various academics to discuss ways to improve their operations. Yuan Mu, Director of the Office of Policy Research of the State Council, urged enterprises to expand overseas to meet the 'World Challenge of Economic and Technical Development' (*HK Economic Times* 12 September 1992). Premier Li Peng also urged state-owned large and medium-sized enterprises to expand into international markets and to strengthen themselves during the process. He further stressed the importance of exploring the many opportunities afforded by the international markets (*Economic Report* 25 November 1991). Deng Xiaoping visited Guangdong in January 1992 and called for faster and further development of the export-oriented economy, especially for the SEZs (*Bauhinia Magazine* March 1992). In March 1992, the Mayor of Shenzhen also responded to Deng's speech and asked some 80 or more overseas enterprises from Shenzhen to meet new performance targets in the year to come. The Director of Foreign Economic Relations and Trade in Foshan, a municipality in the Pearl River Delta area of Guangdong province, also encouraged enterprises with the necessary resources and capabilities to set up manufacturing bases overseas, to avoid discriminatory import measures imposed by the host government (*Wen Wei Po* 14 March 1992). Relevant authorities from other provinces, and from municipalities such as Liaoning, Hubei and Xiamen, expressed their intention to further increase their FDI (*Hong Kong Economic Journal* 23 March 1992; *Wen Wei Po* 11 March 1992; *Xiamen Daily* 27 November 1991).

At the Fourteenth National Congress of the Communist Party, held in Beijing on 12 October 1992, Jiang Zemin, general secretary of the Central Committee of the Party, clearly promised in his report 'to open wider to the outside world and make more and better use of foreign funds, resources, technology and management expertise and to encourage enterprises to expand abroad, as well as trans-national operations' (*Beijing Review* 26 October–1 November 1992: 20). All of these factors encouraged PRC enterprises to invest overseas.

Official figures for China's FDI for the first six months of 1993 are not available at the time of writing, but it is widely acknowledged to be on the increase, as demonstrated by the following statistics obtained during the author's visit to Shanghai in August 1993. By the end of July 1993, the cumulative number of non-trade overseas subsidiaries set up by Shanghai enterprises was 164, with total cumulative contracted investment of US$14 million. The number of non-trade overseas enterprises set up during the first seven months of 1993, and the whole of 1992, is equal to the number of overseas enterprises set up during the past 11 years (*Xinmin Wanpao* 15 August 1993: 1).

Jiansu, an important province in China, whose industrial output value is the highest of all China's provinces, has set up 300 non-trade enterprises in more than 50 countries, half of which were established in 1993 alone. Total contracted investment is US$130

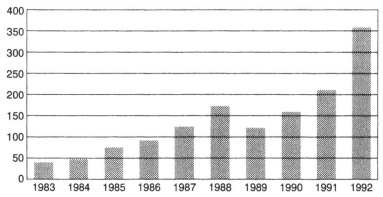

Figure 5.2 Number of non-trade PRC firms established abroad: 1983–92
Source: MOFERT

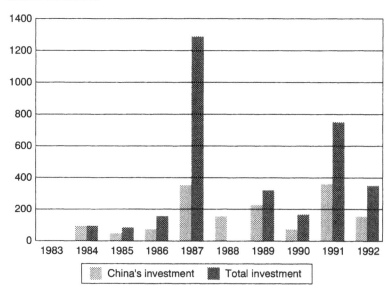

Figure 5.3 PRC outward direct investment in non-trading activities:
1983–92
Source: MOFERT

million (*Wen Wei Po* 9 August 1993). China's FDI in non-trading
activities from 1983–92, in terms of both the number of overseas
enterprises set up and the investment values (i.e. total contacted
investment and investment contributed by PRC enterprises), is
shown in Figures 5.2 and 5.3 respectively. The total contracted
investment value, and the value of investments contributed by PRC's

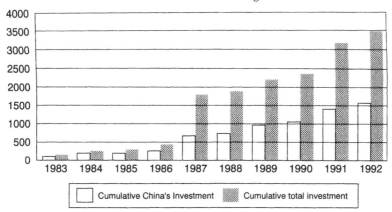

Figure 5.4 PRC cumulative outward direct investment in non-trade firms: 1983–92
Source: MOFERT

enterprises, from 1983–92 are compared in Figure 5.3. Cumulative investment values (i.e. cumulative total investment, and cumulative Chinese investment) from 1983–92 are shown in Figure 5.4.

PRC INVESTMENT IN HONG KONG

According to 1990 MOFERT statistics, by December 1990, the PRC had set up 764 non-trading overseas enterprises, mostly in the form of joint ventures. Total contracted investment was US$2.3 billion, of which PRC enterprises contributed US$1 billion. The overseas enterprises covered 90 countries/regions, including Hong Kong/Macau, the United States, Thailand, Australia and the former USSR. In terms of the number of overseas enterprises, Hong Kong/Macau was top of the list. The above figures include PRC investment in the Hong Kong/Macau region (*Wen Wei Po* 14 December 1990).

However, according to the *Far Eastern Economic Review* (23 June 1988), up to that date, the PRC's cumulative direct investment in Hong Kong alone could be estimated at US$10 billion. The corresponding cumulative total for Japan was US$8 billion and for the United States US$7 billion. At that time, the number of enterprises with PRC capital was estimated at about 3,000. After several crackdowns by the PRC government, this number has been greatly reduced. The Hong Kong Chinese Enterprises Association was set up in April 1992 initiated by China Resources, the Bank of China Group, China Travel and China Merchant. Membership is open to only 'genuine' PRC enterprises in Hong Kong (enterprises with proper approval from the relevant authorities in China and registered with MOFERT) and up to March 1992, 955 PRC enterprises had joined (*The Hong Kong Chinese Enterprises Association* 1992: 5).

According to 1992 MOFERT statistics, there are 1,701 enterprises with PRC capital in Hong Kong. The author was told by one MOFERT officer that this figure is updated from the HK Chinese Enterprises Association membership directory. The exact number of PRC enterprises in Hong Kong and the total investment values are, then, not known. It is estimated that the investment value totals from US$12–20 billion (*Hang Seng Economic Monthly* October 1993).

According to 1991 MOFERT statistics up to September 1991, the PRC has set up 927 non-trading overseas enterprises. Total contracted investment is US$2.8 billion of which PRC enterprises contributed US$1.37 billion. The overseas enterprises covered 101 countries. (*International Business Daily*, Beijing, 2 November, 1991)

It is interesting to note that 1991 and 1992 MOFERT statistics on PRC outward investment (mentioned at the beginning of this article) exclude Hong Kong and Macau. This is because some PRC enterprises remit funds to Hong Kong through other unofficial channels and MOFERT is therefore unable to obtain accurate figures.

Historical development

The development of PRC enterprises in Hong Kong can be divided into three periods. The first period is from 1949 to 1978; the second is from 1979 to 1991 and the third is from 1992 to the present.

First period: 1949–78

The first generation of enterprises in Hong Kong was set up before the Communist Party took over China in 1949. Among them were the China Resources Co., the China Merchants Steam Navigation Co. and the Hong Kong branches of the Bank of China. Since the establishment of diplomatic relations between the new China and Britain in 1950, these enterprises have been owned by the PRC government. Some private enterprises such as Tien Chu Ve-Tsin Chemical Industries and Nanyang Brothers Tobacco Company Ltd were also owned by the PRC government because their parent companies in China were transformed from private status to public–private cooperatives and finally to state enterprises.

From 1949 to 1978, and especially after 1956 when reforms to the foreign trade system were complete, a Soviet-style centralized foreign trade system emerged. The PRC enterprises in Hong Kong, reporting to their respective ministries in China, carried out very specific and monopolistic business functions, e.g. the so-called 'four heavenly kings', namely the China Resources Co., the China Merchants Steam Navigation Co., the Hong Kong branches of Bank of China, and China Travel (Table 5.2).

During this period, these traditional Chinese enterprises were dominant among PRC firms in Hong Kong. Only a few new PRC enterprises were set up, such as the Po Sang Bank Ltd (1964) and the Hua Chiao Commercial Bank (1965).

It is interesting to note that Fujian (1975) and Tianjin (1976) set up overseas enterprises in Hong Kong during this period. The

Table 5.2 Four leading PRC enterprises in Hong Kong and their reporting ministries

Name	Reporting ministries	Core business(es)
China Resources	MOFERT*	Sole agent of China import & export corporations in Hong Kong specialized in import & distribution of fresh, live and frozen foodstuffs, grains, edible oil and textile, light industrial products, export essential materials & equipment for China reconstruction.
China Merchants Steam Navigation Co.	Ministry of Communication	Concentrated on shipping between mainland China & Hong Kong.
China Travel	Overseas Chinese office, state council	Travel related business for overseas Chinese visiting China.
Hong Kong branches of Bank of China	People's Bank of China	Concentrated on foreign exchange activities in various aspects of foreign trade as well as acceptance of remittance by Hong Kong Chinese.

Source: Thomas M.H. Chan (ed.) *Directory of Companies with PRC Capital in Hong Kong*, Hong Kong: CERD Consultants
Note * Now MOFTEC

setting up of these enterprises broke the monopoly of foreign trade held for many years by China Resources.

Second period: 1979–91

In December 1978, when Deng Xiaoping and his supporters gained power during the Third Plenum of the Eleventh Central Committee of the Communist Party of China (CPC), economic reform and the open-door policy were implemented in order to achieve the so-called 'Four Modernizations' by the year 2000. This allowed the state council, ministries, provinces and municipalities (even in Tibet) to set up enterprises in Hong Kong. Their aims in so doing were clear:

- To expand foreign trade.
- To attract foreign capital and technology and to seek out potential business partners to invest in China.
- To obtain market information and familiarize themselves with Western management practice.
- To perform business exercises in trading, shipping and finance (including raising debt and equity capital).

The names of some of the most important enterprises, and their date of registration in Hong Kong are given in Table 5.3

The first-generation PRC enterprises in Hong Kong have had to adapt, and now also seek to attract foreign capital and technology and potential partners to invest in China. In addition, they need to obtain market information, familiarize themselves with Western management practice and respond to competition from their sister organizations from the PRC provinces and municipalities. They have had to restructure their organizations and adopt new business strategies. In the case of China Resources Ltd, each individual department became a strategic business unit responsible for specific operations such as shipping, transportation, warehousing and retailing, or a specific product such as light industrial products, food etc. and its profitability. A holding company, China Resources (Holdings) Co. Ltd, was thus formed in July 1983. The company also became horizontally integrated, began operating several supermarkets and emporia and engaged in industrial production, such as investing in canned products via a joint venture with NamSoon. In 1984, it also formed a subsidiary called Sun Keng Enterprises Co., with the Bank of China Group, to purchase a 34.8 per cent share of Conic Electronics (*Hong Kong Economic Daily* 22 January 1984).

Table 5.3 Major PRC enterprises registering in Hong Kong: 1979–86

Company name	Identification	Date established
China International Trust & Investment Corporation HK Ltd [CITIC (HK) Ltd]	Directly under state council core business in investment & trade.	14–5–1985
China Everbright Holding Co. Ltd	Directly under state council. Specialize in trading, investment (include properties, securities, manufacturing concerns).	10–5–1983
Guangdong Enterprises (Holdings) Ltd	Under Guangdong provincial government. Acting as the sole agent in Hong Kong of all the economic organizations and foreign trade enterprise of Guangdong Province. Specialize in trading, technical imports, banking and finance, house construction, insurance, tourism, transportation, packaging and advertising.	Spring 1981
Fujian Enterprises (Holdings) Co. Ltd	Under Fujian provincial government. Sole agent in Hong Kong of all the economic organizations and foreign trade enterprise of Fujian Province. Core businesses include trading, finance, construction, insurance, tourism, advertisement, manufacturing etc. One of its subsidiaries, C.C. Toys (HK) Co. Ltd, is planned to be listed in Hong Kong Stock Exchange by end of 1994.	26–9–1980
China Liaoning Ltd	Directly under Liaoning government. Core businesses is import and export trade business of Liaoning.	20–9–1985
Henan Hong Kong Enterprises Ltd	Directly under Henan government. Core business is import & export trade business of Henan.	23–8–1985
Zhejiang Fuchuen Co. Ltd	Directly under Zhejiang government. Specialize in import/ export trading. Introduction of foreign capital, advanced technology & equipment, tourism transportation, shipping & shipping agency, international & Chinese investment.	18–8–1986
Hunan Trading Co. Ltd	Under government of Hunan Province. Carry out import & export trade business of Hunan.	2–7–1985

Table 5.3 Continued

Company name	Identification	Date established
China Shandong Co. Ltd	Under government of Shandong Province. Specialize in import & export business of Shandong Province.	4–10–1985
Yue Xiu Enterprises Ltd	Under municipal government of Guangzhou. Specialize in import & export trade business of Guangzhou.	28–12–1984
Shanghai Industrial Investment Co. Ltd	Under municipal government of Shanghai. Import & export trade business of Shanghai. Tourism, investment.	17–7–1981
Shum Yip (SZ) Trading Co. Ltd	Under municipal government of Shenzhen. Import & export trade business of Shenzhen.	27–5–1983
Zhuhai International Ltd	Under municipal government of Zhuhai. Specialize in import & export business, contractual manufacturing or compensation trading; joint venture or contractual cooperation of industrial projects, etc.	12–1–1985
Scriver Trading Ltd	Under municipal government of Beijing. Specialize in import & export business of Beijing.	1–6–1979

The purchase was thwarted and the company suffered big losses for several years, showing a profit again only in 1991 ('Target' intelligence report, vol. 26, 6 July 1988; *Wen Wei Po* 8 February 1992). In August 1992 China Resources Holdings increased its stake in Winland Investment Ltd from 26.4 per cent to 33 per cent, and renamed itself China Resource.

The Hong Kong branches of the Bank of China also carried out horizontal integration with Hong Kong's 12 other PRC banks (namely, Communication, Nanyang Commercial, Kwangtuong Provincial, Sin Hua, China and South Sea, Kincheng, China State, National Commercial, Yien Yieh, Po Sang, Hua Chiao and Chiyu), forming the Bank of China Group. Detailed information about the Bank of China Group is given in Table 5.4. The Group expanded and diversified the business from foreign exchange activities to direct borrowing, syndicated loans, and involvement in industrial projects. The Group also engages in leasing, introduction of foreign capital and technology and real estate, and even invests in industrial and

Table 5.4 Information about the Bank of China Group

Bank	Place of registration	No. of HK branches	Total assets (in billions)	Ownership
1. BOC	Beijing	23	12,151.0	PRC
2. Communication	Beijing	26	1,110.4	People's Bank of China
3. Nanyang Commercial	Hong Kong	39	414.2	Partly owned by BOC
4. Kwangtung Provincial	Beijing	23	415.3	40% owned by PRC
5. Sin Hua	Beijing	42	495.0	BOC
6. China and South Sea	Beijing	20	272.1	BOC
7. Kincheng	Beijing	27	479.7	BOC
8. China State	Beijing	19	246.0	BOC
9. National Commercial	Beijing	21	300.0	BOC
10. Yien Yieh	Beijing	21	208.1	BOC
11. Po Sang	Hong Kong	11	488.0	Partly owned by BOC
12. Hua Chiao	Hong Kong	22	220.4	Partly owned by BOC
13. Chiyu	Hong Kong	16	136.6	Partly owned by BOC
Total		310	16,936.8	

Source: Forbes 8 May 1992

infrastructure projects in mainland China. For example, during the recent visit of the Governor of Jiansxi province to Hong Kong, the Bank of China Group agreed to invest US$130 million in a power station, a ceramics factory and a bridge in the province (*Tai Kong Pao* 21 May 1992).

The Group is the second largest bank in Hong Kong. The business operations of the Group have also made tremendous progress. From 1979 and 1990, group deposits increased almost nineteenfold, loans almost twenty-fivefold, and total asset value by nearly thirty-seven-fold. Business volume increased some 84.3 times, and the number of branches and sub-branches by 1.2 times. The number of employees also, of course, increased, nearly doubling (*Bank of China Group Report* 1990).

China Merchants Ltd also expanded its shipping-related businesses to transportation, shipbuilding and repairing, hotels, manufacturing, infrastructure (such as a wharf and terminals in Hong Kong, and the development and construction of the Shekou industrial zone) and retail businesses (a duty-free shop in Hong Kong airport). It became a holding company – China Merchants Holdings Co. Ltd. (CMH) – in 1985. CMH purchased the Union Bank of Hong Kong in June 1986 through Modern Concepts Ltd, whose shares are predominantly held by CMH. In April 1987, CMH established the first corporate bank in China. In May 1988, the first corporate insurance company in China – Ping An Insurance Company – started business in Shekou with CMH as one of its investors; in August of the same year, CMH successfully completed its purchase of a British insurance company, a British insurance broker and a Hong Kong-based insurance company, from Orient Overseas (Holdings) Ltd. Consequently, finance and insurance have now become an important and indispensable part of CMH (*China Merchants Holding Report* 1991). The China Merchants Bank will soon set up its representative office in Hong Kong and will be upgraded to a full licensed bank by 1997 (*Min Pao* 18 April 1992).

PRC investment in the HK manufacturing sector

According to the statistics from the Hong Kong Industry Department's report, by 1990, PRC investment in manufacturing industry in Hong Kong amounted to HK$330 million. PRC is the third largest investor in Hong Kong after Japan and the United States. There are 40 manufacturing concerns in the colony with PRC capital. Most of the investments were carried out after 1985 (before 1985, there were only 13 manufacturing concerns with PRC capital in Hong Kong). Of the 40 manufacturing concerns only 25 per cent are wholly owned, with the remaining 70 per cent operated as joint ventures with Hong Kong investors; 5 per cent are joint ventures with foreign capital. This is very different from Japanese and US investment in Hong Kong's manufacturing sector. Clearly, PRC firms invest in the hope of learning production and management skills (*Hong Kong Industry Department Report* 1990 and *Economic Reporter* 2264). In January 1994, during a land lease-signing ceremony in Hong Kong, Shanzhen Electronic Group (SEG) announced that the company, with foreign and Hong Kong partners, would be investing HK$230 million to manufacture special-use integrated circuits. This is a capital-intensive advanced technology project, motivated by the desire to acquire new technology (*Hong Kong Economic Times* 4 January 1992).

Public listing on the Hong Kong Stock Exchange by companies with PRC capital

In order to learn how to raise equity capital through financial markets, PRC enterprises also seek public listing either through acquisitions or new listings.

The first case is the acquisition of Conic Electronics by Sun Keng Enterprises Company, owned by China Resources and the Bank of China Group, in 1984. The acquisition was a bitter experience, as mentioned before. The main motive for the acquisition of Ka Wah Bank in April 1986 by CITIC (HK) Ltd, and of the Union Bank by China Merchants Holdings Ltd in June 1986, was to help the Hong Kong government to restore the stability of the colony's financial system.

In 1987, Guangdong Enterprises (Holdings) Ltd, through one of its 100 per cent-owned subsidiaries (Winland Investment) acquired a listed company, Union Globe. The New Cathay Hotel was then injected into the listed company in exchange for new shares. The listed company then changed its name to Guangdong Investment.

Fujian Investment Ltd, a financial company from Fujian Province, set up a joint-venture bank, the Xiamen International Bank, in Xiamen Special Economic Zone, with Pan India International Finance Co. Ltd. (PANIN), a listed company in Hong Kong. However, when PANIN suffered great financial loss, Fujian Investment acquired the listed company and then changed their name to Min Xin Holdings.

In 1986, Yue Xiu Enterprises Ltd, general agent of the Guangzhou Foreign Trade Company, acquired Wah Shing Toys Consolidated Ltd, which had a record of profit over a number of years. The company was then listed on the Hong Kong Stock Exchange in 1987.

Fu Hui Jewellery, a joint venture between Gold Dragon of Hong Kong and the Fujian Jewellery Import and Export Corporation in Fujian Province, was set up in 1985 to design and market a variety of precious jewellery for both overseas and local markets. After five years of profitable operation, the company was listed on the Hong Kong Stock Exchange in 1990.

In 1988 CITIC purchased a 12.5 per cent stake in Cathay Pacific Airways for HK$2 billion. In 1989 CITIC (Hong Kong) purchased a 20 per cent stake in HK Telecom for HK$10 million. In 1990 CITIC increased the share holding in Dragonair to 38.3 per cent to become a major share holder. In 1990, CITIC took over Tylfull, a listed company in Hong Kong, and injected the 38.3 per cent of Dragonair into Tylfull, changing the name of the company to CITIC-Pacific. In 1991, CITIC-Pacific purchased a 52 per cent stake of Hang Cheong, and in 1992 took over another 45 per cent of the same company, for HK$1.8 billion. Hang Cheong is an old-established conglomerate in Hong Kong engaged in retailing, motor agencies, etc., and was the takeover target of several Chinese groups. It is a general belief that Hang Cheong will contribute significantly to CITIC-Pacific's profits. CITIC-Pacific has become one of the top 20 stocks on the Hong Kong Stock Exchange.

From the above, we note that PRC enterprises have sharpened their skills in the financial market, following the Conic Electronics disaster, resulting in successful operations and listing in the case of Fu Hui, and successful and profitable operations in the case of CITIC (Hong Kong).

Third Period: (1992 to the present)

During this period, PRC enterprises in Hong Kong were further motivated:

1 To obtain foreign capital through listing on the Hong Kong Stock Exchange.
2 To use Hong Kong as a base to internationalize their operations further (i.e. to set up overseas offices, assembly plants and full manufacturing facilities, as well as using Hong Kong as a base for exports)

At the beginning of 1992, especially after Deng Xiaoping visited south China, the PRC enterprises in Hong Kong became very high profile, in contrast to their habitually more discreet presence. China Travel donated millions of dollars to the Chinese New Year firework display, partly to inaugurate China Travel Year 1992, but mainly to enhance its public image in preparation for its future listing on the Hong Kong Stock Exchange. Hong Kong's PRC enterprises had always been shy of talking to the media for various reasons; now, however, they took an active role in telling the news media their business, performance and strategic plans. The chairman of Fujian Enterprise (Holding) Ltd told the *Hong Kong Economic Report* the company's strategic plan for 1992 (the article appeared in the 16 March 1992 issue). The company is a conglomerate with interests in shipping, tourism, manufacturing, finance, engineering, construction and trading. The two main objectives were stated as:

1 To attract foreign capital and technology to invest in China, especially Fujian Province
2 To use Hong Kong as a base to internationalize their operation. They have set up seven companies in the United States, Canada, Japan, Australia, Thailand and Argentina, and also a joint venture fishing and fish products company in Peru, where the company has ten fishing vessels. The fish meat and powder are processed in Peru, then re-imported to China. Total sales for last year amounted to US$9 million.

In May 1992, the chairman told the *Hong Kong Economic Times* that its subsidiaries in toys, manufactures, tourism, finance and shipping would be listed on the Hong Kong Stock Exchange sometime that year (*Hong Kong Economic Times* 14 May 1992).

Similarly, the managing director of China Resources told reporters on 19 March 1992 that the enterprise was preparing for its subsidiaries to be listed on the Hong Kong Stock Exchange in the near future (*New Evening Post* 19 March 1992). One Hong Kong analyst foresees that China Resources will make use of Winland Investment (see above) in order to have some of its businesses listed. However, the same analyst commented that the management of China Resources is relatively conservative. The expansion may not be as aggressive as that of CITIC or Guangdong Investment (see below) (*Hong Kong Economic Times* 21 March 1992). China Resources also made use of Hong Kong as a base to internationalize its operations. It has set up several overseas offices after careful planning, including Ng Fung Hong Inc., Teck Soon Hong Trading (USA) Inc., Chinese Arts & Crafts (New York) Inc., The China Carpet (USA) Co. Ltd, and The Pearl River Merchandising Corporation in the United States; Intraco Resources Trading Pte Ltd in Singapore; and Thai Resources Holdings Co. Ltd, Changchun Development Ltd, the International Exhibition Centre and the New City Golf Development Company in Bangkok, jointly funded with Thailand. It has also invested in the development of virgin forests in Indonesia, in conjunction with Indonesian firms, and has set up branches in Australia, Japan, South Korea, the United States and Canada, and an office in Austria to handle trade, retail business and real estate development (Enterprise Groups (Corporation) in China Editing Committee 1990, *Enterprise Groups in China* vol. 1, Beijing: Economic Science Publishing House). On 29 June 1992, during a public seminar, the director and deputy general manager of Guangdong

Table 5.5 Expansion of Guangdong Investment through acquisitions:
1987–91

Month/year	Properties
2/1987	New Cathay Hotel and Sladen Investment Limited
2/1991	HK Environmental Pollution Control Services
6/1991	Cameron Commercial Centre
10/1991	Citybus Limited
12/1991	Guangdong Tours
12/1991	Supertime (Guangzhou Malting)
12/1991	Panyu Site
6/1991	Shenzhen brewery, Guangdong Hotel in Shenzhen; properties

Source: Proceedings of the Listing of PRC Enterprises in Hong Kong 1992

Investment gave a detailed account of the company's successful expansion through a series of acquisitions (Table 5.5):

Guangdong Enterprises (Holdings) Ltd, the parent company of Guangdong Investment, has established its own corporations or joint ventures, some 15 in all, in the United States, Canada, Australia, Britain, France, Germany and Thailand, engaged chiefly in the export of Guangdong products, and the import of materials that are not easily available in Guangdong. It is now building a Chinatown in Paris.

The director and deputy general manager of China Merchants Ltd (CMH) told reporters that in consultation with their financial consultants, the company was planning to have its subsidiaries, such as its chemical and electronics concerns in Shekou, listed on the Hong Kong Stock Exchange (*Hong Kong Economic Times* 11 May 1992).

In July 1992, Hai Hong Holdings Company Ltd, a wholly-owned subsidiary of CMH, was listed on the Hong Kong Stock Exchange. The company manufactures paint, and the entire operation is located in the PRC. It set up a holding company in Hong Kong (the first time that a PRC firm with its entire operation in mainland China was directly listed in Hong Kong), and the issue raised HK$91 million, and was 374 times oversubscribed. The offered price was HK$1.5 per share. However, during the first day of trading on 15 July 1992 the price went up to HK$4.5 per share.

In August 1992, China Overseas Land and Investment Ltd (a wholly-owned subsidiary of the China State Construction Engineering Corporation), with businesses in property development and investment in both Hong Kong and China, offered 820 million shares at HK$0.10 each, or HK$1.03 per share to the public. The issue was many times oversubscribed and shares were traded at HK$1.74 per share during the first day of trading.

In 1992, the following nine state enterprises were identified by China's State Council for listing on the Hong Kong Stock Exchange in 1993:

Qing Dao Breweries
Shanghai Petrochemical Complex
Yizheng Joint Corporation of Chemical Fibre
Kunming Machine Tool Plant
Maanshan Iron & Steel Company
Dongfang Electric company
Tianjin Bohai Chemical Industry Co.
Beijing Renmin Machinery General Plant.
Guanzhou Shipyard International Company Limited

According to Charles Lee, Chairman of the Hong Kong Stock Exchange, the enterprises must meet the Exchange's listing requirements and follow international standards. In particular, their financial statements had to be prepared in accordance with internationally accepted standards (*Hong Kong Standard* 7 October 1993).

To sum up, there are five ways in which a PRC firms can be listed in Hong Kong:

1 By acquisition of a listed company in Hong Kong, and the injection of assets into the listed company (reverse takeover), e.g. CITIC's takeover of Tylfull and Guangdong Enterprise's takeover of Union Globe.
2 By acquisition of a company that fulfils the listing requirements, e.g. Yue Xiu Enterprises Ltd's takeover of Wah Shing Toys Consolidated Ltd in 1986.
3 By setting up a holding company registered in Hong Kong, which owns the assets in China, e.g. the Hai Hong Holdings Company Ltd.
4 PRC firms registered in China seek listing on Hong Kong Stock Exchange, e.g. the nine state-owned enterprises mentioned above.
5 Setting up a company in Hong Kong for three to five years, and meeting the other listing requirements, e.g. Fu Hui Jewellery.

In the first two examples, looking for a takeover target may be very difficult and the cost of acquiring a 'shell' company may be very expensive. In the case of the fifth option, waiting for three to five years is very time consuming. More and more PRC firms will make use of the third and fourth alternatives. However, difficulties are posed by the need to meet international accounting standards and exchange requirements. For those existing PRC enterprises in Hong Kong, the fifth method may prove easier.

Despite difficulties in meeting international accounting standards, six PRC firms (Qing Dao Breweries, Shanghai Petrochemical Complex, Kunming Machine Tool Plant, Maanshan Iron & Steel Company, Beijing Renmin Machinery General Plant and Guanzhou Shipyard International Company Limited) were successfully listed on the Hong Kong Stock Exchange in 1993, and were many times oversubscribed.

Though buying a 'shell' company in Hong Kong may be very expensive, the acquisition of such firms by PRC interests has increased rapidly. From Table 5.6, we can see that there were 14 acquisitions by PRC interests from August 1992 to May 1993, as compared with only five from 1986 to 1990.

CHARACTERISTICS OF PRC OUTWARD DIRECT INVESTMENT

According to two surveys carried out by the Multinational Corporation Research Centre of the Foreign Trade University of Beijing, the characteristics of PRC outward direct investment are as follows:

1 The growth rate of PRC outward direct investment is much higher than that of the other developing countries in their first ten years of development.
2 Total investment value is relatively small. Average investment value of overseas production enterprises is US$2.87 million of which PRC average equity participation is US$1.237 million. Only a few investments are more than US$100 million. However, PRC enterprises in Hong Kong are mostly in the form of conglomerates.
3 Investment is mainly in the form of joint venture (partners are mainly Overseas Chinese). PRC enterprises are mainly minority share holders.
4 Overseas enterprises are mainly greenfield, complemented by acquisition.

In addition to this, the present author carried out a survey on the same subject, based on the author's interviews with MOFERT officials in the summer of 1992. Up to June 1992, China had set up

Table 5.6 China's GDP growth

Date	Mainland interest	HK takeover target	Transaction
1986	CITIC HK	Ka Wah Bank	92% stake taken, then diluted holding to relist in 1988
	China Merchants	Union Bank	62% stake taken
1987	Guangdong Enterprises	Union Globe renamed Guangdong Investment	Took 63.5% from Amchamp Trading
	Fujian Investment and Enterprise Corp	Panin Holdings now called Min Xin Holdings	Became single largest shareholder, no details
1990	CITIC HK	Tylfull renamed CITIC Pacific	51% taken from Chao Kuang-piu
1992			
Aug	China Resources	Winland renamed China Resources	33%, $501 million stake
Oct	Shougang Corp	Tung Wing Steel	51%, $239 million stake with Cheung Kong
Nov	China Resources	Hong Kong Chinese Bank	15%, $174 million stake
Dec	Jinchuan Non-Ferrous Metals Corp	Paladin	30%, $162 million stake
1993			
Feb	Shougang Corp	Eastern Century	25%, $164 million stake
Feb	China Poly Group CITIC Development	Continental Mariner	61%, $287 million stake
March	China Resources	HK Toy Centre	7%, $34 million stake
March	China National Non-Ferrous Metals Ind Corp	Laws Property	68%, $682 million stake with Jinhui
April	Shougang Corp	Santai Manufacturing	68%, $314 million stake
April	China Resources	Hong Kong Building and Loan	10% stake with Hong Kong Chinese Bank
April	Shougang Corp	Chevalier Intl	Negotiations in progress, no details
April	China Aerospace Industrial Corp	Conic Investment	51%, $233 million stake
May	Ministry of Foreign Trade & Economic Cooperation*	First Pacific Bank	33.75%, $362.1 million stake
May	China National Cereals, Oils and Foodstuffs Import & Export Corp (CEROIL FOOD)	Seabase International Holdings	55%, $382.75 million stake

Note * It was renamed from Ministry of Foreign Economic Relations and Trade (MOFERT) during the Eighth National People's Congress opened in March 1993

1,171 non-trade enterprises overseas. Total contracted investment was US$3.359 billion of which PRC enterprises contributed US$1.485 billion. In terms of equity contribution, PRC enterprises contributed 44.2 per cent. Out of 1,171 enterprises there were only 27 overseas enterprises with over US$5 million investment contributed by PRC enterprises. This accounted for 2.3 per cent in terms of number of overseas enterprises and 65.7 per cent in terms of investment value. This indicated that PRC's overseas enterprises are mostly small and medium-sized.

China's outward FDI has also become more diversified in terms of destination (host countries). At the end of 1985, Chinese overseas enterprises were located in 45 countries and/or regions but were mostly concentrated in Hong Kong and Macau (host to 54 enterprises), the United States (21), Thailand (11) and Japan (11). This accounted for 63 per cent of the total number of Chinese overseas enterprises. By 1988, Chinese overseas enterprises had spread to 79 countries and regions of which more than 240 were in Asia, more than 80 in Africa, more than 50 in Europe, nearly 40 in Oceania and more than 20 in north America and Latin America (Ye Gang 1992). Up to the end of 1991, Chinese overseas enterprises had spread to more than 112 countries/regions, mostly concentrated in the following countries (in descending order): Hong Kong, the United States, former Soviet Union, Thailand, Australia, Japan, Canada, Australia, Singapore and Germany. The number of overseas enterprises in these countries (651) accounting for 65 per cent of total number of Chinese overseas enterprises. The investment value in these countries was US$1.188 billion, accounting for 85 per cent of total investment. This reflected the fact that PRC overseas investment is concentrated in north America and the Asia-Pacific region. Investment in America, Canada and Australia accounted for 85 per cent of total investment (from interview with MOFERT officers).

PRC enterprises have invested in various industries and continue to diversify into different sectors abroad. At the end of 1985, there were 45 manufacturing and agricultural projects, accounting for 24 per cent of all projects; 14 extraction projects (8 per cent of the total), 19 construction projects, 15 restaurant and transportation projects, and projects combining industrial and trading activities. By the end of 1988, manufacturing and agriculture accounted for about 40 per cent of all projects (50 per cent if extraction projects are included) (Ye Gang 1992: 126).

In terms of investment value, extraction projects accounted for

29.4 per cent of total investment; and industrial and agricultural production accounted for 51.6 per cent of the total investment. The following accounted for 81 per cent of the total investment: engineering contracting, technical development. Other services (restaurants and cafeterias, tourism, finance, medical/ health care and transportation) accounted for 19 per cent of total investment (from interview with MOFERT officials, based on 1991 statistics).

SUMMARY AND CONCLUSION

PRC enterprises started their FDI in 1979. During the first six years (1979–85), only state-owned import and export corporations, under MOFERT and Provincial and Municipal International Economic and Technological enterprises, under the Commission of Foreign Economic Relations and Trade, were eligible to invest overseas. In 1985, MOFERT allowed enterprises under other ministries to invest overseas, including the Parent Companies Research Institute, and big transnational corporations such as China National Metals and Minerals Import and Export Corporation, China National Chemical Import and Export Corporation (Sinochem), and Capital Iron & Steel Company (Shougang Corporation). After measures taken to readjust the overheated economy in the year 1988–9 (especially just before and after the Tiananmen Square incident), China's economy started to pick up. The Chinese government started to pay attention to the development of the 'external oriental economy'. Enterprises are now encouraged to participate in the world economy and invest overseas, particularly following Deng Xiaoping's visit to the south in early 1992, and the CCP Chief Jiang Zemin's promise during the Party's fourteenth National Congress to open China wider to the outside world and encourage enterprises to expand their investment abroad and their transnational operations. Apart from large and medium-sized state enterprises, many small enterprises, including small private and township enterprises, have also set up overseas. (This can be seen in the large number of overseas enterprises and relatively small investment value in 1992).

Guangdong city is the greatest single source of investment, followed by Fujian and Shanghai, and the same cities are also the leading host sites for FDI within China. The following calculation shows the ratio of inflow of foreign capital into China, and outflow of Chinese capital abroad:

Without taking into account investment in Hong Kong

Up to 1991
$$\frac{1.395}{23.348^3} = 0.0598$$

Up to 1992
$$\frac{1.590}{34.358^4} = 0.0463$$

Taking into account the investment in Hong Kong

For the year 1991 (investment in Hong Kong is estimated at US$12 billion)

$$\frac{12 + 1.395}{23.348} = 0.57$$

For the year 1992 (investment in Hong Kong is estimated at US$14 billion)

$$\frac{14 + 1.59}{34.358} = 0.45$$

Without taking into account the investment in Hong Kong, the ratio is lower than that of developing countries (1:0.13), developed countries (1:1.4), and the world average (1:1.1). However, taking into account investment in Hong Kong, the ratio is much higher than that of developing countries but still lower than developed countries and world average.

China is the world's most populous country, and has 1.17 billion people, accounting for about one-fifth of the human race (*Time Magazine* – special report on China, 10 May 1993, 19: 17). The economic growth (GDP) in 1992 was 12 per cent, and touching 14 per cent for the first quarter of 1993 (*Businessweek* 17 May 1993: 20). China's GDP growth is shown in Figure 5.5. Both of the above magazines predict China as 'the next superpower' and 'the emerging economic powerhouse of the 21st century'.

In May 1993, the International Monetary Fund calculated China's GDP at nearly US$1.1 trillion, using a new method that revalued the economies of developing countries (see Chapter 10). This made China the third largest world producer, behind the United States and Japan (*South China Morning Post*, Business Section: 4 May 1993).

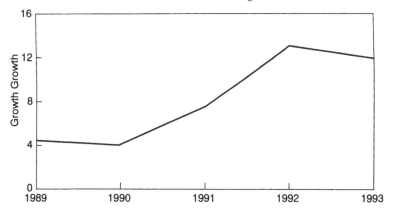

Figure 5.5 China's GDP growth: 1989–93
Source: China State Statistical Bureau

No doubt, China will become a major economic power in the world. FDI from China is still very insignificant when compared with that from other more developed countries; but with its present growth rate, PRC multinationals will definitely increase in number and in size and play a significant role in the world economy.

NOTES

1 The 8th National People's Congress held in March 1993 decided to rename the Ministry of Foreign Economic Relations and Trade, the Ministry of Foreign Trade and Economic Cooperation (MOFTEC).
2 'Bean curd, also known as bean cheese, is a soft vegetable cheese extensively eaten in the Orient that is prepared by treating soy bean milk with magnesium chloride, dilute acids or other coagulants and draining and pressing' (*Webster's Third International Dictionary*: 191).
3 *Statistical Yearbook of China* 1992: 64
4 *ibid.*; *Business China*, 28 June 1993: 4.

BIBLIOGRAPHY

Sun, Wei Yan (1992) 'Development Strategies for the Transnational Operation of Chinese Enterprises', *Management World* 1: 44–8
Tseng, C.S. (1992) 'Entrepreneurship: Challenges for the 21st Century', *Proceedings of the ENDEC World Conference on Entrepreneurship*, August 1992
Ye, Gang (1990) 'China's Overseas Enterprises Participating in International Markets' *International Economics and Management* 133, January: 15–19
Ye Gang and Deng Qinmin (1990) 'Characteristics and Superiority of

Shanghai in Developing its Overseas Enterprises', *International Economics and Management* 137, May 1990: 2–5

Ye Gang (1992) 'Chinese transnational corporations', *Transnational Corporations* 1, 2, August: 125–33.

6 The distribution system in China

Past, present and future

Tseng Choosin, Paula Kwan and Fanny Cheung

INTRODUCTION

Since the commencement of economic reform in 1979, China has gradually evolved from a sellers' market to a buyers' market. The reform policies are reinforced in a report made by Jiang Zemin to the Fourteenth Congress of the Chinese Communist Party in October 1992.[1] The distribution system has also undergone a series of vigorous changes in terms of structure, forms of operation, products offered and functions performed, in order to meet the emerging needs of the consumers.

This chapter studies the centralized Chinese distribution system prior to economic reform, the changes made up to the present moment, and anticipated future trends with the aim of providing useful insights for prospective foreign investors in China.

Marketing has been defined as a human activity directed at satisfying needs and wants through exchange processes (Kolter 1994). Normally, the exchange is the act of obtaining a desired product manufactured in the factory, by the offering of money. Goods are delivered from the manufacturer to the consumer through the distribution channel. To meet the demands of the consumer, the channels of distribution must be capable of accommodating timely and efficient flows of goods. The recent reforms in China have resulted in an increase in people's income and a subsequent rise in purchasing power. In order to meet soaring consumer demand, producers are having to diversify and improve the quality of commodities on offer. To cope with these changes, reform in the distribution channels and retailing pattern is inevitable.

STRUCTURE OF THE DISTRIBUTION CHANNEL PRIOR TO ECONOMIC REFORM

Shortly after the founding of the People's Republic, several measures were introduced by the central authourities, aimed at discrediting and abolishing the practice of individual commerce in China. Private wholesalers were largely replaced, either by state- or collectively-owned wholesale agencies. Parallel to the above changes, private retailers were transformed into joint state–private commercial units, or cooperative groups (Tung 1982: 50). The trading and distribution of consumer goods were thus monopolized by the state. Supply and demand were controlled from the centre. This arrangement posed a number of problems. With no direct link between producers and consumers, consumer demand could only be estimated, and enterprises were instructed to produce accordingly. However, the state lacked sufficient information in order to estimate demand accurately, hence the composition, quality and specification of commodities were by no means a reflection of the prevailing market conditions (Shen Yang 1984). The high costs incurred as a result of markups at every stage of the distribution channel, and the extreme length of the channel itself, were also problematic. Therefore, goods produced were not marketable and customers were deprived of desired products. Tie-in selling,[2] was the most common method of reducing the surpluses of unmarketable goods (*Summary of World Broadcasts–Far East*: 1986). Retail distribution under such a system functioned primarily to ensure the supply of basic goods, and was producer-driven rather than consumer-led.

Before the commencement of reforms in 1978, the Ministry of Commerce held overall responsibility for regulating the supply of consumer goods. Under the ministry there existed various specialized corporations divided along product lines to handle a specific category or group of goods. For instance, the distribution of household electrical appliances was under the control of the Metals, Transport, Electrical and Chemical Companies, a corporation under the Ministry of Commerce (China Handbook Editorial Committee 1984).

Interviews were conducted by one of the present authors with government officials in Shanghai, Hangzhou and Guangzhou in early 1993, in which information about the distribution system before reforms was revealed. The distribution system was a three-tier structure comprising the First-Level Purchasing and Supply Enterprises (FLPSEs); the Second-Level Purchasing and Supply Enterprises

(SLPSEs) and the Third-Level Wholesalers (TLWs). The FLPSEs were located in just three cities, namely Tianjin, Shanghai and Guangzhou. Reporting to the Ministry of Commerce in Beijing and the local commercial bureau, the FLPSEs purchased goods from all over China, accepted imported goods and then distributed to the second tier of the system, the SLPSEs. The SLPSEs operated at the provincial level and reported to the commercial bureau of the province, as well as to the local government department taking charge of commercial matters. They were normally located at provincial capitals and were responsible for the purchase goods from FLPSEs, and their distribution and transportation to the third-level wholesalers in the various cities and counties, who in turn redistributed to local retailers (normally state-owned enterprises). The supply and distribution of goods in rural areas were under the control of the Supply and Marketing Cooperatives. A significant characteristic of this system was regional protectionism. The retailers were only allowed to buy from wholesalers within the dictated region; supplies from elsewhere were brought in only as a very last resort. Therefore, there was hardly any prospect of supply meeting demand effectively and efficiently.

RECENT DEVELOPMENT

Since 1979, then, China has gradually moved from a centrally planned, product-based economy to a more market-oriented, highly decentralized economy. The establishment of the SEZs, the opening-up of the 14 coastal cities, and the preferential treatment given to foreign investors have resulted in the soaring number of foreign investments. Moreover, China has gradually loosened its import controls in preparation for GATT readmission; import trade has also been accelerated. As a result, the inherited centralized distribution system could no longer cater for market needs, either in terms of trade volume or the variety of commodities. Consumers have become more affluent and their demand for goods more selective. Goods produced under the centrally planned system could no longer satisfy their needs, and changes were urgently needed (*Almanac of China's Commerce* 1984: 15–16).

Decentralization of distribution authority

The trading and distribution of goods in China are no longer under the exclusive control of the Ministry of Commerce. Private individuals, collectives, producers and other government units can all buy and sell freely. Producers can no longer market their products exclusively through state wholesale channels, but must find their own customers, at least for goods that do not come within the scope of the state plan. Therefore, members of the distribution channel all need to pay great attention to consumer needs. They have to attract customers by providing a greater variety of products, of better quality and at competitive prices. This is the essential first step in China's move from a supply driven to a demand-led market.

Management reform in retail outlets

Before the reforms, complaints about the rudeness of sales people in retail stores were very frequent. The egalitarian wage system and guaranteed job security meant that sales staff were neither rewarded nor punished for their performance; there was no motivation at all to provide better services to the customers. Reforms in the management of retail stores have since changed matters, however. The majority of small-scale, state-owned enterprises are now operated under a contractual-responsibility system. Larger units in the commercial system were put under a new scheme of management. Whilst remaining state-owned, they are now accountable. They are allowed to select their sources of purchasing and to decide on their own reward and punishment system for staff. They also retain some of their profits and distribute bonuses to the staff based on individual performance. With rewards linked to performance on the part of both individuals and the store as whole, both parties are, it seems, trying hard to attract customers by providing better services.

Elimination of the fixed price policy

The pricing of commodities, except a small number that are still subject to planned allocation, is no longer under state control. Therefore it is natural for wholesalers and retailers to seek products with higher margins and greater market potential. Retailers are free to choose their suppliers and they may even buy goods directly from the manufacturers or import agents. This will shorten the channel of distribution and thus minimize the overall handling cost. Moreover, the shortening of the communication link between the retailers and manufacturers can help the latter to get updated market information and be more adaptable to the needs of consumers.

Since implementation of the above measures, the members of the distribution channel have had more freedom to choose their suppliers; to own and use their self-raised funds; to fix the prices of their commodities within the range set by the state. However, the retail enterprises still have a certain amount of their business decided by responsible higher authorities and approved by China's industrial and commercial administration. Retail enterprises can be divided into three basic types: comprehensive, specialized and general.[3] In order to facilitate the administration and distribution of raw materials and commodities, the Ministry of Domestic Trade was proposed as a replacement for the Ministry of Commerce and the Ministry of Materials and Equipment in 1993 (*South China Morning Post* 16 March 1993). In short, the retail business in China consists of a variety of economic sectors, from state-run enterprises, to supply and marketing cooperatives, to collectives and individually owned businesses. In cities and rural areas alike, they help to deliver the goods from manufacturers to consumers (Ma 1990: 374–6).

Under the reformed distribution system, the retail trade has seen a dramatic increase, as reflected by the figures in Table 6.1. Moreover, the number of individual traders has increased drastically, as shown in Table 6.2. This reflects the fact that the reforms in the distribution system have provided a better business environment for individual traders.

Table 6.1 Development of China's retail sector: 1978–92

	1978	1980	1985	1989	1990	1991	1992
No. of retail outlets (000s)	1,048	1,463	7,783	8,413	8,710	9,241	10,063
Retail employment (million)	4.47	6.37	17.96	20.33	20.91	21.98	24.34
Total sales (rmb billion)	136.4	176.8	327.2	600.9	612.7	690.3	792.2

Source: Statistical Yearbook of China 1993: 584 and 607

Table 6.2 Number of individual traders: 1978–92

	1978	1980	1985	1989	1990	1991	1992
Number (000s)	108	378	6,189	6,892	7,232	7,773	8,511
Percentage to total no. of retail outlets	10.3	25.8	79.5	81.9	83.0	84.1	84.6

Source: Statistical Yearbook of China 1993: 590

Lifting of restrictions in retailing

The rigid structure of China's distribution system changed after the implementation of the new measures. However, foreign investors entering the Chinese market were still prevented from setting up their own marketing distribution channels, no matter which entry mode they had chosen before the economic reforms. Both imported goods and goods manufactured by wholly foreign-owned companies had to be distributed by local wholesalers and retailers. For foreign investors, therefore, the selection of the distribution agent was of paramount importance. The effectiveness and efficiency of distribution were very much dependent on the networking of the import agency and its working relationship with government officials. For companies choosing exports as their entry mode, such as Nestlé, it was essential to pick an influential local partner capable of establishing a beneficial relationship with the other members of the distribution channel. Thus, the company could achieve better market coverage and acquire a better position for product display. This was also true for companies opting to set up joint ventures. General Food could influence retailers and have its products displayed in prominent positions, while its competitors' products were placed in the inconspicuous positions.

In 1991, Yaohan Department Store, a Japanese retailer, marked a milestone in the retailing business in China. With a total investment of US$1.25 million, and accounting for 49 per cent of shares, Yaohan set up a department store in Shenzhen with a local partner. This was the first time that China had allowed a foreign investor into its retailing business. Shortly after this, China announced the opening up of a further ten cities, for the setting up of joint-venture retailers on a trial basis.[4] In each of these cities, a maximum of two joint ventures would be permitted. These joint-venture department stores are allowed to sell a full range of merchandise, and enjoy import and export rights. They can import goods for sale, limited to general merchandise, to a value not exceeding 30 per cent of their annual total turnover, and they have to balance their own foreign exchange needs (*China Business Review* September–October 1992: 4). In 1992, two more department stores, Shanghai First–Yaohan Department Store and the Beijing–Yansha Friendship Store, were set up as joint ventures between overseas and local partners. Besides Yaohan, there has been an increasing number of foreign investors showing interest in the China retail market. In view of this success, six more cities look likely to be added to the list in the near future

(*Ming Pao* 19 January 1994).[5] This provides an alternative method of access to China's market for foreign investors. Rather than exporting or setting up joint-venture manufacturing plants and having their goods distributed through the existing channels, they can set up a joint-venture retailer to sell the goods direct to consumers. According to a senior government official in the Ministry of Commerce, China is also considering the feasibility of releasing the wholesale trade to foreign investors (*Hong Kong Economic Journal* 19 January 1994).

Joint-venture retailers in China are, then, subject to certain conditions. Nonetheless, the Chinese government has become increasingly flexible in enforcing the policies imposed on the joint ventures. Provided that they can achieve their foreign exchange balance, they are allowed to import more than the set 30 per cent of foreign goods. The Sino-Japanese SCITE shopping centre in Beijing, opened in December 1992, was allowed to generate 60 per cent of its total annual turnover from imported goods. There are also ways of solving the problem of balancing foreign exchange. Joint ventures can buy Chinese products with renminbi and export them for foreign currency. They can also set up joint-venture manufacturing plants to produce goods for both local and overseas markets. Benetton is currently sourcing from factories in southern China that are already producing Benetton clothing for export to Japan (*International Market News* 1993, vol. 96).

Giordano, a Hong Kong clothing manufacturer and chain retailer, also made good use of the new retailing policy. Before the lifting of restrictions on foreign participation in China's retail sector, Giordano had already set up a manufacturing plant in China to produce goods for their retail chains in Hong Kong and Singapore. Shortly after the release of the restrictions, the joint-venture manufacturing plant, which is considered as a local partner, entered another joint venture with Giordano in Hong Kong. By doing so, Giordano was able to extend its retail chain to Shenzhen. One more retail outlet had already been set up in Guangzhou, and together they generated sales of some rmb 400 million (*Far Eastern Economic Review* 2 December 1993).

RETAIL PATTERNS IN THREE SELECTED CITIES

Below is a very brief summary of the findings of a study carried out by one of the present authors on three cities, focusing on retail patterns and consumer behaviour in 1993. The study looked at

Guangzhou and Shanghai, where the first two joint-venture retailers in China were set up, and at Beijing.

Guangzhou

The distribution system for Guangzhou has undergone an important change. Over 100 suppliers and sales enterprises have been approved as distribution reform units on a trial basis for four years. These 'guinea pigs' have full autonomy to manage their business, to choose the scope of their business and to select markets and merchandise. They can also branch out to other provinces in chain operations.

Because of their proximity to Hong Kong, consumers in Guangzhou are more Westernized and are more open to accept new products. They are also the wealthiest group of customers in China and so are more selective when purchasing goods. Hoping to enhance shopper traffic and sales volumes, many state-owned and collectively-owned department stores have recently been renovated. Interviews were conducted with the management of two leading department stores, the Guangzhou and the Nan Fong. It was found that their average daily sales figures were rmb 1.2 million and 1.3 million respectively, a huge figure when compared to the national income per capita. (According to the *Statistical Yearbook of China* 1992, the national income per capita in 1991 was rmb 1,401.)

The retail market has been opened up to foreign department store operators as well. Investors from Hong Kong, Thailand, Japan and Taiwan have already invested or are planning to invest billions of yuan.[6]

With the recent completion of modern traffic networks between Guangzhou and the Pearl River Delta region, the travelling time between the city and the counties has been greatly reduced. This will facilitate the distribution of products as well as the transportation of shoppers. Guangzhou should, therefore, prove an attractive market for retailers.

Shanghai

Because of the reforms in the retail store management, many of the stores in Shanghai have extended their shopping hours to 9 or 10 p.m. Together with the recent refurbishment of the city's two high streets, the Nanjing Ru and Huai Hoi Zhong Ru, the consumer traffic has soared sharply. The inroads made by the Yaohan Group have initiated significant changes in consumer buying behaviour and in the form of competition between retailers. Shopping is no longer being considered as a chore for the obtaining of necessities, but as a major leisure activity. This concept is also widespread in the other two cities. Moreover, the development of Pudong also presents numerous opportunities for investors. Another department store will soon be built in Pudong by the Yaohan & Shanghai No. 1 Joint Venture. Sincere, a famous department store in Hong Kong, has also signed a joint-venture agreement to set up a department store there.

Beijing

Township shopping centres and collective markets are becoming more and more popular in Beijing. People are trying hard to earn more money, and setting up as a self-employed trader is perceived as an easy way to get rich. An increasing number of outlets are available to marketeers, and people with more money are more willing to spend. Investors will find a wealth of opportunities here. The local government will soon restructure and reorganize its commercial administration system, hoping to cut down the bureaucracy. The opening of the Yansha Friendship Shopping City in late 1992 took the retailing industry into a new era; the highly attractive shopping environment here has made the store a focus for leisure, and sales have reached an average of rmb 1.5 million per day (*International Market News* 1993, vol. 92).

FUTURE TRENDS IN THE CHINESE DISTRIBUTION SYSTEM

Clearly, opportunities exist in China's retailing industry. Distribution channels are the key to the traditionally closed Chinese market, and they should be perceived and used by Western or Asia-Pacific investors as competitive weapons. Their impact on a company's performance in the changing Chinese market should not be underestimated. As a consequence, the ability to manage channels strategically and to anticipate future trends is of prime importance to investors. In spite of the remarkable progress since economic reform was introduced, the distribution system remains underdeveloped as compared with developed countries. It is expected that the Chinese distribution system will continue to evolve in a variety of ways, as outlined below.

Structure

The distribution channel will probably be shorter in future as a consequence of reform, bringing both cost and communication advantages to retailers. Timely delivery and low costs are success in the current climate. In order to reduce costs and gain tighter control over the quality and quantity of commodities, wholesalers and retailers are expected to expand both vertically and horizontally. They will almost certainly seek to integrate with other members of the distribution chain in order to reduce purchasing and handling costs. Such integration may be in the form of joint ventures or cooperative agreements between state-owned retailers in different provinces, between wholesalers and wholesalers, and so on. Backward integration will also become very popular among retailers as this can reduce costs and ensure tighter control.

Nature of products to be distributed

According to the focus group study conducted, Chinese consumers are very sensitive to quality, service and promotions. Goods are often purchased for their social symbolism, enhancing and communicating a particular image to others; durability is no longer an important criterion in the purchase decision. Chinese consumers are now more willing to accept new products, and according to one senior official in the Ministry of Commerce, tend to look for 'well-known', 'special', 'quality' and 'innovative' products (*Almanac of China's Commerce* 1991). In response to this, distributors are shifting their focus away from the supply of basic goods, and towards responding to consumer trends.

Retail activity

In order to broaden the range of products offered and keep operation costs down, retailers tend to sell goods by consignment. This also minimizes risk and maintains better cash flow. Faced with increasingly fierce competition, and intent on better market coverage, manufacturers are now much more willing to enter into 'consignment' agreements with retailers.

Services

In order to cope with severe competitive pressures, and the increasingly diverse needs and criticisms of customers, participants in the distribution chain will probably increase their levels of customer service. As discussed above, services provided to customers were, under the old system, very poor. The Nan Fong Department Store pioneered changes in this field by introducing a bonus system for staff (*Almanac of China's Commerce* 1984). Other major department stores, such as Number One Department Store in Shanghai, and Wah Lin Department Store, also followed.

However, most department stores in China still employ old-style methods, and are frequently criticized by customers. Products are still displayed in glass cabinets and can be examined only at a distance; no touching or trying is allowed. Moreover, there are no delivery or installation services for large items. Improvements in delivery services, displays and fitting services would certainly give any store willing to try them the competitive edge.

According to the focus study mentioned above, Chinese consumers do not yet possess sufficient knowledge to distinguish between and select from a variety of models of any given product. Therefore, the provision of an inquiries and information service would also attract customers to a store. This also implies that sales people should possess adequate product knowledge.

Geographic expansion

Another possible development in China's retail sector is the expansion of stores in the suburbs of large cities. As has been seen elsewhere in the world, the development of city centres pushes up the cost of living for city-dwellers and businessmen, with the result that new commercial and residential sectors have squeezed out to the suburbs. The building of more retail networks and shopping centres in these areas is the logical consequence.

Marketing activities

The role of marketing has become increasingly important as a consequence of the intensifying competition between products and the growing sophistication of Chinese consumers. Modern Chinese consumers tend to choose well-known brands and to relate quality with brand. The marketing of Rado and Citizen watches in China provides very good examples of effective ways to capture the Chinese market. Before the products were sold in China a significant amount was spent on advertising in order to build up their image. As the result of strenuous promotion, Rado and Citizen were perceived as prestige, quality brands. Sales soared when they were finally available in the shops (Mun 1988). Walter (1974) has shown that consumers in developing countries tend to spend a disproportionate amount of money on goods that have prestige value or that have been aggressively advertised, and the same is very much true of China today.

Sales promotion tools such as discounts, samples, coupons, cut-price packs and contests will gradually become more popular among retailers. Chinese consumers are basically unfamiliar with many products, and the above are all excellent ways to speed up purchase action and to induce initial trials of new products.

New forms of operation

Western consumers are, of course, well accustomed to a variety of different types of retail outlet, many of which are apt for introduction and development in China.

Supermarkets

The first supermarket in China was introduced as a department of the Friendship Store in Guangzhou in 1981, and accepted only Foreign Exchange Certificates. By 1990, there were around 150 supermarkets throughout the country (Mun 1988). Because of the increase in the standard of living amongst Chinese consumers after economic reform, a wider range of better-quality products is now needed. Shoppers also want to be able to handle products before they buy them. It seems likely that more and more supermarkets will be set up in China, and that the nature of their operations will change as storechains replace single units.

Specialist shops

Chinese consumer attitudes have become more Westernized, associating products with a certain self-image. As the consumers become more affluent, they will be eager to acquire specialist, top-quality products; hence specialized shops will become more popular.

Chain stores

According to Zhang Hao Ruo, the chief of the Ministry of Domestic Trade, chain stores will be the next focal point of development in China's retail industry. Foreign investors are recommended to establish their chain store operations on a joint-venture basis with local Chinese partners (*Hong Kong Economic Journal* 5 November 1993). Dickson Concepts, a Hong Kong-listed up-market retailer selling foreign prestige brands opened its first mainland store in Beijing in May 1993. The chain then opened two further outlets, in Guangzhou and Shenzhen, in October 1993, with another 31 due to be set up in 1994. (*South China Morning Post* 26 October 1993). It is anticipated that more companies will consider operating chain stores on the mainland in the future.

Non-store operations

An increasing number of people have been engaging in part-time or second jobs in China as the result of economic development. People are working at improving their incomes, and jobs as sales agents in direct marketing networks are proving attractive. With the accelerating pace of life in China and the development of efficiency-consciousness, direct marketing is expected to prosper. Avon Cosmetics has a firm foothold in the direct marketing business in China (*International Market News* 1993, vol. 92).

The vending machine also has great potential for development. With the escalating number of shopping centres, vending machine retailing could become more popular. Canteens in universities and schools are likely to be targeted too. Teenagers and children in China today have more money to spend, and freedom of choice; and under the one-child policy, parents tend to be more accommodating to the demands of the only child in the family.

The retailing 'backlash'

According to Mun (1988), the growth in the more up-market retail sector in China will probably bring about a backlash whereby supermarkets and others will move downmarket as the increasing supply of quality goods fuels fierce competition at the top. In the long term, China's new-style retailers will gradually shift their focus from the more exclusive end of the market to more general buyers, in order to broaden the scope of their markets.

CONCLUSION

In order to enjoy long-term success in the increasingly competitive Chinese distribution system, channel members must strategically determine their best marketing mix of pricing, service, quality, product, location and promotion. Retailing in China is fast catching up with the West, but retailers must continue to strive to introduce the following Western practices into a still relatively unfamiliar setting:

• Pricing should remain reasonable, yet generate a perception of 'worth' among customers.
• Service should be personal, building customer loyalty.
• Quality should be excellent and consistent.
• Products should provide variety and choice, with familiar brands, specialist and innovative goods answering emerging consumer needs, and with competing producers well differentiated.
• Promotions should aim to generate store traffic, build store image and create store preference.

NOTES

1 Accelerating Reform and Opening-up' (reported by Jiang Zemin at the Fourteenth National Congress of the Chinese Communist Party, on 12 October 1993), *Beijing Review* 1992: 20.
2 Tie-in selling obliges consumers to buy additional commodities in order to purchase the product desired.
3 Comprehensive retail enterprises sell a wide range of daily necessities, but offer little choice. Specialized retail enterprises handle one large category of goods, such as clothing shops, or deal in various kinds of commodities needed by certain consumers, such as 'women's shops'. General retail enterprises carry a wide variety of goods, combining the extensiveness of the comprehensive store with the choice of goods of the specialized store (Ma 1990: 376).
4 The 11 cities open for joint venture retailers are Beijing, Shanghai, Tianjin, Dalin, Qingdao, Guangzhou, Shenzhen, Xiamen, Zuhhai, Shatou and Hainan.
5 The following cities are also now open: Wuhan, Shenyang, Chongqing, Xian, Nanjing and Harbin.
6 Some major investments include:

• Yaohan's joint venture retail store set up in 1991 (*Hong Kong Economic Journal* 5 November 1993);
• Seibu, a Japanese retail giant, has pledged to invest US$103 million to set up a 3000 m² store (*Hong Kong Economic Journal* 5 November 1993);
• Chi Tai, a large conglomerate from Thailand, has committed rmb1.5

billion to constructing a large shopping centre in Guangzhou (*Sing Tao Yat Pao* 3 October 1993).

BIBLIOGRAPHY

Almanac of China's Commerce (1984) Beijing: Economic Management Press
—— (1991) Beijing: Economic Management Press
China Handbook Editorial Committee (1984) *Economy*, Beijing: Foreign Language Press.
Findlay, A.M., Paddison, R. and Dawson, J.A. (1990) Retailing Environments in *Developing Countries*, London: Routledge.
Holton, R.H. and Sicular, T. (1991) 'Economic Reform of the Distribution Sector in China', *The American Economic Review*, 81, 2, May.
Kolter, P. (1994) *Principles of Marketing*, New York: Prentice Hall.
Ma, H. (ed.) (1990) *Modern China's Economy and Management*, Beijing: Foreign Language Press.
Mun, K.C. (1988) 'Chinese retailing in a changing environment', in Kaynak, E. (ed.) *Transnational Retailing*, New York: Walter de Gruyter.
Qiang, G. and Harris, P. (1990) 'Retailing Reform and Trends in China', *International Journal of Retail and Distribution Management*, 18, 5.
Shen Yang (1984) 'New Changes and New Problems in Beijing Market for Manufactured Daily Necessities', *Jingji Guanli*, 4.
Statistical Yearbook of China (1992) State Statistical Bureau.
Summary of World Broadcasts – Far East (1986) 30 July.
Tung, R.L. (1982) *Chinese Industrial Society After Mao*, Toronto: Lexington Books.
Walter, H.G. (1974) 'Marketing in developing countries', *Columbia Journal of World Business* 9, 4: 29–30.

Part III

Business and social transformation

7 Economic reform, industrial relations and human resources management in China in the early 1990s

Malcolm Warner

INTRODUCTION

It has been pointed out elsewhere that the Chinese labour-management system has not yet developed Western-style industrial relations (Warner 1986; 1991; 1992; 1993; 1994). Chinese trade unions, for example, did not develop along the same lines as their British, continental European or north American counterparts, but followed the Soviet model (Schurmann 1966). Without Western-style (or Japanese) free collective bargaining, Chinese unions emerged for the most part as a politicized response to the modernization process, particularly in an economy where only a minority of the total workforce were to be found in the industrial sector, and where a labour market existed in only a very limited sense.

Conceptually, Chinese industrial relations may be regarded as *sui generis*, although they resemble the 'command economy' collective-representation model more than any other (Pravda and Ruble 1987). Such unions fit into an industrial relations system in Dunlop's (1958) sense, although not quite resembling the Western variant, and even in their pre-reformed state, Chinese enterprises operated clearly identifiable *personnel administration* procedures. Since the mid-1980s, these have been transformed considerably. We must first delineate how the new system is evolving out of the old one, why the reforms have come about, and where they are leading. It should, however, be noted that organized labour in China has traditionally been *reactive* to changes in the direction of economic policy since the PRC was established in 1949, and tends to follow Party direction both centrally and locally.

ECONOMIC REFORMS SINCE 1979

Any discussion of China's dramatic changes since the death of Mao
Tsetung in 1976 must therefore take into account the new 'open-
door' policies to the West (and Japan) and the 'Four Modernizations'
(of Agriculture, Industry, Science and Technology, and Defence).
Such strategic shifts have had important implications for the Chinese
economy, and in turn for its management and labour supply (White
1991).

First, we need to describe and discuss the extent of economic
growth in China since the reforms were launched in 1979. For much
of the time, the average rate of growth was over 9 per cent per
year, and this was the longest period of sustained growth since the
founding of the People's Republic (Watson 1992: 1). China's economy has nearly tripled since the reforms were introduced; by the
year 2002 it could well be eight times the 1979 level. If the events
of June 1989 led to a relative regression, this appears to have been
ironed out subsequently. In the early 1990s, the reforms intensified
once more and were given a further boost in early 1992. Rapid
economic growth once again manifested itself, in sharp contrast with
the rest of the world, where the major industrial powers were faced
with recession.

At the last five-yearly CCP Congress in Beijing in October 1992,
the assembled 2,000-or-so delegates had little option but to endorse
Deng Xiaoping's revival of the economic reform programme pur-
sued since 1979. The economy had been in the doldrums from the
end of 1988; when faced with inflation and trade deficits, the State
Council initiated a policy of retrenchment. Its goal at the time had
been to damp down an overheated economy and calm the waves of
decentralization. In 1992 the Party's paramount leader rekindled the
torch of change, with a new agenda for economic reform and personnel changes. In 1993 these reforms were being implemented in
over 100 pilot state-owned enterprises. In 1994 economic reform is
still prominently on the agenda (*Beijing Review* 10 January 1994).

Such new steps toward economic reforms in turn prompted a
qualitative change in industrial relations and the management of
human resources (Warner 1986; 1991; 1992; 1993; 1994). These innovations had been at hand since the mid-1980s, but gained a boost
from the new emphasis in economic policy. The collapse of the
former Soviet Union and the backwash of the Tiananmen Square
repression have left China's leaders in a determined state of mind,
but conscious of the fact that economic growth via decentralization

may be the best way to retain authority. Compared with the former Soviet Union, however, China has had *perestroika* but little *glasnost*. Political reform therefore remains in the shadows.

CHINESE TRADE UNIONS

Trade unions in the People's Republic of China have traditionally been vertically organized, in keeping with Leninist ideology and Soviet 'industrial' principles of organization (Brown 1966; Poole 1986; Pravda and Ruble 1987). Craft and occupational structures were also found, based on the older 'guild' tradition which traditionally characterized master–apprentice relations (Ma 1955; Chesnaux 1969). Reform of the economy led to rationalization of industrial relations: 'The labour movement has ... been restructured to harmonize with government ministries on industry lines, while regional federations of unions are linked with the Party structure on a geographical basis' (Lansbury *et al.* 1984: 57).

There were only around 100,000 primary trade unions in 1951-2; now there are over 600,000. There were only just under 2.5 million union members in 1949, but this had grown to over 100 million by the end of the 1980s. As there is a virtual closed-shop, this aggregate is not too meaningful. Even so, Article 1 of the All China Federation of Trade Unions (ACFTU) Constitution (1988) states that: 'Membership in trade unions is open to all manual and non-manual workers in enterprises, undertakings and offices, whose wages constitute their principal means of livelihood'.

The ACFTU is the 'apex' organization that integrates the constituent parts. There are 15 national unions respectively organized by trade in the following industries: railways, civil aviation, seamen, road transport, post and telecommunications, engineering and metallurgy, petrochemicals, coal-mining and geology, water and electricity, textiles, light industry, urban development and building materials, agriculture and forestry, finance and trade, and education. The Federation's eight departments are currently organized as follows: economy, technology and labour protection, labour and wages, women workers, propaganda and education, international liaison, organization, finance and accounts and auditing. The ACFTU 'advises' the government and the Party on new legislation and then helps to interpret its application.

Shop-floor relations have long been the responsibility of both trade unions and elected workers' congresses, representing the workforce and staff with, in theory at least, one representative for ten or 12 workers. In large enterprises, the basic unit is the union team, centred on the work-group, meeting once a fortnight, or monthly, as distinct from the worker's congress, which is convened between one and four times a year depending on 'custom and practice'. The full-time union committee in the workplace provides continuity of contact when the congress is in abeyance.

The *danwei*, the all-important officially designated work-unit and 'building block' of Chinese society, has, for the last half-century, dominated both managers' and workers' lives, inside and outside work, and provided cradle-to-grave welfare services. Trade unions in such work-units stressed production rather than consumption values, but nonetheless have had to look after the everyday welfare interests of their members. They have also played other social roles, such as enforcing and monitoring birth-control policies, through their surveillance of women workers in the factories and offices.

The trade union's role may be said to centre on 'labour productivity, worker morale and welfare rather than the interpretation of national policy' (Henley and Nyaw 1986: 648). The trade union does not bargain freely, or fix wage-levels as in Western countries, but in contracted or leased enterprises it helps determine the allocation of funds and the arrangement of working schedules. Normally, trade unions are supposed to help implement the resolutions passed by the workers' congress in these areas. In the everyday work of the enterprise, union officials are also expected to defuse conflicts between the workforce and management. If the latter behave unacceptably (for example by reducing bonuses), or there is a stoppage by the workers involved, the union is asked to intervene. In recent years, Chinese trade unions, on the state's initiative, have promoted a system of so-called 'collective agreements' (Gong 1989). These accords are drawn up by individual enterprises in order to anchor labour-management relations and define the respective roles of managers and unions; they should, however, be distinguished from collective bargaining (Warner 1993).

The role of the Party secretary in the enterprise remains central whatever the changing institutional arrangements, be they managerial or representative (Walder 1989). The Party committee is responsible for 'guaranteeing and supervising' policy implementation (Child and Xu 1989: 10). In this sense, the full-time union cadres may be seen as influential *vis-à-vis* policy-making bodies with the enterprise, as they reflect the Party line, regardless of whether the factory director officially has more or less power. On key issues such as dismissals, management is more likely to meet with the union officials representing the workers' congress rather than with the Party committee (Child and Xu 1989: 28), but it is doubtful if the unions play a particularly independent role in the factory. Greater union participation to protect workers' rights has been proposed.

Indeed, Ni Zhifu, chairman of the ACFTU and vice-chairman of the Standing Committee of the NPC was reported as telling local trade union leaders:

> that trade unions at all levels must actively participate in the country's reforms and protect the workers' interests on the basis of safeguarding the general interests of the state. He said that it is necessary to get the ordinary workers involved in the reforms in such areas as housing, social security and medical care for the success of the reforms lies in the support of the workers. He urged enterprises, especially the large and medium-sized state enterprises, to set much store by the initiative and wisdom of the workers in revitalizing their management and improving economic performances. He also urged the full implementation of the 'enterprise law' which provides the power of the workers' representative congresses. Democratic management is not merely a form, but an important system that calls for the full reliance on the workers and ensures their rights as masters of the enterprises, he stressed.
>
> (*Summary of World Broadcasts* 1991)

The workers' congress sessions are, however, often mere formalities; workers elected to them are inevitably drawn from the union faithful (Warner 1993).

The precise role the unions will play in the post-Tiananmen Square phase of reforms has yet to be clarified, but it is very likely that they will continue to follow the 'official' line as previously. One observer (Korzec 1992) fears that the reforms are set to fail because they break the 'social contract' set up after 1949 between the state and the workers. Under this arrangement, 'the enterprise, with its comprehensive welfare and political functions, is that State in miniature. Moreover, this identity based as it is on long-engrained habits of dependency remains popular' (Howe 1992: ix). It was just this *status quo* that the Chinese trade unions institutionalized. Others see the possible emergence of a form of 'corporatism' as a result of the economic reforms, with an enhanced representative role for the unions 'within limits' (Chan 1993: 44).

LABOUR MARKET REFORM

As a lynch-pin of China's human resources management system, the 'iron rice-bowl' employment policy had its roots in the early 1950s (Schurmann 1966: 250ff). It was originally intended to protect skilled workers, but eventually spread to cover the majority of urban workers. After leaving school, young Chinese workers were allocated jobs by the local labour bureau, in most cases with little reference as to where they wanted to work or what they wanted to do. They were then assigned to a work-unit which registered their citizenship status (or *hukou*).

The wage grade system – usually eight levels for factory workers – had been taken over from the Soviet model. Citizenship registration was thus anchored in its initial placing and labour mobility was minimal. Urban dwellers without hukou were non-persons. Dismissal was rare; motivation was low. As has been said of other Communist economies, 'they [the cadres] pretended to pay us, and we [the workers] pretended to work'. For much of the time, and especially during the Cultural Revolution, an egalitarian wage-payment system was common, and incentives were limited. The characteristics of the old-style, existing system and the model aspired to by the reformers are set out in Table 7.1.

An interesting, but by no means unique, feature of the post-1950s Chinese employment system had been the practice of 'occupational inheritance' (or *dingti*). When a worker retired, he or she could recommend a close relative for the job. This practice led to overmanning on an extensive scale (Howe 1992: ix). Steps to scale down this system have met with mixed results, as Chinese state enterprises

Table 7.1 Reform of China's labour-management system

System characteristic	Existing	Reform
Strategy	Status quo	Reformist
Employment	Iron rice-bowl	Labour market
Conditions	Job security	Labour contracts
Mobility	Job assignment	Limited flexibility
Rewards	Egalitarian	Meritocratic
Wage system	Grade-based	Performance-based
Promotion	Seniority	Skill-related
Union role	Consultative	Coordinative
Management	Economic cadres	Professional management
Party role	Central	Advisory
Work organization	Taylorist	Flexible
Efficiency	Technical	Allocative

have been pressed to adopt the labour contract system, with more open job recruitment. As early as 1984, the present writer found the number of apprenticeships cut back in several large firms visited and raw recruits hired on contracts (Warner 1986: 361). On the other hand, Granick (1991: 274) found that open inheritance of jobs was still very prevalent in the early and mid-1980s, with over 90 per cent of posts in this category. It was, as he put it, 'automatic', 'legal' and 'real' (1991: 274). Although the *dingti* arrangements were formally cancelled in 1986, later reports still indicated that the practice was prevalent through labour-device companies set up by local labour bureaux. With rising youth unemployment, it is likely to continue 'in legal or semi-legal guise' (Korzec 1992: 25).

Given the scale of the problems, the rationale of Deng-ist reforms was to introduce greater efficiency into the system by the use of market mechanisms. The trade-off was to be between efficiency and equality (Hsu 1991: 106ff). Efficiency was to be seen not only as technical efficiency in terms of the best input–output ratios, but also as *allocative* efficiency in terms of optimizing use of resources. The Chinese leadership saw China at a primary stage of economic development and was therefore willing to see increasing inequality continue for some time. Equality has thus been reinterpreted as 'flexibly' for the time being. Discussions of wage-related issues had long focused on the Marxist dictum of 'distribution according to labour', but some economists concluded that differentials were not too great once other factor-contributions were taken into account. Reforms had to be designed to give both enterprises and individuals the greatest autonomy and initiatives possible. Economists such as Jiang Yiwei (1980), Dong Fureng (1986) and Liu Guogang (1987) set out plausible efficiency-centred strategies.

Even as late as 1988, a polemic ensued regarding a proposal to create a 'labour market', since not all economists agreed that labour was a commodity under socialism. Earlier, the Maoist vision of 'distribution according to labour', conditional on 'each according to his labour', had become controversial. Many Chinese economists supported the notion that the total wage-fund of the enterprise should be a reflection of its performance on both macro- and micro-grounds. Growth of aggregate wages should not go beyond national income and productivity; at the micro-level, the new approach was intended to increase the incentives of both firms and employees. For this to happen, however, other changes, such as price reforms, must take place, allowing an enterprise's profits to reflect its performance. Some went on to argue that it was wiser to open up the labour market and let the market determine wage levels. The caveat was advanced, however, that profits were not created by labour alone. Thus, if wages were geared to profits rather than labour productivity, workers might become work-shy and seek illicit ways to boost profits to increase their wages. Others wanted a half-way house, where there was a fixed wage plus a bonus reflecting increases in enterprise profits. One idea was to merge the wage-fund, bonus-fund and welfare-fund as a 'labour contract-fund' which would be part of the costs of production. When total production costs fell, with higher labour productivity, the fund would increase, and vice versa (Hsu 1991: 167).

As price reforms were introduced, many everyday items, particularly food, became more expensive. Allocative efficiency was enhanced, and although wages were indexed, this was at least an *overt* rather than a *covert* subsidy. Some economists did not want national indexation, but rather a selective subsidy or a local adjustment. There was, to sum up:

> no consensus among Chinese economists on price and wage reforms. Because China's price reform has been postponed, so has serious wage reform. However, China's recent price-wage discussion does illustrate functional economics at work – its attempt to include wide-ranging micro- and macro-concerns and its pragmatic pros and cons weighing approach with greater sophistication.
>
> (Hsu 1991: 169).

Partly as a result of such thinking, material incentives were introduced. The 'floating wage' became more important as a method of rewarding effort and productivity. Whilst such new practices were welcomed by some workers who stood to benefit, others who were potential losers were resentful. In effect, many managers paid all employees a bonus in order to placate them and to avoid any conflict and disruption to production, thus defeating the purpose of the innovation, in the eyes of critics. So-called 'red-eye disease' (jealousy) has been quite general as a result of the economic reform policy. Greater economic rationality led to discrepancies in rewards between groups of workers in the same firm or between firms, but these were not perceived as a return for greater effort (Thompson 1992: 241-4).

Another consequence of the reforms has been a move away from the Soviet-style grading system, and the incorporation of greater rewards for flexibility (Takahara 1992). Promotion was previously by seniority and political fidelity rather than acquired expertise and motivation. Previously, all wage levels were fixed by the state. In principle, the system rewarded 'each according to their labour'. There had long been a minimum wage system, based on the cost of subsistence for two people, and the actual sums paid to each of the various ranks of a particular enterprise were fixed by the local district labour bureaux, following provincial and industrial-level bureaux guidelines. Fringe-benefits, housing subsidies and the like were ascertained accordingly. The system was criticized for 'low wages, high employment', but fundamentally meant gross overmanning. It was criticized as inefficient not only internally, but also by foreign investors. Reacting against this, the reforms were intended to introduce rewards; in principle at least, the 'iron rice-bowl' was to be 'smashed' (Leung 1988: 69). By 1993, what the Chinese call a 'labour-force market' had been widely introduced (Gao 1994: 12–16).

By the late 1980s, the State Economic Commission had launched extensive wage reforms. In future, state enterprises could decide their own reward levels. There would be a basic wage, topped up by bonuses and productivity deals. Such reforms were not welcomed by economic conservatives, whether lobbying at macro- or micro-levels, and were not well received in trade union circles. Piecework, which had been used a great deal in the 1950s in state enterprises, then banned in the Cultural Revolution, was reintroduced. Covering only one in ten state enterprise employees by the mid-1980s (Granick 1991: 283), it was particularly common practice in coal-mining and the docks. Piece-work rates were mostly used to compensate for low bonuses and because they could be paid out of costs rather than profits.

According to a survey carried out by the ACFTU, using a sample of 210,000 workers from over 400 enterprises, only around one in eight (12.2 per cent) were able to display a high level of 'enthusiasm' in their work since the labour reforms were introduced, while seven out of eight (87.8 per cent) displayed only mediocre motivation. More than one in three (36.3 per cent) felt disempowered as 'masters' in their enterprises, and half (51.5 per cent) thought workers' status was unduly low, while the rest felt they had virtually become 'hired hands'. Low enthusiasm for the labour reforms among workers was principally reflected in the following:

1 low attendance rates
2 low utilization rate of working hours (i.e. not above 50 per cent)

3 poor motivation at work and unwillingness to learn professional skills
4 low labour productivity
5 low political enthusiasm, with workers unwilling to join the Youth League or the Party, preferring to pursue their own 'material' interests.

Based on various surveys, the causes leading to low motivation among workers are summed up as follows:

> The system of labour contracts has affected the enthusiasm of workers and staff members. . . . With a sense of being 'second-class workers', workers employed under labour contracts generally consider themselves inferior to others, feel insecure and lack the sense of having a stable job. As a result, their initiative and creativity in work are declining.
>
> The unfair distribution has hurt the enthusiasm of workers and staff members. The sharp contrast between the high income of self-employed businessmen and the low income of workers in state-owned enterprises has had a great impact on workers. More-over, state-owned enterprise workers also earn much less than those working in joint ventures or foreign-invested enterprises. . . .
>
> The improper management of enterprise leaders has also impaired the enthusiasm of workers and staff members.
>
> *(Summary of World Broadcasts* 1992)

Under the old labour system, dismissals were virtually impossible, and very rare. Today, they are somewhat easier in principle but are, in reality, minimal – less than 2 per cent, taking several different forms, from temporary suspension to outright sacking depending on the gravity of the offence. In joint ventures, workers who perform poorly may sometimes be transferred to a 'labour-service' company owned by the same enterprise group, or to a non-joint-venture plant on the same site – 'one factory, two systems'.

Redundancies are another novel feature of the economic reforms. As state enterprises are made more economically responsible, the less productive ones are shedding labour, particularly on 'pilot' or 'experimental' sites selected to test the new enterprise contract responsibility schemes. In the case of mergers and contractions, older workers, or the less competent, are shed, transferred or retrained. Precise numbers for these redevelopments are not available, but are likely to be small. Large numbers of peasants have also been displaced from the countryside, with estimates running into tens of millions (Thompson 1992/3). Any traveller to the PRC today is immediately struck by the vast numbers of peasants in transit on buses and trains – clear evidence of this rural exodus.

'Disguised unemployment' has long been a feature of economic development. Overmanning in both the rural and urban sectors in China testifies to this phenomenon. 'Frictional unemployment', due to job changes, is possible to a small extent in the relatively more mobile sectors of the labour market and was, until the early 1990s, very low in the state sector where job allocation meant inbuilt rigidities. The rate of job transfer is now increasing for professionals and technically-skilled personnel in state-owned firms (*Beijing Review* 1 February 1993: 12). 'Premature unemployment' also exists, especially where perhaps as many as one in ten of young people are 'awaiting assignment', as the euphemistic Chinese phrase puts it (Warner 1994).

Officially, China has had a 'three-in-one' policy, using established labour bureaux, labour service firms and a mixture of informally organized networks that encourage exchange in sectors such as self-employment (Thompson 1992: 246). A pioneer in the last of these categories is the Beijing Talent Exchange Centre. In 1989, it launched the Spring Labour Fair, bringing together 130 firms and 6,000 potential workers. By 1992, attendance had grown tenfold. There are also unofficial labour markets for rural migrants such as young women seeking jobs as domestic servants (Thompson 1992: 246). Job transfers have become easier: over 1 million technical and managerial personnel registered at personnel exchange centres in 1993, in order to seek relocation. According to a recent estimate, as many as one in three professionals would like to move their place of employment: the actual transfer rate is probably around 2.5 per cent. Many qualified young graduates would like to work in joint ventures. Nearly half the staff in Shanghai's 1,000 foreign-funded enterprises were hired by such personnel agencies (*Beijing Review* 1 February 1993: 13).

A significant feature of the changes in the labour market brought about by the economic reforms of the 1980s has been the proliferation of the use of employment contracts. By the end of the decade, it was estimated that at least one in ten workers in the industrial labour-force was employed on a contract basis rather than having a 'job for life'; and many consequently saw themselves as second-class employees in a 'two-tier' labour-market (White 1986; Leung 1988; Granick 1991). By the end of 1993, contracted employees were estimated to account for over one in five of the workforce in state-owned firms (*Beijing Review* 14 March 1994: 26). A recent Chinese estimate states that as many as 50 per cent of labour-force resources (excluding agriculture) was allocated by the market (Gao 1994: 12–16).

While labour contracts are to be found in the state enterprises, they are more common in other economic organizations, such as township industries, joint ventures and privately- and/or foreign-owned firms. The labour-force in these instances is more likely to be young, and/or female, as well as of recent rural origin (Jacka 1992). Reduced social costs mean lower labour costs for enterprises, while higher money wages may be offered to compensate such recruits for their limited tenure. The notion of using temporary 'contract-labour' was originally imported from the former Soviet Union in the mid-1950s, and was at first used quite extensively on construction projects, subsequently spreading to other types of workplace. Contract-labourers had reduced status, lacking the security, privileges and perks of state employees. During the 1960s, the widespread resentment among contract-labourers provided eager recruits for the Red Guard during the Cultural Revolution. Currently, temporary contracts coexist with labour contracts of short, medium or longer-term duration. Such practices reflect a greater degree of convergence with other east Asian labour-markets. Chinese enterprises are able to take advantage of the plentiful supply of workers to offer cheap labour to foreign firms, such as Hong Kong entrepreneurs. The latter are thus willing to use their capital, and their managerial expertise, to tackle and rectify problems of low productivity and poor quality control. In theory, such joint ventures or wholly-owned enterprises exist to provide an export-base along the coastal periphery of China (Vogel 1991).

STATE INDUSTRIAL ENTERPRISES

A major policy shift signalled in early 1992 – confirmed by the late spring, legitimated in the autumn of that year, and extended in 1993 – has been the reform of the state industrial sector. This part of the economy had long been the favoured recipient of government support, heavily subsidized and staunchly protected. The reason for this special treatment was its vanguard role in the modernization process since 1949. It was also a major contributor to state funds, as tax revenues could be gathered from the more productive sub-sectors.

State-owned enterprises (officially 'owned by the whole people') have long been the work-horse of Chinese industry. Large and medium-sized firms in this sector number over 100,000 (out of a total of some 1,300,000) and used to produce the bulk of the total gross value of industrial output – nearly 80 per cent in 1980. However, their contribution was nearly 55 per cent of this total by the early 1990s. By this date, large state firms had grown, while small state firms had shrunk dramatically. State enterprises were still inefficient and overmanned, with just under half of the 100 million state workers employed in the large and medium-sized enterprises (State Statistical Bureau 1992). It was not uncommon to find an enterprise employing over 100,000 people on one site. Such large firms display all the apparatus of Chinese labour-management relations, with a consistent set of personnel practices (Warner 1994). They have almost complete unionization, with workers' congresses as well as branch union committees. Examples of these large state enterprises are to be found in cities such as Shanghai, Shenyang, Wuhan and other major conurbations (Leeming 1992: 115).

Since 1986 they have grown at around 7.5 per cent a year and the volume of state subsidy has become not only a drain on resources that could be best used elsewhere, but also anomalous in an emergent, if still regulated, market economy 'with Chinese characteristics'. Previously, this sector had not been appreciably open to market forces. By spring 1992, the government had decided on the basis of policies formulated in May and September of the previous year to steer these enterprises into the market, holding them responsible for their profits and losses, even to the point of bankruptcy. A further reform of the labour and personnel system was announced at the same time.

The Commission for Restructuring the Economy, the Ministry of Personnel and the ACFTU put forward a 12-point proposal for deepening reform of the system of administration of labour and personnel, wage distribution and social insurance in enterprises in early 1992. The gist of this document was as follows:

1 Earnestly follow the guidelines of the State Council circular on stopping unnecessary inspection and appraisal of enterprises, and non-interference in the internal structure of enterprises. A comprehensive review of the various regulations and policies governing enterprises, formulated in recent years, should be conducted. Any contents which do not conform to the enterprise law and other relevant state provisions concerning improving enterprises should be revised or abolished. It is necessary to take effective measures to resolutely do away

with unnecessary activities on inspection, appraisal, target-fulfilment, promotion and examinations; thus enabling enterprises to devote their undivided attention and efforts to improving production and operation.

2 Strengthen in a practical way the internal economic responsibility system in enterprises, and strive to establish and perfect various rules and regulations.

3 Carry out reform of the personnel system in enterprises, and gradually implement an appointment system for management and technical personnel.

4 Consolidate and improve the labour contract system.

5 Gradually implement a full-time labour contract system.

6 Strengthen wage management and improve formulas for linking total wages to economic efficiency; gradually evolve from wages linked to a single target, to wages linked to multiple-target performance. It is essential to pay attention to maintaining and enhancing the values of state-owned assets, technological advancement and productivity, as well as to improving other comprehensive economic performance indices including the ratio between capital invested and profits delivered, and taxes paid to the state.

7 Implement an independent distribution system with distribution according to work, and overcome egalitarianism. A wage system based on the skills of a certain section of a production line should be gradually introduced, provided it is within the limits of the total wages determined by the state, and carried out on a voluntary basis among enterprises.

8 Make strenuous efforts to improve the quality of labour contingents in enterprises, and adhere to the principle of training prior to both employment and promotion. Newly-recruited technical workers should undergo professional training and strict assessment.

9 Continue to implement the reform of pension and social insurance systems and gradually establish a multi-tier insurance system, integrating basic insurance provided by the state and supplementary insurance provided by enterprises with personal savings in insurance.

10 Continue to expand the scope of existing insurance and improve the system of on-the-job insurance.

11 Speed up reform of the labour planning system and implement autonomy in personnel appointments and wage distribution among enterprises.

12 Strengthen democratic management among enterprises and bring the role of the workers' congress into play.

(Warner 1994)

In order to deal with the problems of the state industrial sector (particularly the large number of loss-making enterprises), the establishment of a social security system (i.e. unemployment insurance) was announced to cushion the blow to the displaced workers. The state would at the same time develop employment in the service industries to absorb surplus labour and raise wages for both workers and government employees. The goal of these cuts was to deal with the low levels of economic efficiency, excessive overmanning and unduly high indirect employment costs due to the generous welfare provisions provided in state industrial enterprises, referred to, as we saw earlier, as the 'iron rice-bowl'.

Over 500 enterprises were thus designated as experimental sites. Greater competition was to be introduced and life-time tenure for cadres was to be abolished to encourage freer transfer of workers, and performance-based remuneration. Some enterprises are even experimenting with the selling of shares to employees. Enterprises with long-term losses are to be merged, shut down or declared bankrupt.

Firms would have to recruit through examinations. Senior staff who fail the tests would be assigned menial jobs, and successful junior employees would be promoted. Enterprises would also be able to hire staff from abroad, an unprecedented innovation. Wages would be fixed by enterprises according to performance levels as well as regulations, with freedom to arrive at the total sum for bonuses. Empirical investigations by the present author in state-owned enterprises in Beijing and the north-east in mid-1993 indicated that although the 'comprehensive' reforms were being implemented, there was a gap between intent and practice as is often the case in China (Warner 1994).

COLLECTIVELY- AND PRIVATELY-OWNED ENTERPRISES

Collectively-owned industrial enterprises in urban and rural areas (owned, that is, by major administrative units and municipalities) now employ over 50 million workers and produced over 35 per cent of the total gross value of industrial output during fast expansion at the end of the 1980s. Since 1986, they have grown at around 18 per cent per annum. In principle, they may recruit freely according to their production needs, but the larger ones often resemble state-sector enterprises and are run by lower-level government bodies seeking to provide as many local jobs as possible. Such firms used to have 'controlled' wages but may now reward workers and managers more flexibly. On paper, there are nearly 20,000 trade union branches with 3 million members in this sector. It is not known, however, how many enterprises described as 'collective' are indeed 'private'. Some entrepreneurs find it 'politic' to turn over a minority of the shares to staff members, or pay substantial bonus payments, thus registering their firms as 'collective' enterprises (Young 1992: 66).

In 1978 there were only 150,000 licensed individually-owned firms (although many more were illicitly run). By 1993, there were over 20 million, but there is still believed to be a vast number of unregistered enterprises. Most of these are in small-scale commercial trade, or in services such as catering or repairs. Little capital, labour or skills is needed. Many operate either in 'grey' or even 'black' markets, and have dubious reputations. Yet they probably account for around 20 per cent of retail sales. Individually-owned firms, in both urban and rural areas, are said to employ just under 25 million workers and to make around 5 per cent of the nation's goods measured by gross value of industrial output. Small family concerns are registered as individual industrial and commercial households (*getihu* or *geti gonshanghu*) and were initially supposed to employ no more than seven people, plus five apprentices. Larger privately-run enterprises (*siying giye*), defined as having more than eight employees, are now legalized (Young 1992: 64). They have greater leeway in their employment practices and in effect operate in more flexible ways than the state-owned and collective enterprises. Small firms are, however, less well-researched than the others (for an exception, see Nee 1992).

JOINT VENTURES

Joint ventures and wholly foreign-owned firms have become increasingly more common in the PRC. Between 1978 and 1991, the PRC signed contracts totalling US$48.6 billion, of which less than half was eventually invested. By the end of 1991 there were at least 20,000 joint ventures (*Beijing Review* 3–16 February 1992: 20), and in 1992, 47,000 new joint ventures were set up. By 1993, an estimate of 100,000 firms was suggested, but many of these were said to be small (*Financial Times* 14 June 1993: 2). In recent years their output (together with that of private firms) has grown by over 50 per cent a year. Joint ventures produce a small but growing percentage of the value of industrial output but are important for technology and knowledge transfer. Joint ventures and wholly foreign-owned firms now account in total for about 5 per cent of gross industrial output by value, employing more than 5 million workers. They are also able to recruit their own employees, in theory at least, by examination and selection techniques; but in the early days, labour was allocated. Some of these firms may have trade unions, but not necessarily workers' congresses. Union militancy here has not been noteworthy, to date. In the SEZ, and large coastal cities such as Dalian and Shanghai, it is claimed that around half the foreign-funded firms have minimal trade union representation, although this may be only a stated ACFTU aim rather than fact, and many have been described as little more that 'sweat-shops' (Chan 1993). Situated mostly on the eastern sea-board, joint ventures have to pay more to attract better-qualified workers and to compensate for the higher cost of living there. These enterprises have greater autonomy in their labour-management policies than state enterprises. They can 'hire and fire', and enforce their own disciplinary measures and work practices. Stricter supervision and greater managerial control is common in such firms.

There are clearly attractions in working in foreign-funded ventures:

> In the summer of 1991, the Hangzhou BC Foods Co Ltd, a joint venture with the US Coca Cola Co, advertised for four secretaries. Unexpectedly, more than 500 people applied for the positions. A situation where one person is to be selected from 100-plus applicants is quite common now in foreign-funded businesses, namely Sino-foreign joint ventures, cooperative, and exclusively foreign-owned enterprises
>
> (*Beijing Review* 16–23 November 1992: 21)

The relatively high income of such employees gives them a standard of living well above their counterparts in other fields of work. However, there are drawbacks, for unsatisfactory performance may lead to a drop in wages, demotion or dismissal.

Wages and bonuses are unquestionably higher in monetary terms in the SEZs than inland. Higher wage costs are nonetheless balanced by higher productivity. Additional labour costs are incurred by the foreign investor, but these are not paid to the worker. The local labour-service company takes this percentage of total labour costs in order to cover both direct and indirect costs of labour supply, such as social insurance and so on. Joint ventures also often supply dormitory accommodation in order to house these mainly rural, frequently temporary and/or contract-employed migrants, as was traditional in the first days of industrialization in both China and Japan (Chan 1993).

The adoption of Western management practices in joint ventures has not been universally welcomed. Foreign managers of some joint-venture enterprises have widened salary differentials and abolished some accommodation and service facilities for employees.

Yanh Zhijun, the vice-general manager of the Babcock and Wilcox joint venture in Beijing argued that:

> overseas management methods could not be copied as easily as technology. Foreign partners should not disregard China's traditional culture and ways of work ... the Western style of management has its advantages, but the Chinese style is good at fostering enthusiasm among employees. Ideally, a blend of the two will be sought
>
> (Cited in Warner 1994)

CONCLUSION

As the enterprise reforms unfold, the nature of industrial relations in Chinese factories will no doubt evolve further as state-owned firms become less prominent. One observer (Korzec 1992) fears that the reforms are set to fail because they break the 'social contract' set up after 1949 between the state and the workers. Under this arrangement, 'the enterprise, with its comprehensive welfare and political functions, is that State in miniature. Moreover, this identity based as it is on long-engrained habits of dependency remains popular'. In all the areas outlined in this chapter, trade unions and worker congresses (where one or both are actually present) will no doubt have had their say, but the evidence is that they are becoming marginalized and increasingly by-passed or over-ridden whenever enterprise directors are granted greater discretionary powers (Warner 1994). Outside the state sector, their influence is already very limited, or non-existent. Institutional adaptation will no doubt proceed on pragmatic lines, neither old-style Maoist, Western nor Japanese.

ACKNOWLEDGEMENTS

I am grateful to Mr Martyn Wright and Dr Peter Nolan (both at Cambridge) for their useful comments.

BIBLIOGRAPHY

Brown, E.C. (1966) *Soviet Trade Unions and Labour Relations*, Cambridge, Mass: Harvard University Press.

Chan, A. (1993) 'Revolution or Corporatism? Workers and Unions in Post-Mao China', *Australian Institute of Chinese Affairs*, 29: 31–61.

Chesnaux, J. (1969) *The Chinese Labour Movement, 1919–27*, Palo Alto, CA: Stanford University Press.

Child, J. and Xu, X. (1989) *The Communist Party's Role in the Enterprise Leadership at the High-Water of China's Economic Reform*, Working Paper, Beijing: China–EC Management Institute (CEMI), 50 pp mimeo.

Dong Fureng (1986) 'On the Labour System and Whether Labour is a Commodity', *Guangming Ribao*, 4 October: 4.

Dunlop, J.T. (1958) *Industrial Relations Systems*, New York: Holt.

Gao, S. (1994) 'Market Economy and the Labour Force Market', *Beijing Review*, 3 January: 14–16.

Gong, Y. (1989) 'Chinese Trade Unions' Function of Democratic Participation and Social Supervision', *Chinese Trade Unions* 2: 2–5.

Granick, D. (1991) 'Multiple Labour Markets in the Industrial State Enterprise', *China Quarterly* 126, June: 269–89.

Henley, J.S. and Nyaw, M. (1986) 'Introducing Market-Forces into Managerial Decision Making in China', *Journal of Management Studies* 23, 6: 635–56.

Howe, C. (1992) 'Foreword', in Korzec, M. (ed.) *Labour and the Failure of Reform in China*, London: Macmillan and St Martin's Press.

Hsu, R.C. (1991) *Economic Theories in China 1979-1988*, Cambridge: Cambridge University Press.

Jacka, T. (1992) 'The Public–Private Dichotomy and the Gender Division of Labour', in Watson, A. (ed.) *Economic Reform and Social Change in China*, London: Routledge.

Jiang Yiwei (1980) 'The Theory of an Enterprise-based Economy', *Social Science in China* 1, 1: 48–70.

Korzec, M. (ed.) (1992) *Labour and the Failure of Reform in China*, London: Macmillan and St Martin's Press.

Lansbury, R.D., Ng, S.K. and McKern, R.B. (1984) 'Management at Enterprise-level in China', *Industrial Relations Journal* 15, 1: 56–64.

Lee, L.T. (1986) *Trade Unions in China: 1949 to the Present*, Singapore: Singapore University Press.

Lee, P. (1988) *Industrial Management and Economic Reform in China, 1949–1984*, Oxford: Oxford University Press.

Leeming, F. (1992) *The Changing Geography of China*, Oxford: Blackwell.

Leung. W, (1988) *Smashing the Iron Rice-Pot: Workers and Unions in China's Market Socialism*, Hong Kong: Asia Monitor Resource Centre.

Liu Guogang (ed.) (1987) *Ways of Reform: Opening and Development of China's Socialist Economy*, Beijing: Economic Management Press.

Ma, C. (1955) *History of the Labour Movement in China*, Taipei: China Cultural Service.

Nee, V. (1992) 'Organizational Dynamics of Market Transition: Hybrid Forms, Property Rights and Mixed Economy in China', *Administrative Science Quarterly*, 37: 1–27.

Poole, M. (1986) *Industrial Relations: Origins and Patterns of National Diversity*, London: Routledge.

Pravda, A. and Ruble, B.A. (1987) (eds) *Trade Unions in Communist States*, London: Allen & Unwin.

Schurmann, F. (1966) *Ideology and Organization in Communist China*, Berkeley, CA: University of California Press.

State Statistical Bureau (1992) *Statistical Outline of China*, Beijing: SSB.

—— (1993) *Statistical Outline of China*, Beijing: SSB.

Summary of World Broadcasts (1991) 7 August, London: British Broadcasting Corporation

—— (1992) 21 March, London: British Broadcasting Corporation.

Takahara, A. (1992) *The Politics of Wage Policy in Post-Revolutionary China*, London: Macmillan.

Thompson, P. (1992) 'Disorganized Socialism: State and Enterprise in Modern China', in Smith, C. and Thompson, P. (eds) *Labour in Transition: The Labour Process in Eastern Europe and China*, London: Routledge.

Thompson, S. (1992/3) 'Afloat in a better sea', *China Now* 143, winter: 26–8.

Vogel, E. (1991) *The Four Little Dragons*, Cambridge, MA: Harvard University Press

Walder, A.G. (1989) 'Factory and Manager in the Age of Reform', *China Quarterly* 118, June, 242–64

Warner, M. (1986) 'Managing Human Resources in China', *Organization Studies* 7, 4: 353–66

—— (1991) 'Labour Management Relations in the PRC: The Role of Trade Unions', *International Journal of Human Resource Management* 2, 2, 205–20.

—— (1992) *How Chinese Managers Learn: Management and Industrial Training in the PRC*, London: Macmillan.

—— (1993) 'Human Resources Management with Chinese Characteristics', *International Journal of Human Resource Management* 4, 1: 45–65.

—— (1994) *The Management of Human Resources in Chinese Industry*, London: Macmillan.

Watson, A. (ed.) (1992) *Economic Reform and Social Change in China*, London: Routledge.

White, G. (1986) 'Labour market reform in Chinese industry', in Warner, M. (ed.) *Management Reforms in China*, London: Pinter: 113–26.

—— (1991) (ed.) *The Chinese State in the Era of Economic Reform*, London: Macmillan

Young, S. (1992) 'Wealth but not security: attitudes to business in the 1980s', in Watson, A. (ed.) *Economic Reform and Social Change in China*, London: Routledge.

8 Total quality management and the future of China

Wan Waichai and Wong Yuklan

INTRODUCTION

The decade of the 1990s has been characterized by extended, intensive global competition in the products and resources markets. In order to stay profitable and competitive, firms are forced to find better ways to meet the needs of their customers, to reduce costs and to increase productivity. In the leading industrialized countries, total quality management (TQM) has long been recognized as the crucial synthesis of these objectives and their practical realization. TQM can be defined as the total involvement of all participants in the quality-supplying process, and the making of continuous improvements to meet customers' escalating expectations through the establishment of a new organizational culture, not forgetting the extension of that culture to all suppliers. On the one hand, a system perspective and a holistic approach are essential in the identification and elimination of resources duplication and non-global maximization outcomes. On the other hand, the culture of continuous improvement in every activity is crucial to the firm's capacity to meet the customers' requirements.

On a theoretical level, TQM can enhance the competitive position of a firm because it offers not only the direction of change but also the guiding principles for practical implementation. The core concept is to take business organization as a system of processes aiming to create value in the market through exchange.

CUSTOMER SATISFACTION

Given this view, the direction of change should be market-oriented organizational practice. Accordingly, the production of goods and services has become a secondary aspect, to be promoted only after customers' needs have been properly defined and satisfied.

This explains why firms that are concerned only with specification fail to achieve TQM results. Firms that concentrate their efforts solely on improving their technical and other operational efficiency will also fail. Such firms all overlook continuous customer satisfaction as the most important part of the whole value-added chain. Value, repeated customers, and profits will follow only after we have customer satisfaction.

CONTINUOUS IMPROVEMENT

While the direction of change is clear, there are many different possible ways to organize the planned changes. In other words, TQM offers a broad framework, within which many different approaches are possible, and this is reflected in the various existing practices of excellence in firms in the leading industrialized countries. Within the broad framework, one central idea is the continuous improvement of the firm and everyone in it, in every sphere and part of its activity. Doing better and better is more important than whether the current result is good or bad.

We are faced, then, with an open system. There is a continuous interaction between the organization and its environment, and the business system will adopt different states dependent upon the input conditions defined by the environment. Hence, today's optimum will be tomorrow's sub-optimum; continuous improvements are essential if a company's competitive position is to be maintained. A sluggish market leader can be overtaken by its ever-improving competitors.

EXTENDED SYSTEM

Another possibility is to set up a dynamic network of quality suppliers through cooperation and partnership arrangements. The relationships should be close and permanent enough to permit the interchange and sharing of vital resources including information, storage space, training facilities, and so on. The role of this dynamic network is important in the complex and changing competitive environments of the 1990s. Such an arrangement can lead to a more efficient use of resources and a guarantee of quality results. The customer is perceived as being served directly by the network as a whole, rather than the individual firm.

PEOPLE MAKE QUALITY

In order to carry out and sustain the process of change, we also need to focus on the role of human resources. It is clear that systems, standards and technology themselves will not automatically result in continuous improvement and customer satisfaction. Therefore, leadership, teamwork and motivation are the major turnaround strategies in building a quality culture.

CHINESE EXPERIENCE OF TQM

On a practical level, current processes of TQM as guided by Deming and others have accounted partially for the Japanese economic miracle. The significance of the process is that the international competitiveness of an economy will be shaped by its ability to assimilate the broad framework offered by TQM.

However, few Chinese firms have gone so far as to implement the strategic perspective of quality; far more frequently, we find a less-developed focus. The simple declaration that TQM is being implemented does not inform *a priori* about the characteristics of the quality programme being applied. Only when we know precisely which objectives, policies and measures have been implemented can we discover whether management of quality in a firm has focused on technical or social aspects, and whether it has been limited to the production process, or constitutes part of the firm's total business strategy.

On one hand, the pressure of increasing costs, and the prospect of greater competition after readmittance to the GATT, together with more demanding customer requirements, have pushed Chinese firms towards implementing TQM. And the Chinese government, well aware of the importance of quality improvement to the international competitiveness of the local economy, has an added incentive to participate actively in promoting and facilitating the TQM efforts of Chinese firms. The government has set up institutions such as CQCA, CAST, CSBTS and so on, which act as innovation centres, encouraging the spread of TQM across the region or throughout the country, disseminating information, facilitating inter-company relationships, providing training and sometimes even subsidies.

This chapter is a survey study on 83 manufacturing firms in Guangtung Province. It aims to explore empirically the effectiveness of their TQM programmes. Top managers are interviewed. Two types of effectiveness measurements are used; conclusions are drawn

Table 8.1 Mean values of firms participating in TQM study: 1993

	Median	Mean	Standard deviation
No. of employees	145	161.3	197.5
Long-term assets ('000 rmb)	8,237	9,546	7,963
Sales ('000 rmb)	79,766	125,306	130,546
% export on sales	70.5	81.3	14.3

on the achievement and performance of TQM in these firms. A group of high-performance firms was selected from the sample and was compared with the entire sample so as to isolate the decisive factors for the success of the programme in these Chinese firms.

The basic problem facing this research was how to measure the effectiveness of the quality programmes implemented by the sample of firms. Objective measures, such as quality cost, cannot be used because the data is not available in most of the firms and, more importantly, quality cost can in fact be measured in various ways. One possible solution was to rely on the managers' subjective estimates of those results attributable directly to the quality programme. Specifically, two different measures of effectiveness were used. First, the managers were asked to specify the objectives of their programmes, and then to rate their satisfaction level with the achievement of each of the objectives, on a Likert grading scale from 1 to 5. Second, managers were asked to estimate the direction and size of the changes in a number of variables over the past year, which had directly resulted from their programmes. The variables included: sales, absenteeism, suggestions received, training, rate of customer complaints, labour productivity, production equipment productivity, ratio of defective products to total output, unit product cost, stock volume, profits and quality culture.

EFFECTIVENESS OF THE TQM PROGRAMME

The first part of the survey studied the effectiveness of the TQM programme in the Chinese context. The attributes of the 83 sample firms are shown in Tables 8.1 and 8.2.

Table 8.3 represents the data corresponding to the level of top managers' satisfaction with the achievement of the different objectives of the programme. It shows that top managers are generally satisfied with the overall achievement of the programmes, with a mean estimated achievement of objectives of 2.95, on the 1–5 scale. The most popular objective is the achievement of customer consoli-

Table 8.2 Industrial sectors of participating firms

	Number of firms	*% of total samples*
Textile	16	19.3
Garment	14	16.8
Footwear	13	15.7
Toys	10	12.0
Food	9	10.8
Furniture	7	8.4
Paper	6	7.2
Ceramics	4	4.8
Metals	4	4.8
Total	83	100.0

Table 8.3 Stated TQM objectives and estimated achievement of them

Objectives	*Percentage of firms which included this objective*	*Estimated achievement of this objective (on a scale of 1 to 5)*
Improvement in work environment	54.2	3.23
Products standardization	88.0	3.21
Managers' motivation	72.3	3.15
Customer consolidation	96.4	3.14
Management system improvement	84.3	3.08
Work system improvement	78.3	3.06
Improvement in external communication	74.7	3.04
Product innovation	66.3	3.00
Employee motivation	60.2	2.97
Productivity improvement	88.0	2.97
Production process innovation	71.1	2.94
Profits improvement	90.4	2.91
Traditional market share improvement	85.5	2.83
Access to national markets	74.7	2.81
Improvement in internal communications	72.3	2.81
Access to foreign markets	90.4	2.63
Labour relationships	51.8	2.32

dation, with 96.4 per cent of firms pursuing this objective. Its mean of satisfaction is quite encouraging (3.14). The objective recording the highest level of satisfaction was 'improvement in the work environment'. This is due to the emphasis in many firms on introspective analyses and investment in new production facilities. Table 8.4 shows that the measures employed by these firms to implement their quality programmes are mostly technically oriented. We can

Table 8.4 Measures already applied to implement the TQM programme

Measures	Percentage of firms
Employment of technical staff	68.7
Production equipment investments	61.4
Quality control department created	59.0
External audits	55.4
Employee training by consultancy firm	54.2
Quality diagnosis by consultancy firm	54.2
Manager training by consultancy firm	48.2
Product design changes	45.8
Promotion of team work	39.8
Economic incentives to improve quality	38.6
Job redesign	32.5
Employee training by internal staff	30.1
Quality laboratory	30.1
Participative style of management	27.7
Quality manual design and implementation	24.1
After-sales service set up	21.7
Statistical process control	18.1
Quality management committee set up	14.5
Quality cost analysis	2.4
Suggestions box	2.4

Table 8.5 Positive effects achieved by the TQM programme during 1993

Effects	Percentage of firms experiencing this effect
Increase in sales	84.3
Improved ratio of defective products to total output	68.7
Decrease in customer complaints	66.3
Increased profits	59.0
Improved training	56.6
Reduction in unit production cost	55.4
Improved labour productivity	54.2
Improvement in production equipment productivity	53.0
Increased number of suggestions	51.8
Development of a quality culture	48.2
Stock volume reduction	31.3
Reduced absenteeism	30.1

see from Table 8.4 that many firms prefer these measures, e.g. employment of technical staff, production equipment investments, external audit, training and diagnosis provided by consultancy firms. Such external resources are heavily used because Chinese firms are generally lacking in expertise and experience in the implementation of TQM.

Table 8.6 Difficulties encountered in implementing the TQM programme

Difficulty	Mean of importance given (on a scale of 1 to 5)
Quality department given sole responsibility for quality	3.89
Lack of experience in quality management	3.82
Lack of commitment of top management	3.70
Resistance to change	3.64
Lack of resources	3.43
Emphasis on short-term objective	3.34
Quality systems based on detection	3.08
Operatives given sole responsibility for quality	2.89
Barriers between departments	2.60
Production department given sole responsibility for quality	2.41
Lack of objectives and strategies	2.39
Excessive reliance on the quality manual	1.61

Table 8.5 demonstrates the estimated changes in a number of variables of performance resulting from the programme. Generally speaking, the top managers did not find that the introduction of TQM brought with it many adverse effects. The most frequently experienced result was an increase in sales, as experienced by 84.3 per cent of the sample. However, we should note that it is hard for the managers to distinguish the effect of the TQM programme from that of the booming economy in southern China. The strong growth of sales and customer bases are largely caused by the overall economic growth in south China; TQM is not the only contributing factor. Furthermore, we should not overlook the effect of high inflation rates in Guangtung Province on the nominal sales figures.

Overall, TQM has enjoyed only moderate success in southern China. Many firms still consider quality to be a series of standard specifications that they have to achieve if they wish to enter a particular market. They fail to consider TQM as a means of better satisfying the needs and demands of the customers, and therefore they do not take a strategic view of it. They do not see TQM as an asset for the firm and as a source of competitive advantage.

Basically, the lack of a strategic and global focus on the management of quality is reflected in the various problems encountered by managers in implementing the TQM programme: excessive reliance on the quality department, lack of experience in quality manage-

Table 8.7 Effects of quality programme on labour productivity

Improvement registered	No. of companies	Percentage of total sample
More than 30 per cent	1	1.20
21–30 per cent	3	3.61
11–20 per cent	5	6.02
Up to 10 per cent	16	19.28
Positive response but no estimate	20	24.10
Negative response	16	19.28
No response/don't know	22	26.51
Total	83	100.00

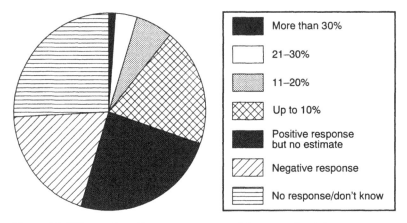

Figure 8.1 Effects of quality programme on labour productivity

ment, lack of commitment, resistance to change, etc. Although China has adopted an open-door policy since 1978, Chinese managers know very little of quality management, not to mention the experience of implementing TQM. Chinese management tends to stress tactical issues and short-term performance. Another reason for the unsatisfactory results of TQM implementation is the misconception of quality. Chinese managers believe that quality problems can be tackled by post-operational detection activities rather than by building quality into the processes.

For the successful implementation of TQM, firms need to design a quality system based on prevention. However, it is not easy to

Table 8.8 Effects of quality programme on customer complaints

Improvement registered	No. of companies	Percentage of total sample
More than 30 per cent	4	4.82
21–30 per cent	6	7.23
11–20 per cent	8	9.64
Up to 10 per cent	20	24.10
Positive response but no estimate	17	20.48
Negative response	13	15.66
No response/don't know	15	18.07
Total	83	100.00

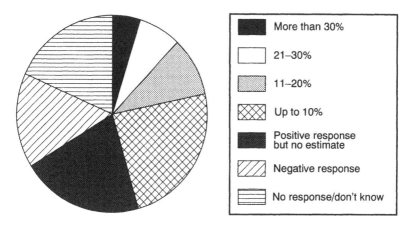

Figure 8.2 Effects of quality programme on customer complaints

move from a system based on detection to a system based on prevention, and the former is a serious obstacle to the implementation of TQM programmes. In other words, the predominant focus should be on the process itself rather than on the output. The better the knowledge of the firm's processes, the more thorough the corresponding TQM programme designed for them, and the lower the fluctuation in output.

In Tables 8.7–8.16 and Figures 8.1–8.10, we can see in more detail the firms' estimates of the effect of the programme on a number of performance criteria. The missing cases in these tables represent those firms that stated a positive effect but did not estimate an exact

Table 8.9 Effects of quality programme on production equipment productivity

Improvement registered	No. of companies	Percentage of total sample
More than 30 per cent	3	3.61
21–30 per cent	3	3.61
11–20 per cent	6	7.23
Up to 10 per cent	12	14.46
Positive response but no estimate	20	24.10
Negative response	25	30.12
No response/don't know	14	16.87
Total	83	100.00

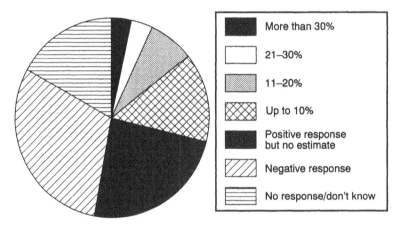

Figure 8.3 Effects of quality programme on production equipment productivity

value. Some of the results are quite spectacular, bearing in mind that they represent only one year. These data show conclusively that for some firms at least the quality programme has been very effective.

After analysing the general results of the sample, we aim to isolate the main determinants leading to the success of the TQM programme. The high performance group, with sales improvements of over 10 per cent in the year 1993, is compared with the overall sample. There are many different ways to quantify the TQM pro-

Table 8.10 Effects of quality programme on defective products ratio

Improvement registered	No. of companies	Percentage of total sample
More than 30 per cent	5	6.02
21–30 per cent	7	8.43
11–20 per cent	13	15.66
Up to 10 per cent	12	14.46
Positive response but no estimate	20	24.10
Negative response	12	14.46
No response/don't know	14	16.87
Total	83	100.00

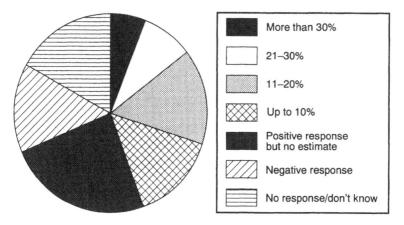

Figure 8.4 Effects of quality programme on defective products ratio

gramme performance. However, the sales growth figure is used as a proxy in this survey study because sales figures were considered to be a more reliable estimate than other criteria, and revenue income adheres closely to the central objective of TQM (continuous customer satisfaction). Clearly, the most successful group had placed a greater emphasis on innovation than the rest of the sample: innovation in products, markets, processes and production equipment.

Table 8.17 compares the perceived level of achievement of objectives in the most successful firms with that in the rest of the sample. If we calculate the difference between the means, we find that innovation in the production process, access to national markets

Table 8.11 Effects of quality programme on profits

Improvement registered	No. of companies	Percentage of total sample
More than 30 per cent	3	3.61
21–30 per cent	5	6.02
11–20 per cent	9	10.84
Up to 10 per cent	12	14.46
Positive response but no estimate	20	24.10
Negative response	22	26.51
No response/don't know	12	14.46
Total	83	100.00

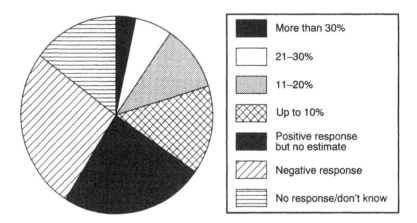

Figure 8.5 Effects of quality programme on profits

and innovation in the products themselves were the objectives recording the biggest differential in their perceived achievement between the successful firms and the rest of the sample. Thus, the broad frame of quality management was given a more innovative bias by the small group of successful firms than by the firms in the rest of the group.

The second interesting aspect of the results is the intensity of change that took place in the firms as a result of the introduction of a quality programme. Table 8.18 shows the managers' estimates of the intensity of these changes, in means, for the 'top' group of 23 firms as compared with the sample as a whole. It is clear that the

Table 8.12 Effects of quality programme on suggestions received

Improvement registered	No. of companies	Percentage of total sample
More than 30 per cent	3	3.61
21–30 per cent	5	6.02
11–20 per cent	8	9.64
Up to 10 per cent	9	10.84
Positive response but no estimate	18	21.69
Negative response	27	32.53
No response/don't know	13	15.66
Total	83	100.00

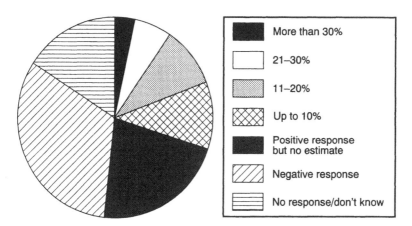

Figure 8.6 Effects of quality programme on suggestions received

difference between the levels of change in most of the variables is considerable, and the successful companies have made greater changes in almost all of the aspects considered. We can therefore conclude that the TQM programmes of the small group of firms can more properly be defined as programmes of change than can those of the sample as a whole.

Once again, differences are greatest in the innovative aspects of the programmeme. As Table 8.18 shows, the changes showing the greatest differentiation between the most successful group and the sample as a whole were: the introduction of new lines, the purchase of new production equipment and changes in the pro-

Table 8.13 Effects of quality programme on sales

Improvement registered	No. of companies	Percentage of total sample
More than 30 per cent	6	7.23
21–30 per cent	7	8.43
11–20 per cent	10	12.05
Up to 10 per cent	15	18.07
Positive response but no estimate	19	22.89
Negative response	13	15.67
No response/don't know	13	15.66
Total	83	100.00

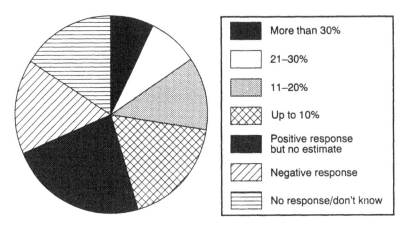

Figure 8.7 Effects of quality programme on sales

duction process, especially with the introduction of automation. The difference in improvements in management skills between the two groups is also notable. From the data, we can also conclude that the quality programmes that led to the highest increase in sales were also those that involved the greatest changes within the firms. The successful programmes focused far more on innovation, technology, product renovation and openness to new markets. These programmes also improved management skills and motivation to a higher degree. Their innovative nature and improved management have in turn contributed to the programmes' success.

Table 8.14 Effects of quality programme on production costs

Improvement registered	No. of companies	Percentage of total sample
More than 30 per cent	1	1.20
21–30 per cent	4	4.82
11–20 per cent	7	8.43
Up to 10 per cent	14	16.87
Positive response but no estimate	20	24.10
Negative response	23	27.71
No response/don't know	14	16.87
Total	83	100.00

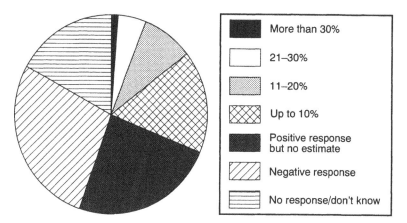

Figure 8.8 Effects of quality programme on production costs

SUMMARY AND CONCLUSIONS

The firms on which this study is based are pioneers in the quality management field in China. They have placed a great deal of emphasis on training and external consultancy, and based their programmes on education and training in general. Nevertheless, most of the programmes reflect a lack of strategic perspective, and they are mostly oriented towards the technical aspects of quality assurance. We have also seen that better sales results are achieved by those firms that are prepared to innovate and embrace considerable changes in processes, equipment, products and markets, and to encourage greater improvements in management skills and motiv-

Table 8.15 Effects of quality programme on stock volume

Improvement registered	No. of companies	Percentage of total sample
More than 30 per cent	1	1.20
21–30 per cent	3	3.61
11–20 per cent	5	6.02
Up to 10 per cent	7	8.43
Positive response but no estimate	10	12.05
Negative response	41	49.40
No response/don't know	16	19.28
Total	83	100.00

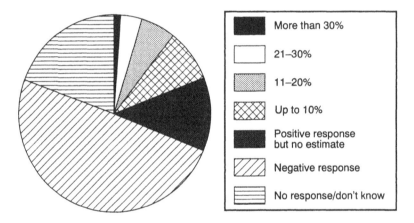

Figure 8.9 Effects of quality programme on stock volume

ation. While TQM is not a guarantee for success, it is a broad framework, within which many different approaches and practices coexist. The pattern of approaches and practices chosen by each firm will govern whether or not that firm becomes competitive. In this chapter, we have analysed the results of TQM implementation within 83 firms in Guangtung Province, evaluating the effectiveness of the programme. To do this, we relied on the subjective opinion of the top managers and also two different measures of the effectiveness: the level of top managers' satisfaction with the achievement of the different objectives of the programmes, and the estimated

Table 8.16 Effects of quality programme on absenteeism

Improvement registered	No. of companies	Percentage of total sample
More than 30 per cent	1	1.20
21–30 per cent	3	3.61
11–20 per cent	6	7.23
Up to 10 per cent	9	10.84
Positive response but no estimate	6	7.23
Negative response	40	48.19
No response/don't know	18	21.69
Total	83	100.00

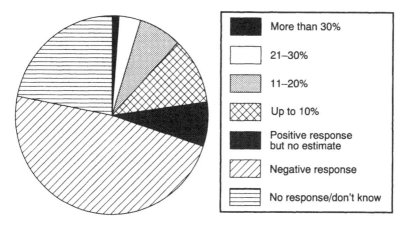

Figure 8.10 Effects of quality programme on absenteeism

changes in a number of variables of performance resulting from the programmes.

We have seen that the overall achievements of the programs were perceived by managers to be quite high, and that the estimated changes in the different variables of performance as a consequence of the implementation of TQM were very positive from some of the firms in the sample.

Focusing on the estimated increase in sales as a consequence of the implementation of TQM, the group of firms with the highest performance was selected and comparisons with the whole sample were made. It was concluded that the successful groups placed

Table 8.17 Difference in perceived achievement of objectives

Objectives	Successful firms (scale of 1 to 5)	Whole sample (scale of 1 to 5)	Difference
Production process innovation	4.13	2.94	1.19
Access to national markets	4.00	2.81	1.19
Product innovation	4.17	3.00	1.17
Managers' motivation	4.20	3.15	1.05
Access to foreign markets	3.67	2.63	1.04
Traditional market share increase	3.83	2.83	1.00
Standardization of products	4.17	3.21	0.96
Customer consolidation	4.00	3.14	0.86
Productivity improvement	3.75	2.97	0.78
Profits improvement	3.03	2.91	0.72
Improved labour relationship	2.80	2.32	0.48
Improved internal communications	3.25	2.81	0.44
Improved work system	3.38	3.06	0.32
Improved external communication	3.04	3.00	0.04
Employees' motivation	3.00	2.97	0.03
Improved work atmosphere	2.83	2.81	0.02
Improved management system	3.00	3.08	−0.08

more emphasis on innovation, in products, markets, processes and production equipment, that their managers were more highly motivated by the programme, and that their skills improved more. It was also seen that the intensity of the different changes experienced within the programmes was higher. Therefore, it can be said that the innovative nature of the programmes, the intensity of the different changes, and the improved management techniques have proved decisive to the success of the programmes.

Table 8.18 Difference in intensity of change

Change	Mean intensity of change (1 to 5): successful firms	Mean intensity of change (1 to 5): whole sample	Difference
New product lines	4.67	2.82	1.85
New production equipment	4.43	2.85	1.58
Automation of production process	4.00	2.76	1.24
Other changes to production processes	4.38	3.21	1.17
Increase in market share	3.71	2.61	1.10
Improvement in management skills	4.00	3.06	0.94
Reduction in product prices	3.17	2.38	0.79
Improved product design	4.00	2.22	0.78
Reduced workshop errors	4.13	3.35	0.78
Improved training	3.88	3.18	0.70
Maintenance of machinery	3.14	2.54	0.60
Increased job variability	3.14	2.56	0.56
Improved internal communications	3.57	3.06	0.51
Supplier base	2.83	2.42	0.41
Publicity methods	2.50	2.28	0.22
Employee participation	2.86	2.69	0.17
Distribution	2.29	2.13	0.15
Tighter relationship between production and marketing	3.00	2.92	0.08
Redundancies	1.60	1.77	−0.17
Team work	2.00	2.20	−0.20

BIBLIOGRAPHY

Kanji, G.K. (1990) 'Total Quality Management: The Second Industrial Revolution', *Journal of Total Quality Management* 1 (1): 3–14.

Pall, G.A. (1987) *Quality Process Management*, Englewood Cliffs, N.J.: Prentice-Hall.

Price, F. (1984) *Right First Time – Using Quality Control for Profit*, Aldershot: Gower.

Wong, Y.L. (1993) 'Quality Strategies of Small Businesses in Hong Kong', *Proceedings of the 2nd Asian Congress on Quality & Reliability*, Beijing: IAP.

9 Growth, stability and reforms in China

Conflicting goals?

Wolfgang Klenner

INTRODUCTION

Economic reforms are usually initiated whenever it is expected by decisive social groups that a change in economic systems will result in a higher level of welfare. Thus, the crucial test of China's economic reforms will be whether expected welfare gains will indeed materialize. This chapter attempts to judge China's economic results and perspectives from this point of view.

In the following approach a very simple welfare function will be selected which consists of three broad goals, each with two sub-goals:

- *High economic growth*
  generated mainly by productivity gains
  geared towards individual preferences
- *Economic stability*
  in the short run: no inflation pressure
  in the long run: steady growth
- *Social stability*
  providing an adequate social network
  limiting income differentials

Evaluating China's economic performance on the basis of these goals would usually require a quantitative macro-economic analysis. This chapter, however, will attempt to look more closely at structural details and their relevance to China's future development. Therefore, a sectoral approach based on qualitative assessments[1] will be chosen. Three sectors will be distinguished:

1 The rural sector, with more than 400 million workers, mostly engaged in agriculture

2 The private sector, including foreign-funded firms and collective and state-run enterprises contracted to private managers
3 Medium-sized and large state-owned enterprises

ACHIEVEMENT OF GOALS WITHIN THE RURAL SECTOR

China's government initiated its reform programme in the countryside, where most of the population is engaged in agriculture. The basic idea of reform policy was to link economic rewards more directly to individual efforts, hence the measures applied quite successfully about two decades ago, when a high degree of centralization had almost eliminated individual incentives. Land use rights were assigned to individual peasants, and the principle of free markets on which selected agricultural products could be sold was accepted. More recent reforms, however, have further stressed that there was no intention to re-establish the old commune system.

Under these new conditions, peasants worked harder and longer, in order to raise family incomes. Output per capita, output per hectare and thus agricultural production and income as a whole increased. Moreover, the whole population was better off than before, since the acceptance of free markets for agricultural products, and the introduction of changes in state and collective distribution networks geared production more closely to the needs of consumers.

There are no signs that economic stability was seriously jeopardized by the severe inflationary pressure generated by developments in the countryside: the increase in rural income was based on an increase in real production, and output was geared to individual preferences. Commodities, therefore, did not end up in unsaleable stockpiles in state-run warehouses, but satisfied consumers' demand. Moreover, individual peasants faced hard budget constraints, since banks and credit cooperatives were usually unwilling to extend loans for projects and transactions that had little chance of showing a profit, and were indeed under no political obligation to do so.

Nevertheless, the Central Bank authorities were faced with considerable problems. The communes were replaced by several hundred million individual farmers, bringing an increase in cash payments and, correspondingly, a decrease in the amount of remittances. This resulted in drastic changes in money demand and its structure. Since these changes were difficult to predict, the Central Bank was certainly not always able to match the money demand with an adequate money supply.

As far as the stability of economic growth is concerned, it remains to be seen whether output will be increased further. There are two problems closely connected with the abolition of communes. The handing out of land to individual families is equivalent to a greater fragmentation of agricultural inputs, which in many cases complicates the modernization of agricultural production. Moreover, productivity gains in the future might be limited because it is unclear who will pay for and take care of infrastructure projects. During China's pre-reform period, peasants were allocated tasks relating to the maintenance of infrastructure and production. Post-reform, however, farmers are primarily interested in achieving immediate production results, and tend to neglect investment in infrastructure; it is, therefore, sometimes argued that the growth of production in recent years was mainly the result of the disinvestment of that which had been built up during the Mao Tsetung era.

Social stability might be hampered by drastic structural changes in the near furture. The enormous amount of surplus labour in the countryside was, until recently, camouflaged by the commune system. According to some estimates, surplus labour might total 30 per cent of the rural labour force. This would amount to more than 100 million peasants for whom new jobs had to be created.

With a population as vast as that of China, even small percentages, expressed in absolute figures, are staggering. However, we guard against dramatizing this, because China has several large cities able to absorb a certain amount of labour migrating from the countryside. The continual influx of surplus labour to large cities in Japan and South Korea in the 1950s and 1960s, for instance, helped local industries to maintain low wages and become competitive on world markets. Thus, China's abundant labour could enable it to pursue its export-orientated policy – as long as world markets remain open for Chinese products. However, many of China's cities are already overpopulated and provide miserable housing conditions. Massive floods of peasants into the cities would enlarge all these problems. The task ahead might be eased if capital were transferred to the countryside, rather than peasants into the cities. Indeed, there are many examples of Chinese and foreign enterprises investing in remote areas to take advantage of cheap labour. However, should China be unwilling or unable to maintain its previously tight restrictions on rural migration, a growth of suburban slums is unavoidable.

The erosion of social stability could be prevented by establishing a social network for those who are unable or no longer able to produce for the market. A rudimentary network was built up as part of China's cooperative movement which provided health care, education and a kind of pension scheme, but under present conditions many of these services no longer exist. Nowadays, the family has again become the centre of gravity of 'social' welfare. However, if families are impoverished, they will not be able to lend support to their members.

Reforms have helped the majority of rural households to raise their income, but this has also increased income disparities between individuals and regions. Those close to large cities have far greater opportunities to work and acquire wealth than peasants living far from 'good' markets, who still live in poverty. These differentials alone are not necessarily harmful to social stability, but could cause serious problems in the case of adverse developments arising.

ACHIEVEMENTS OF GOALS WITHIN THE PRIVATE AND COLLECTIVE SECTOR

The linking of economic rewards to individual effort was also taken as the basis for the transformation of China's small-scale state and collective enterprises in industry, services and transportation. Small-scale state enterprises were contracted to managers who, almost like private owners, could decide on inputs and outputs, earn profits and were responsible for losses. As a result, production was geared to individual preferences and grew rapidly. Productivity increased, although mostly within the limits of existing traditional technology. Excellent results, as well, were achieved by private enterprises, financed by locals or foreigners. But technological achievements were probably less than expected since the bulk of foreign investment was directed towards exploiting China's cheap labour force, with less advanced technology.

Specific structural elements that could generate inflationary pressure cannot be identified since collective and private enterprises usually face hard budget constraints. Neither their investment nor wages would be financed from the state coffers, and banks lend to private and collective firms according to business principles and not political guidelines.

Further growth will certainly require structural adjustments and modernization. However, most of these changes could be accomplished within the already established basic framework, so that economic stability would not be put at risk.

As far as social stability is concerned, two different effects can be expected. Further growth of this sector will contribute to providing additional workplaces for surplus labour from the countryside. On the other hand, state regulations on wages and working conditions are still very poor. What critics of capitalist countries might call 'exploitation' seems quite common within this sector. On the other hand, successful owners and managers can earn high incomes which, because of China's inefficient tax system, are usually not levelled off by personal taxation. For the time being, however, it seems that these income differentials are tolerated, as long as they are based on personal effort and not on corruption.

ACHIEVEMENTS OF GOALS WITHIN THE STATE SECTOR

Only after visible reforms had been achieved in the rural and more traditional industrial sectors did China's reformers turn, more determinedly, to medium-sized and large state-run enterprises. Here, conditions were quite unlike the structures of the rural, private and collective sectors, where it had been possible to draw on the results of experiments with comparable concepts in the early 1960s, or even in China's pre-socialist period, characterized by the existence of millions of individual farmers and private small-scale entrepreneurs.

Most of these enterprises were built during China's pre-reform period and structured according to the requirements of the country's centralized administration. The experience of reform in the early 1960s, or of managing large-scale private firms before socialization, therefore, was not of much help.

Looking at China's concrete reform measures, various policies can be distinguished, all aimed at creating independent economic units. First, attempts were made to provide material incentives: enterprises were allowed to retain a certain portion of their profits. At the same time, permission was granted to produce more than was stipulated by the Plan, and to sell the additional products on the market. This measure still guaranteed Plan fulfilment, but also incited managers to use resources more efficiently and to gear 'overplan' production to market needs. However, the resulting two-tier price system for homogeneous products generated welfare losses – at least when compared with a market system. Compared with the former totally planned system, however, results could be said to be 'better'.

Another measure entailed the abolition of quantitative targets for a few selected commodities, setting only prices. Enterprises were free to produce commodities in any amount, provided that, under given prices, profits were maximized. This was not exactly the 'Konkurrenzsozialismus' that Lange and Lerner had described in the 1930s, since it did not provide for the setting of scarcity prices by the state.[2] However, the basic ideas were comparable. Finally, selected medium-sized enterprises were allowed to produce and sell whatever they expected to be profitable. As a result of these measures, China's state sector was transformed into an extremely heterogeneous and complex amalgam of market and planning mechanisms created by reformers on the one hand, and maintained by planners on the other.

The effects of these reforms on economic growth within the state sector are not too convincing. Statistics show that despite a few isolated impressive results reported in the press, overall performance as far as productivity and market-orientation are concerned remained rather poor. Thus, it comes as no surprise that the state sector's share of total industrial output dropped from about three-quarters to just a little over half within one decade of reforms.

The poor results of reforms within the state sector have been caused mainly by inadequate regulations for capital and labour. It had been intended to liberalize these inputs in order to enable enterprises to respond flexibly to market developments. However, it was realized that under China's existing conditions, consequent reforms of factor markets would have put social stability in jeopardy. But half-hearted reforms of capital markets, while not putting social stability at risk, did adversely affect economic stability. The economic changes instigated were coupled with two-digit rates of inflation that could be controlled only by administrative rationing of capital. Thus, it transpired that within the state sector high economic growth and economic and social stability were conflicting goals. China's solution to this conflict has been, for the time being, to sacrifice consequent reforms as well as economic stability for the sake of social stability, as elaborated below.

By partly reforming the existing banking system and establishing rudimentary markets for shares, capital markets were already replacing the handouts that were formerly disbursed from the state coffers according to the Plan. These measures enabled enterprises to respond flexibly to the market and expand their capacities without having to ask the administration for permission. As a result, there was a considerable growth in the numbers of profit-motivated firms.

This posed the problem of how to restrict expansion in order to avoid an overheating of the economy. In a planned economy, restrictions are applied by strictly limiting donations to the amounts stipulated by the Plan. In market economies, control is exerted indirectly within a system that could be described as 'three linkages' and 'two non-linkages'. 'Three linkages' refers to the classic 'textbook' relations between the market and firms, firms and business banks, and business banks and the Central Bank. The term 'non-linkages' refers to the minimizing of connections between the Ministry of Finance and the Central Bank, and between the Ministry of Finance and enterprises: the Ministry of Finance should not give orders to the Central Bank to cover budget deficits by new money, and the Central Bank should not cover firms' losses.

This kind of system would be required in China if it were to decide to liberalize capital and leave its allocation almost entirely to the market. However, we find close connections between China's Ministry of Finance, the Central Bank and Chinese firms, rather than 'non-linkages'. The Central Bank is still subordinated to the Ministry of Finance which thereby has easy access to money; and it is quite common for the Ministry of Finance or its subordinate local bureaux to extend financial help to loss-making enterprises. Under these conditions the kind of linkages between markets, enterprises, banks and the Central Bank that are required for the functioning of market mechanisms cannot be developed.

Considerable effort and time are necessary in order to establish a system in which market participants submit to monetary and financial discipline. However, problems in overcoming these difficulties are not the sole reason for the still inadequate functioning of China's capital markets. China's government is afraid to risk sowing the seeds of social instability, should capital allocation become based strictly on market principles.

In order to understand this reasoning, we need to examine the structure of China's state enterprises, of which about one-third are loss-making. If these loss-making firms were exposed to the market they would have extreme difficulty in surviving. Many of them would go bankrupt and would have to dismiss their workers, numbering some several dozen million. This would not be the only negative effect on employment. Since most firms are heavily overstaffed (estimates of disguised unemployment within China's state industry put it at around 30 per cent) even more workers would lose their jobs should state enterprises be compelled to minimize costs. The employment of a large proportion of the working population within state enterprises, and their integration into social 'units', was an important political goal of China's pre-reform government. Managers of firms grumbled whenever they were forced to extend their staff and provide additional social services, but they were not in a position to oppose this policy. Finally, they could live with it because workers were on the payroll of the state; wages did not have to be earned on the market. In view of this staggering degree of potential urban unemployment, China's decision to emphasize social stability and its reluctance to concentrate solely on reforms and economic stability are quite understandable.

How to deal with these conflicting goals? A possible way out of this dilemma seems to be the establishment of a safety net that is no longer based on the affiliation of workers to a specific state enterprise, but organized on a country-wide basis. Most of the social responsibilities of the state-run enterprise, including the providing of housing facilities, could be transferred to specific organizations.

Of course, social security would certainly become an extremely heavy burden in view of the fast-growing number of people who, with reforms in progress, might lose their jobs and need supporting. However, compared with the present practice of subsidizing enterprises, this would be less expensive, since dismissed personnel would recieve transfers lower than their former wages. On the other hand, there would also be definite positive effects: enterprises would be freed from their social obligation to employ people they don't need, and to provide housing and other social services. They could be fully exposed to the market and be forced to minimize costs and adjust their production to individual preferences. Capital allocation could be left to the market which, together with an appropriate institutional framework, would help to realize price stability and steady economic growth. Under these conditions, a further privatization of state enterprises would make sense.[3]

NOTES

1 for statistics on China's economy see *China Statistical Yearbook* (various issues), Beijing: State Statistical Bureau of the People's Republic of China.
2 See Oskar Lange, 'On the Economic Theory of Socialism' in *The Review of Economic Studies*, 4 (1936–37): 53–71 and 123–142.
3 Private capital would be lured by the capitalized value of the potential returns of the production facilities of an enterprise, and not by the value of its housing stock, which is extremely high in China's large cities.

10 The impact of current economic development in China on the market entry strategies of foreign consumer goods manufacturers

Tseng Choosin, Paula Kwan and Fanny Cheung

INTRODUCTION

Since 1978, a series of reforms has taken place in China transforming her from a centrally planned economy to a more market-driven mechanism. Recently, foreign investment in tertiary industries has been encouraged, though with some limitations. This is indeed a great opportunity for foreign investors to get into the tertiary industries[1] in China – a previously restricted area. This chapter will examine and discuss the various market entry strategies available to foreign manufacturers of consumer durable goods who wish to enter the Chinese market under the prevailing economic and political environment. China's readmission to the GATT, yuan reform, and cultural and social factors will also be discussed.

Before 1978, China was a rather closed market, the supply and demand of goods in the 'key industries' including coal, electricity, petroleum, machinery, and so forth were put under the control of the central planning authorities (the State Planning Commission, the Economic Commission, the State Council and central ministries). Other, non-key, industries were controlled by the local planning authorities (the bureaux of the State Planning Commission, the Economic Commission and industrial ministries). Involvement in international trade was very minimal and foreign investment was prohibited. Goods would be imported only if planned supply fell short of planned demand, which might be the result of natural disasters, shortage of domestic resources, or inadequate technology for domestic production.

In 1978, China began its economic reform. In 1979, the central government decentralized the foreign trade authority to 12 newly formed national foreign trade corporations. The establishment of SEZs on the south-east coast of China in 1980, and the subsequent designation of 14 coastal cities as 'open cities' in 1984, marked a drastic change to China's traditionally closed economy.[2] Preferential treatment was given to foreign investors who showed interest in the Chinese market.

By the mid-1980s the Ministry of Foreign Economic Relations and Trade (MOFERT) had approved the creation of 800 separate import and export corporations, each authorized to engage in international trade transactions within specified product ranges. The numbers of trade corporations soared to more than 5,000 in 1990.

After Deng Xiaoping's visit to southern China in early 1992, the country's accelerating economic reform and increasing openness to the outside world were once again affirmed, as reflected in the China Communist Party Central and State Council Document No. 2 (in connection with accelerating economic reform) issued in March 1992, Document No. 4, regarding the further opening-up and acceleration of reform in the coastal region issued in May 1992, and Document No. 5, regarding the acceleration of the development of tertiary industries in June 1992. In the report to the Fourteenth Congress of the Chinese Communist Party (CCP) in October 1992, General Secretary Jiang Zemin proclaimed China's long-term intention to open up to the outside world, and to attract foreign investment in accordance with the national industrial policy. In the Third Plenary Session of the Fourteenth Central Committee of the Communist Party of China, held in November 1993, decision was made to establish a socialist market economic structure and to accelerate the reform and opening-up of China's international economic relations. China's determination and eagerness to participate more fully in international trade regime is, then, not in doubt. Under the open-door policy, China is a market of great potential to foreign investors.

China is one of the world's fastest-growing economies. Efforts in 1988 and 1989 to deal with unacceptably high inflation caused a brief decline in growth to 4 per cent, but this was still 'boom' level by Western standards. Growth accelerated again to 7 per cent in 1991 and to 12.8 per cent in 1992. Real GNP growth in China (1980–92) is shown in Figure 10.1.

In May 1993, the International Monetary Fund (IMF) recalculated China's GDP – an estimation based on the goods and services a particular country's currency will buy, as compared with the purchasing power of other currencies (the earlier method measured each country's output by valuing its goods and service in US dollars, using international exchange rates). China's GDP was nearly US$1.7

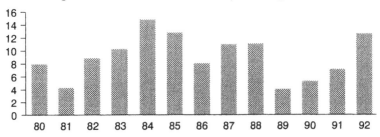

Figure 10.1 Real GNP growth in China, post-reform: 1980–92 (percentage)
Source: State Statistical Bureau

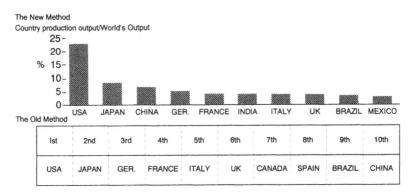

Figure 10.2 The top ten world economic powers in GDP terms, on old and new IMF calculations

trillion. This made China the third largest world economy, behind the United State and Japan (*South China Morning Post* 21 May 1993). Figure 10.2 shows the ranking of world economic powers by both methods.

China is the world's most populous country, with nearly 1.2 billion people. It is a market of great potential to foreign investors. Foreign investment into China is on the increase. By the end of 1992, the total cumulative contracted foreign investment in China was US$114 billion, with about US$58 billion being contracted in 1992 (*Business China* 28 June 1992: 4; 13 July 1993: 101).

There is, then, a great variety of business opportunities in China, especially for foreign investors. Businessmen have so far responded with various different entry strategies into the Chinese market, including exporting, licensing, franchising, management contracts, turn-key contracts, contract manufacturing/international sub-contracting; industrial cooperation agreements; contractual-joint ven-

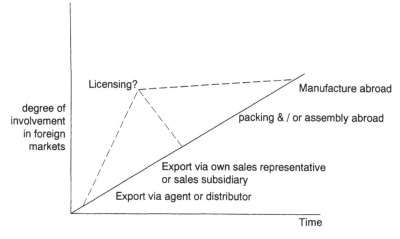

Figure 10.3 The internationalization process

tures, equity joint ventures and wholly owned subsidiaries. (Young, *et al.* 1989). For manufacturers of consumer durables, the most common modes are exporting, licensing, equity joint venture and wholly owned subsidiaries.

Firms expanding into foreign markets will normally follow a recognizable path, the 'internationalization process', beginning with exports and then extending into other forms of international involvement such as licensing and foreign manufacture. According to Cavusgil (1984), internationalization can be classified into three stages: the experimental involvement stage, the active involvement stage, and the committed involvement stage. Research by Johonson and Valhne (1977) on Swedish firms expanding abroad, and Buckley *et al.* (1983, 1988) on UK and continental European investors also supported this.

However, in early 1980, when China began to open up to the outside world, the actual development of foreign investors' involvement in the Chinese market was not quite in line with these theories. The initial stages of the internationalization process were often omitted – export was not always the chosen entry mode for companies eyeing China's market potential. Many investors experienced difficulties in exporting to a centrally planned economy. China had set up a system of import and export licensing as a means to control the volume and commodity composition of trade, as the scope of central foreign trade planning dwindled. The import licence is issued by MOFERT on a case-by-case application basis. Provincial governments with delegated authority can also issue licences to import within their own area. In 1992, there were 53 kinds of product requiring an import licence, including some consumer products. Import licences serve several economic functions, playing a key role in balancing the rising demand for imports and the limited sources of foreign exchange, and protecting specific domestic industries against foreign competitors. Besides import licences, tariffs are used to control the volume and commodity composition of imports. In general, imported goods in China are far more expensive than locally made ones and may be less attractive to price-sensitive consumers. The very size of the Chinese market means, however, that the small percentage of people able to afford imported products is still numerically significant. But because of the aforementioned restrictions imposed by the Chinese government, exporting was not difficult during the 1980s.

Licensing is one alternative method of entry into the China market, and it requires less investment than direct manufacture. For example, DuPont have set up a licensed plant in Shanghai manufacturing Teflon pans. The critical factors to be considered in any licensing agreement are the enforcement of the contract and the policing of the operation, hence transaction costs are high due to China's underdeveloped, albeit now reformed, legal and regulatory system in China (Buckley 1987). The protection of information and technology under the licence agreement, which is of prime importance for foreign investors, could not be fully enforced, thus discouraging foreign investors from choosing this particular entry strategy.

Joint ventures are the most commonly adopted strategy for entry into the PRC, representing another departure from the standard internationalization process. Although joint ventures in China have to overcome considerable obstacles in communications and human resources management (Davidson 1987), there are many advantages. They are able to capitalize on China's low production and labour costs, with less capital injection than direct manufacture. More importantly, Chinese joint-venture partners can help firms to operate more effectively when dealing with the bureaucracy, and to achieve smoother working relationships with government agencies in China. Key players in this category include Squibb, Ingersoll-Rand, Rank Xerox and S.C. Johnson.

Some companies prefer, for various reasons, to set up their own wholly owned enterprise. For instance, Hilton International and W.R. Grace seek to maintain their American culture and style of management in Chinese operations, and believe that they can do this only within wholly owned units. 3M set up its wholly owned plant in China following difficulties in picking a joint-venture partner capable of handling its various and diverse product lines. (*The Wall Street Journal* 24 October 1988). However, this option for entry requires huge capital injection, and is only really open to large multinationals with ample investment ability. Smaller companies and those unwilling to take high risks will continue to depend on direct exporting or licensing.

China's business environment is dynamic and fast-changing. Business enterprises need to monitor the following political, social and economic changes with great care in order to formulate an effective entry strategy.

Readmission to the GATT

Recent radical changes in China have facilitated her increased involvement in international trade, the most significant being the application for readmission to the GATT. China had been striving to re-enter the GATT since it joined the World Bank and the IMF in 1980. In 1982, China received observer status and officially applied for membership in 1986. In October 1990, a working group was set up to consider China's trade regime and to determine the conditions under which China could rejoin the GATT. As an original signatory to the GATT, China views its current bid as a resumption of her membership, which was withdrawn by Taiwan after the Communists gained control of the mainland in 1949. The GATT is founded on free market economics, i.e. on the assumption that trade responds to prices and that prices reflect demand and supply in world markets. Although China is now less reliant on central planning, it is still not a free market economy, and many issues need to be resolved by China before its readmission can be seriously considered. Douglas Newkirk, GATT's principal negotiator on the protocol for China's entry, indicated that five broad points must be incorporated into the protocol:

- A unitary national trade policy, so that imports receive the same treatment at every entry point
- Full 'transparency', so that all regulations, licence requirements and quotas are explicitly spelled out
- Elimination, over time, of non-tariff barriers to trade
- A commitment to move to a full market-price economy

- A temporary 'safeguard system' to protect against 'surges' in Chinese exports.

(The China Business Review May–June 1992)

To pave the way to GATT membership, and to prove China's sincerity in opening up its domestic market, MOFERT announced on 12 April 1992 that the numbers of import permits issued for various products would be reduced from 53 to 37 (Table 10.1) and that this number would be further reduced to no more than 12 within two or three years. Moreover, local authorities in cities and autonomous regions can trade with foreign companies under the system of contractual obligation and self-responsibility for profit and loss. These regional trading companies would act as agents, looking after import procedures and documentation. Foreign companies are allowed to choose their own agents or trading companies according to their scope of business. On the other hand, China would make its import system more 'transparent'. To achieve this, it would clear all of its 'internal' documents concerning import management, and all legislation and documentation relating to foreign trade would be centralized and announced by the MOFERT. In order to facilitate the economic reform, MOFERT was restructured as the Ministry of Foreign Trade and Economic Co-operation (MOFTC) in 1993 *(South China Morning Post* 16 March 1993). Although the readmission of China to the GATT is now only a matter of time, the actual date of readmission is very much dependent upon the smooth implementation of China's trade agreement with the US, and the resolution of human rights issues. According to the GATT regulations, the tariff reductions can be phased in over a period of years, so that China would not be required to reduce all tariffs immediately upon entry. Therefore exporters to China would not benefit in the short term. However, in the long term, these measures would reduce the price differential between imported and domestic products, making China a better market for foreign exporters, especially those less willing to take risks, and small or medium-sized enterprises.

The GATT does not explicitly require contracting parties to make their currencies freely convertible, though members are pledged to consult with the IMF about foreign exchange problems and to accept the Fund's determination on whether their country's convertibility policies are in accordance with IMF policies. The inconvertibility of the renminbi may allow China to continue to control import levels by restricting access to foreign currency and forcing up the prices

Table 10.1 Commodities subject to PRC import licence: 1982–93

Year	Import goods	Year	Import goods
1982	21	1988	53
1983	21	1989	53
1984	21	1990	53
1985	18	1991	53
1986	18	1992	37
1987	45	1993	37

Source: MOFERT, MOFTC

of many foreign goods beyond the means of Chinese people. This is one way in which China can circumvent the requirement to open up for imports.

Macro-environment control

Signs of economic overheating appeared in 1992 when China's GDP grew by 12.8 per cent over the previous year. A dangerous 14.1 per cent growth rate was registered in the first quarter of the year and, as a result, the economy saw a huge increase in investment and domestic demand, especially for capital goods. At the same time, surging domestic demand drove prices up, making domestic sales more profitable. In order to cool the overheated growth, the central economic authorities began to strengthen macro-economic control in July 1993. Under the directives from State Council Vice Premier Zhu Rongji, the banks started recalling unauthorized loans. This inevitably tightens money supply and thus the liquidity of enterprises, due to a chain reaction – the banks recall loans borrowed by an enterprise that consequently cannot pay its suppliers, who are then unable to pay the supplier of raw materials. These so-called 'triangular debts' have resulted in the cutting down of institutional purchase (in China, enterprises purchase consumer goods for employees as a kind of incentive), with the result that sales of consumer goods in China, especially imported products, were reduced (*Window* 14 January 1994)

Unified exchange system

Paving the way for re-entry to the GATT, China abolished its double-track exchange system on 1 January 1994, using the floating rate at its foreign exchange swap market to replace its official exchange rate. Before the reform, most investors in China were required to adopt the official exchange rate to pay for their supplies, salaries and rent, thus incurring higher costs (rmb 5.8 per US$ at the end of December 1993) (*Far Eastern Economic Review* 20 January 1994)

Under the new system, there will be only one currency; the renminbi. The Foreign Exchange Certificate (FEC) is to be phased out. Once the renminbi becomes a convertible currency, it will be harder for the black market to make profits. Most important, the new rate unofficially depreciates the renminbi, which will immediately affect the relative prices of traded goods. Importers also have to pay higher taxes. These price changes will cause a rise in the demand for Chinese exports and a fall in the demand for imported foreign goods. In view of this, export entry mode seems less attractive at the present moment; foreign investors would do better to set up direct manufacturing plants in China, as the depreciation of the renminbi will help reduce rents, wages and the cost of raw materials. Moreover, the finished products can be re-exported to the rest of the world, especially Asian countries such as Thailand and Indonesia.

Social changes

An understanding of consumer behaviour in China is also important when selecting a firm's entry mode. A focus group study was conducted by one of the present authors in the cities of Beijing, Shanghai and Guangzhou in 1993. The findings indicated that consumers in each of these cities are very brand-conscious. In general, brand preference followed a distinct hierarchy, with foreign brands the most coveted, followed by goods made in China by joint-venture factories. Local brands are the least preferred. With reference to the up-market segment of consumer durable goods, potential buyers psychologically feel more comfortable opting for foreign brands. This focus group study also revealed that quality appeared to be the most important criterion in the purchase and evaluation of consumer durable goods. Chinese customers have a strong preference for imported goods because they consider the increasingly differentiated ranges of imported goods as signifiers of social status. Locally made consumer goods are always perceived to be inferior in quality. This belief is firmly held amongst the young generation in particular. Guangzhou consumers are highly influenced by Hong Kong and are comparatively more sophisticated than those in Beijing and Shanghai. They are also relatively wealthier than others and are more willing to spend on imported goods. Shanghai buyers appear to be more 'calculating' despite their preference for foreign brands, and they do not accept that the difference between local and imported brands should be overwhelming. Beijing buyers are more emotional and receptive to the messages of the sales promoters. Other research studies have supported this (*China Business Review* November–December 1992).

Before the economic reforms, China practised a policy of long wage and price freezes, leaving the younger generation at a disadvantage in the distribution of income (*International Journal of Social Economics* 1991, vol. 18: 18–28). The economic reforms, which aimed at a fourfold increase in industrial and agricultural output, trade and per capita income by the year 2000, also resulted in a widening of the gap between individual incomes, thus militating against achieving common prosperity of all members of society. This will most likely increase the purchasing power of the young, creating plenty of opportunities for exporters.

On the other hand, the average annual income of workers in China rose to rmb 2,365 by 1991, from 615 in 1978, according to the State Statistical Bureau. Moreover, the average per capita consumption level of Chinese urban and rural residents increased from rmb 175 in 1978 to rmb 803 in 1991, an average annual growth of 6.5 per cent taking price increases into account (*China Market* 1992, 12: 47). The retail market in China, however, grew more rapidly in 1992. Social retail sales, the comprehensive index to manifest and assess the general scale and orientation of market goods sales, amounted to rmb 1,250 billion in 1992, up 16.1 per cent from 1991. The national retail sales of consumer goods in 1992 came to rmb 1,110 billion, up 15.4 per cent over 1991 (*China Economic and Trade News Digest* March 1993, 97). In response to this increase, the spending habits of Chinese consumers among both urban and rural residents, have begun to change. Various kinds of consumer products, including durable goods, have become popular. Consumption patterns have surpassed mere basic requirements and begun to reflect the transition towards a more comfortable life. There is a new tendency to purchase diverse and up-to-date commodities, implying that foreign investors could feasibly set up manufacturing plants in China that would be able to be more responsible and flexible in meeting domestic customers' frequently changed needs and wants.

The recent changes mentioned above will definitely have great impact on the investment strategy of foreign firms who wish to enter the Chinese market. The case of an American manufacturer of consumer durables will illustrate the complexities of the impact.

The American manufacturer in question was the market leader of a particular range of products. It initially exported its product to China through an influential import and export corporation (who were able to obtain import licences and foreign exchange) in the mid-1980s. The manufacturer's main competitiors are Japanese, many of whom did not want to risk their name and so made use of their agents in Hong Kong and smuggled the goods into one of the SEZs for distribution to other parts of China. The American firm found that it was difficult to compete with the Japanese due to the high tariffs imposed through the official channels, and decided to adopt the Japanese method.   Immediately after the Tiananmen Square incident in 1989, the Chinese government offered preferential terms to the American firm to set up a joint-venture manufacturing plant in China, with the totality of its production destined for the domestic market (normally, 70 per cent of production in such enterprises must be exported). The American firm did not wish to miss this opportunity, and a joint-venture plant was set up early in 1990 in Shenzhen, one of the SEZs near Hong Kong. But because of difficulty in getting acceptable quality components in China, the joint-venture factory could use only imported components, assembling just two simple products. However, given the Chinese consumer's preference for imported products rather than joint-venture products, the company found that its own imported products manufactured in the United States or in other subsidiaries, such as Singapore, enjoyed better sales than those from the factory in Shenzhen.

The recent application for China to rejoin the GATT has forced the American company to reconsider its strategy. Should it expand the product base in Shenzhen, or export more products to China? The American firm predicts that China will gradually reduce the tariff, enabling them to reduce the smuggling of products to China through their Hong Kong agent. The company decided to concentrate on exports and embarked on a frantic promotion in China (giving away free gifts with each purchase of their product, lucky draws, etc.). However, the depreciation of the rmb in early 1993 (from HK$100 to rmb 80, to HK$100 to rmb 130). This has left the American manufacturer in a dilemma as to how next to proceed.

Prospective investors wishing to do business in China should treat the business as a long-term commitment. As shown in Figure 10.1, direct investment is the most 'committed' entry mode, giving the investing enterprise a favourable image and making a good impression on the Chinese government, which always gives preferential treatment to its most committed trade partners. For example, during the tax reforms implemented in January 1994, China's central tax authorities assured foreign investors established before 31 December 1993 that they could apply for rebates under a five-year transitional clause if the new laws resulted in higher taxes.

NOTES

1 According to Chinese definitions, agriculture is a 'primary industry', manufacturing and construction are 'secondary industries' and retail, foreign trade warehousing, finance and insurance, real estate, restaurant, culture, education, health, etc. are 'tertiary' industries.
2 The four SEZs are Xiamen, Shantou, Shenzhen and Zuhai; Hainan was added to the list later. The 14 cities are Tianjin, Dalian, Quinhuangdao, Shanghai, Lianyungang, Nantong, Wenzhou, Ningbo, Fuzhou, Yantai, Qingdao, Guangzhou, Zhanjiang and Beihai.

BIBLIOGRAPHY

Buckley, P.J. (1987) *The Theory of the Multinational Enterprise*, Uppsala: Acta Universitatis Upsaliensis

Buckley, P.J., Newbould, G.D. and Berkova, Z. (1983) *Direct Investment in the United Kingdown By Smaller European Firms*, London: Macmillan.

Buckley, P.J., Newbould, G.D. and Thurwell, J.C. (1988) *Foreign Direct Investment by Smaller UK firms : The Success and Failure of First-Time Investors Abroad*, London: Macmillan.

Cavusgil, S.T. (1984) 'Differences among Exporting Firms based on their Degree of Internationalization', *Journal of Business Research* 12: 195–222.

Chiu, T.C.W. (1992) 'China and GATT: Implications of International Norms for China', *Journal of World Trade*, 26: 5–15.

Davidson, W.H. (1987), 'Creating and managing joint ventures in China', *California Management Review*, 29/4: 77–94.

Johonson, J. and Valhne, J.C. (1977) 'The Internationalisation Process of the Firm – a Model of Knowledge Development and Increasing Foreign Market Commitments', *Journal of International Business Studies* 8, 1, Spring/Summer.

Trade Development Council (1992) *China's Consumer Goods Market*, February.

Young, S., Hamill, J., Wheeler, C. and Davis, J.R. (1989) *International Market Entry and Development, Strategies and Management*, Hemel Hempstead: Prentice Hall.

Part IV
Scenarios for the 1990s

11 Economic reforms in China and India

Some comparative views

Gilbert Etienne

The very fast growth of the Chinese economy compared with the Indian economy, since the early 1980s can be explained by two sets of factors, some geographical and historical, some societal and political. In addition, some common and basic difficulties should be taken into account.

FINANCIAL AND COMMERCIAL EXTERNAL RELATIONS

China's export expansion and growing FDI – two major factors of growth – have been made easier by its geographical location. Neighbouring Hong Kong has played a major role in both since the 1980s. Trade with Japan has also benefited from the proximity of the two countries. And in the 1990s, Taiwan and, to a lesser extent for the time being, South Korea have become important sources of FDI and of exports/imports.

The Chinese diaspora in south-east Asia, which dominates a large part of the economy throughout the region, is also playing an increasing role, providing growing investments from Singapore and even Thailand.

Seen from this perspective, India is clearly in a less advantageous situation. The Indian diaspora (25 million) is much less significant than China's (55 million), and most of its members are far away from India itself, in the UK and the USA.

OTHER DIFFERENCES

The above differences do not entirely explain the large differences in FDI and foreign trade shown in Tables 11.1 and 11.2.

What is striking about China is that in the 1980s many FDIs were relatively small, and about two-thirds came from Hong Kong. Some

Table 11.1 FDI disbursed by China and India: 1980–93 (US$ billion)

	China	*India*
1980–90	19	1
1992	11	0.35
1993*	17	0.60

Note * Preliminary estimates

Table 11.2 Chinese and Indian foreign trade: 1972–93 (US$ billion)

	China		*India*	
	Exports	*Imports*	*Exports*	*Imports*
1972	2.9	2.8	2.0	2.2
1992	86.0	80.0	18.8	22.8
1993*	92.0	104.0	22.5	23.5

Note * Preliminary estimates

European and US multinationals did invest, but in relatively limited numbers. Since 1991 and 1992, however, there has been a rush of big multinationals from the USA, Europe and now Japan (which had previously been active mostly in trade sponsored by public loans). At the end of 1992, Hong Kong and Macao's share in cumulative disbursed investments amounted to US$21 billion, versus US$4 billion for Japan, US$3.2 billion for the USA, US$1.9 billion for Taiwan, US$500 million for Germany. (The total disbursed from 1979–92 was US$37 billion.)

Why such a rush? In Beijing (September 1993) the author gathered the following arguments, among diplomatic and foreign business circles:

1 The potential of the Chinese market is enormous and rising; production immediately creates new needs, new outlets and new business possibilities.
2 One must take advantage of the conditions granted by the government which are very favourable at present, but which might alter.
3 Every multinational thinks it should make haste to beat its competitors.

On the whole, the Chinese are clearly more open to FDI than the Indians, or at least a number of them. In practically all the author's meetings with officials at district, provincial and central government levels, and in no matter what sphere of economic activity, the Chinese all state how much they would welcome FDI.

Of course, China has its share of red tape, tedious procedures, and corruption, but the difficulties for foreigners seem less serious than in India, where most foreign companies feel that much remains to be done in the field of liberalization. Taxation is also heavier in India. There is a ceiling on equities, unlike in China, and practically all industrial sectors are open in China, which is not the case in India.

On the other hand, India enjoys some potential advantages that could be more fully exploited if it were to take a more liberal line, namely its legal system, the use of English, the existence of a large stock of modern elites. In China, the developing legal system is still far from complete, and one hears numerous complaints. Few Chinese, compared to Indians, are fluent in English, and this, added to other cultural factors, often makes inter-personal relations more complicated than in India (those are the comments of foreigners operating in both countries).

India's low foreign trade record remains, then, puzzling. Is it due, to some extent, to the tendency (now declining) for Indian business to restrict its activities to the domestic market? In China, right down to district towns of 100–200,000 inhabitants, one finds more and more medium-sized businesses open to the outside world, importing modern equipment, such as the latest Swiss or Japanese textile machines, and then exporting their goods. In a number of cases, particularly around Canton, there is participation from Overseas Chinese in Hong Kong and elsewhere; however, in the interior the author also came across such factories with no direct participation of Overseas Chinese.

Hong Kong has clearly greatly boosted Chinese exports. Many Hong Kong Chinese businesses have goods manufactured in the coastal areas of China, or import directly from these areas. Hong Kong agents, with their wide network of connections on the world market, have played a significant role up to now.

Foreign debt reached US$70 billion in China in 1993, and US$90 billion in India (February 1994). Foreign exchange reserves amounted to US$19 billion in China (end of July 1993) and US$13 billion in India (February 1994).

In China, stock exchanges are being revived after having disappeared following the coming to power of Mao Tsetung in 1949. In India, stock exchanges have been established for a very long time, and began to expand sharply in the 1980s. The latest economic reforms have contributed to a greater opening to the outside world. During 1993–4, portfolio investments by foreign institutional investors reached US$1.2 billion.

DECENTRALIZATION OF THE CHINESE ECONOMY

Under Mao Tsetung the whole Chinese economy, including banking, was heavily centralized. One of the major reforms has been to increase the powers of provinces and townships. The provinces can keep around 60 per cent of their export earnings for their own imports. They are free to conclude joint ventures of up to US$100 million without Beijing's sanction. Townships and districts are also free to conclude joint ventures without the consent of their province, up to US$5 million.

Credit has been enormously decentralized with the creation of many new banks and financial institutions.This decentralization has released contained energies which have contributed to faster growth and growing competition. It has also gone hand-in-hand with a loosening of price controls for a growing number of goods.

Yet the new system is not lacking serious short-comings. The powers of the People's Bank (China's central bank) have been severely eroded, and provincial and other financial institutions are issuing credit unchecked, a situation that the very efficient vice-prime minister, Zhu Rongji, is trying, with some success, to control. A number of dubious loans have been cancelled, but the situation needs further improvement.

This lack of order leads to overlapping investments and all kinds of distortions. For instance, agricultural banks, instead of supporting farmers, invest in real estate. And funds are lacking for infrastructure investments, while they are available for building hotels or offices. Expenditure is lavished on luxurious administrative buildings, and fleets of big air-conditioned cars imported from Japan, or made in China. All are owned by their enterprises, but used liberally off-duty. No less striking is the number of luxurious hotels, even in provincial towns and, in Guangdong, in every district

China's dual system of exchange had created all kinds of abuses, until it was abolished at the turn of 1993. However, this has led to a considerable rise in costs for foreign companies, hence serious complaints.

There is, no doubt, a 'rebound' factor following a period when little construction work was carried out, under Mao Tsetung. But today, the surge of smart new buildings absorbing so much valuable FDI is questionable in its magnitude. Here again, provinces and townships act with hardly any restraint.

THE LURE OF MONEY AND CORRUPTION

In any developing country, one feels a growing aspiration to earn more money, leading to consumerism, but in China this is even more widespread than in India. One reason is the austerity policy followed under Mao Tsetung, but this does not explain everything. It goes together with a kind of intellectual semi-vacuum. Students are no longer interested in studying literature or philosophy. Many professors and teachers are leaving their jobs for the business world, encouraged, no doubt, by the fact that a university professor on a state salary may earn no more than an industrial worker. Teachers are difficult to recruit, and in the long term the already weak education system may get worse. Even high centres of research are affected. In one of China's top institutes, the Academy of Social Sciences, there is no one is below the age of 45. As to the large number of Chinese students and researchers sent overseas, many delay their return or simply never come back. In all these respects, the situation appears less serious in India.

As for corruption, it is debatable whether this is still more widespread in India than in China. The problem is manifest in everything from back-handers paid for contracts, to the smuggling of cars by the thousand, to daily harassment through petty corruption, as in India, which deeply affects the man in the street. The police in China, as in India, are not particularly virtuous.

There is, however, one difference: the Chinese press often carries reports on people sentenced to heavy punishment for corruption, including death. This is much rarer in India, but the deterrent effect in China has, apparently, been minimal.

Prostitution has also re-emerged in China on a large scale, and the press occasionally carries reports on sales of women, as happens sometimes in India.

AGRICULTURE

One basic factor is frequently forgotten when comparing China and India. Over many centuries Chinese peasants have been used to employing highly intensive techniques in irrigation, seed selection, the use of organic manure (including human excreta) and compost, and inter-cropping. Such techniques are common to all areas inhabited by Han Chinese. In India the picture is much more diverse. In some areas there are highly skilled agricultural castes (Jats, Kurmis, Pattidars, Kammas, etc.) who have practised intensive tech-

Table 11.3 Overall percentage growth of Chinese and Indian food outputs: 1950–90

	China	India
Food grains	166	234
Cotton	225	218
Oilseeds	247	215
Sugar-cane*	648	320

Note * China also has sugar-beet (0.5 to 12 million tonnes, 1950–90)

niques down the ages. But in other areas the land is owned to a large extent by non-agricultural castes with no tradition of hard manual work, such as the Thakurs, Bhumihars, and certain Brahmin castes.

Following the famous enquiry by John Lossing Buck (Buck 1964), and comparing Indian data, in the 1930s yields of paddy and cotton in China were double those of India, and the wheat yield was one-third higher. Although caste behaviours are changing in India (since the late 1970s high-caste small landowners have begun to plough their land themselves), and although new inputs have been intro-duced with the 'Green Revolution', substantial differences remain in yields.

Advanced districts in India have attained wheat yields of 3,000–3,500 kg per hectare, and about the same for clean rice, while good Chinese districts achieve 3,500–4,000 kg for wheat and 4,000 for rice. Few areas in China have such low yields of rice as the eastern plains of India (700–1,000 kg per hectare). Rice in less developed parts of China will rarely fall below 2,000 kg per hectare.

In spite of these differences, the growth rate of food grains has been higher in India than in China (Table 11.3)

The decollectivization of China's agriculture, together with coop-erative and private trade, private transport, and cooperative small industries, boosted agriculture in the early phase of the reforms (1980–5). Since then, the growth rate has been much less spectacular. Public investments have fallen so that in the 1980s agriculture accounted for only 5 per cent of state expenditures versus 11 per cent previously. As a result, many hydraulic works are not properly maintained. Many tubewells (predominant in the northern plains) are out of order, and others lack electricity. The irrigated area has increased by only a few million hectares from 1980–92. Seeds renewal and the supply of chemical fertilizers are not adequate. Some increases in the allocation of funds have been recently intro-duced, but only on a moderate basis.

Table 11.4 Per capita food consumption (in kg) in China and India: 1990

	China	*India*
Food grains	204.0	190.0
Meat	20.0	1.5
Eggs	6.3	1.5
Milk	4.0	6.0
Fish	6.5	3.0

Source: *La Chine et l'Inde en Transition* 1992

As a result, there is growing concern about the future of agriculture. This was already clear on the author's visits in 1987 and 1989, but it has since increased, as was evident in 1993. One must bear in mind that in heavily populated and more advanced parts of China, agricultural holdings range between 0.3 to 0.5 hectares or a little more. Wherever yields are high with double cropping, a family can manage for day-to-day investments, but will be unable to replace a pump or a two-wheel tractor, unless enough members of the family have jobs outside agriculture.

The picture is much improved when it comes to fruit, vegetables and meat, where growth remains high. Meat production (especially pork) rose by 109 per cent in China between 1980 and 1990.

The relative neglect of agriculture in terms of public investment is less pronounced in India, but nevertheless quite obvious (6.7 per cent of public outlay in the Sixth Plan, from 1980–5, 5.8 per cent for 1985–90, 6.1 per cent for 1992–7). The irrigated area has continued to increase substantially, but one still comes across serious short-comings such as poor maintenance of canals, unsatisfactory renewal of seeds, inadequate use and balance of fertilizers, lack of electricity for tubewells.

In both countries, reforms from the end of the 1980s have had a definite, and inevitable, urban bias, but the time has come to pay more attention to agriculture, a fact not fully enough admitted in either Beijing or New Delhi. Agriculture still plays an important role in GDP and for employment. The removal of peasants from agriculture to industry and services remains relatively slow. In China there are practically no landless farmers but a floating population of 50–100 million men working here and there on various agricultural labouring jobs, as well as on construction in the cities, often moving around after jobs. In India, there are some 75 million landless labourers, often underemployed in agriculture.

SMALL AND MEDIUM-SIZED INDUSTRIES IN RURAL AREAS

After the big mess created by the Great Leap Forward (1958–60), the Chinese promoted a systematic and rational policy in favour of small industries in large villages and district towns, usually under collective or township ownership.

This development vastly expanded following decollectivization from 1980 onwards. Such enterprises are now owned by townships or by the *Xiang* (subdistrict, former commune) under various arrangements, some being semi-private. Private enterprises are now flourishing too, especially in services: restaurants, hairdressing, transport, with small firms possessing one or a few trucks or mini-buses.

After visiting the same districts in Guangdong, Hunan, Hubei, Hebei – some of them already in the 1960s, and all of them in 1972, 1982, 1987 and 1993 – the following changes and developments in advanced districts have been observed:

Large increases in the numbers of enterprises and workers

The expansion is particularly striking within a 50–100 km radius around Guangzhou, due to the existence of numerous joint ventures with firms from Hong Kong. Local units either produce spare parts or manufactured goods, such as garments, textiles, leather goods, or processed food. A large part of these goods are then exported by the Hong Kong company. As a result, in Hua district, there are now 150,000 workers outside agriculture, versus 100,000 in agriculture. In addition, and despite a high local population (517,000 people on 509 sq. km), the district has absorbed 50,000 workers from other areas, in industry and services, and 10,000 in agriculture.

No less striking is the fact that in the total district income, the share of agriculture has fallen to 20 per cent. The paddy area is shrinking in favour of richer crops: flowers, vegetables, sugar-cane and horticulture.

In Yuanjiang District (150 km from Changsha, Hunan), growth is less spectacular but there is a growing non-agricultural population and the share of agriculture in the district production is falling.

In Xinzhou District (100 km from Wuhan, Hubei), the same trend is noticeable, with the share of agriculture falling from 33 per cent of the district output in 1986 to 23 per cent in 1992.

In Jin District (55 km from Shijiazhuang, Hebei), agricultural output amounts to 25 per cent of the total output.

Qualitative changes

The enterprises created in Mao Tsetung's days were to a large extent self-reliant, resorting to rather primitive techniques with limited technical know-how. They were usually small units.

Now in all four districts, larger enterprises are being built, relying on modern and even very modern techniques. Many import new equipment from Japan, the USA or Europe and, if necessary, they will send some technicians for training abroad. Occasionally, they may even have some expatriate help for a time.

In all four districts, we met smart local 'bosses' in the district administration and in the factories, usually enjoying high salaries thanks to various allowances out of the profit made, and possibly through other means. There is much corruption and they are not shy, especially in Guangdong, about indulging in the construction of grand administrative buildings and in the purchase of luxurious 'office' cars. We must repeat that such districts are representative of only part of China. Many districts are less advanced, but such development is less and less confined to coastal provinces. All these districts also enjoy a highly advanced agriculture (see above).

The situation in India is more varied. Punjab, in this respect, compares not unfavourably with advanced districts of China. However, modern industries of the kind described above, and the spirit of openness and connections to the world market through imports and exports, are much less common in comparable Indian townships or large villages.

As to the shift from agricultural to non-agricultural jobs, this is less pronounced in India than in China. True, one comes across districts with 32 to 37 per cent of the active population outside agriculture, but in many others, especially in the eastern plains, the percentage of non-agricultural workers is in fact falling, as in Muzaffarpur in North Bihar, where 19.05 per cent of the workforce were engaged in non-agricultural activities in 1981, and just 17.77 per cent in 1991.

If the advanced districts of China and India do indeed point the way to the future – i.e. a falling population working in agriculture and rising numbers working in industry and services – at the national level there is still a long way to go. According to the 1990 census in China, 60 per cent of the active population were working in agriculture, while in India (according to the 1991 census) the figure was 64.9 per cent. Thus the difference is not so large, in spite of China's much faster economic growth rate in the 1980s. We should remember that data are not too reliable, however, and that we do not know where the 50–100 million Chinese workers 'floating' in and out of farms and construction sites were recorded.

INFRASTRUCTURE: ELECTRICITY AND TRANSPORT

Since the mid-1980s both countries have been suffering from a shortage of electricity and transport, but the shortfall is greater in China, because of the faster overall growth of the economy.

In 1993, however, the lack of electricity was less acute in China than in 1989. Yet electrical supply grew by just 9 per cent in 1992, while GDP grew by 13 per cent, and industry by more than 20 per cent. The Chinese are able to fully equip power stations of 300 MW (hydel) and 600 (thermal), but larger ones depend, partly, on imports. A plant supplying 600 MW (hydel) equipment looks likely to be built in Harbin in a joint venture. At present, China's industry is unable to cope with the demand even for power stations of 300 MW, so imports are also required.

If the economy keeps on growing at the present rate (12–13 per cent per year) the shortage will further increase. According to rough estimates by the Ministry of Power, a GDP growth of 7–8 per cent requires an additional capacity of 15,000 MW. The Chinese industry can supply 8–10,000 and, at the moment, the balance comes from imports. The target for 1995–7 is to add 15,000 MW per year to China's own output, which confirms the deterioration of the situation unless the economy slows down. For 1994, the government has indicated a 9 per cent growth in the economy. In the early 1990s, 'power shortages have held back industrial production by 20–40 per cent' (*China Business Review* November–December 1993).

As in India, the operations of the existing networks (production, transmission, distribution) need higher and better maintenance, and the replacement of low-quality equipment. There are big losses all the way from the powerhouse down to the user, including pilfering and 'defaults of charges and fees by electricity consumers' (*China Daily* 5 August 1993). Another problem is the low prices charged, in spite of some recent increases.

Whether all these defects are as serious as in India is difficult to say, but they are certainly signficant. Shortage of money has already reduced the original targets of the Indian Five Year Plan 1992–7, and now even the present target of 30,000 additional MW will not be reached. Industrial losses due to shortage of power are estimated at US\$8 to 10 billion per year, reducing output by one-fifth (*Economic Times* 30 September 1993).

Like India, China is looking for joint ventures, so that in each country 30–40 projects are in the pipeline. Yet, for the time being, agreements are slow to materialize, to a large extent because of the price at which electricity should be sold. Again, a similar problem exists in India.

So far China has mainly relied on coal (76 per cent of energy supply), but hydel stations are now expanding faster in central and southern regions, with the aim of creating 40,000 MW of hydel power by the year 2000. Two nuclear stations have been constructed and a third one should come on line around the year 2000. Three projects are currently being studied. Coal should nevertheless remain for a long time the main source of energy (output 1.1 billion tonnes in 1992, 1.5 billion tonnes expected in 2000). In India, coal's share of total commercial energy comes to 67 per cent (output in 1992–3, 238 million tonnes).

Unlike India, China enjoys a surplus of oil (output 140 million tonnes in 1992), an advantage which may come to an end rather soon, unless major discoveries occur. So far, after ten years, offshore exploration has been disappointing. Now the great hope is the Takla-makan Desert in the heart of Xinjiang, but the real size of the oilfields is not fully ascertained and the costs of exploitation will be enormous. The pipeline bringing oil from here to the industrial areas of China may amount to US\$10 billion alone.

As for the allocation of funds to electricity, for many years they have been too limited in both countries. For 1993, power projects in China will probably get about 10 per cent less funds than planned.

In the field of transport, China still suffers from its low starting point in 1949, compared to India. Even today, after doubling the extent of its track, the railway network has reached only 54,000 km versus 62,000 km for India. Yet, in the 1980s, Chinese investment in the railways amounted to 1.4 per cent of its GDP compared to 2 to 3 per cent in countries like South Korea, India or Brazil. The shortage of investments remains in the 1990s. The losses to the economy due to delays and bottle-necks are estimated at US\$45 to 55 billion per year. 100,000 km of railway lines is considered the minimum required. The network should reach 60,000 km in 1995. The difference with India is worse for roads: about 1 million km for China, double for India.

While motor vehicles and road traffic were much curtailed under Mao Tsetung, they have expanded enormously since then, so that the slow pace of road construction and improvement has fallen far behind requirements. In big cities, in spite of a number of fly-overs and tunnels, traffic jams are very bad, and far worse in Beijing than in New Delhi. In the former the number of taxis increased from 6,200 in 1991 to 51,000 in 1993. Traffic outside the cities varies. In fast-growing regions such as the coastal provinces, the situation is continually deteriorating. Already in 1987, in the hinterland of Shanghai, the author was unable to drive above 27 km per hour. In the wealthier districts of other provinces, the same was also true in 1993.

A large programmeme of express roads is under construction, but it will take a few decades to complete. Present road construction is not always adequate. Some new highways in Shandung, or the Beijing–Shijiazhuang expressway (not yet completed) are already showing cracks and potholes, whether due to malpractices on the part of the contractors, or plain bad construction is unclear. In 1993 expressways amounted to 1,300 km, and 1,000 km more should be completed in 1994. By 2000 the Chinese expect to have 18,500 km of major highways, one-third of which will be expressways (*China Daily* 8 February 1994 and 20 February 1994).

As regards India, the pressure on railways is perhaps not as severe as in China. India currently has the lead concerning roads, but for how long? In progressive areas (Bombay–Ahmedabad, the Great Trunk Road from Amritsar to Delhi) traffic congestion is bound to become almost unbearable in a few years' time. Of perhaps greater concern is that programmes for expressways in India seem slow to take off. There are far fewer projects in progress than in China. Four-lane expressways should amount to 1,400 km around 2000. However, shortage of money even for adequate maintenance of existing roads is striking.

Other problems are rather similar between the two countries, such as overloading of trucks, which damages the roads. Motor vehicle accidents are appalling in both countries: around 60,000 deaths per year each, in spite of a still limited density of motor vehicles compared to Europe and the USA, where the ratio of deaths to vehicles is much lower and falling, while it is rising in China and India.

There is, however, one clear advantage for China compared with India, namely its river transport system which, mostly because of geographical conditions, plays an important role in the economy. Considerable progress has occurred since Mao Tsetung's death, by which time river traffic was strikingly low.

To sum up, the requirements of both countries in terms of power supply and transport are enormous. Native industries will not, in spite of continuing progress, be able to meet the full demand for equipment, new power stations and transmission lines. This means that the Chinese, Indian and other Asian markets for foreign enterprises involved in power supply are bound to expand much further. Much foreign participation is also needed in transport and communications.

SOCIO-POLITICAL FACTORS

China's political system enables the government to take more radical decisions than in India. Yet the Chinese authorities do not have a completely free hand, either, and still proceed very cautiously with reforms to the public sector. Only now have some enterprises reduced their overstaffing. Many public sector enterprises remain in the red, and are supported by all kinds of costly subsidies – again a situation well known in India. There is, however, a sizeable difference. The share of the public sector in industry, although falling, is larger than in India, where it amounts to 50–55 per cent of output versus 80 per cent in 1980.

Another issue refers to the opening up of the country to the outside world. There are, in India, xenophobic tendencies, and fear of foreign competition by private and public companies. (Witness the latest swadeshi trends of the BJP.) The various incidents affecting Cargil, for example, have culminated in their withdrawal from a US$30 million project for salt manufacturing. Such currents should not be given too much importance, but they cannot be disregarded either, especially when there are so many opportunities in other Asian countries.

Such attitudes are not to be found in China, but some recent statements do refer to 'hostile forces ... which take advantage of policies of reform and openness to get hold of our political, economic and scientific secrets, hence the need to be vigilant' (*People's Daily* 11 October 1993 quoted in *The Economist* 16 October 1993). The row between China and the USA on human rights and arms supplies from China, and Beijing's failure to get the Olympic games, do account for some of these reactions. It seems doubtful, however, that such feeling could be particularly widespread, since the Chinese economy is now so much involved in world trade and FDI. On the other hand, the issue of human rights and trade relations between the USA and China is obviously a matter of concern.

Beyond these types of events, which may affect the economy of either country negatively, but which will not lead to drastic changes or a return to old policies, one must raise more fundamental issues.

Since the fall of the Empire in 1911, China has never been able to create a stable legitimate political system. The great hopes raised with the advent of Communist rule in 1949 have been broken. Almost no one still believes in Mao Tsetung's ideology, but, as seen at Tiananmen Square, the system remains fragile. Institutions remain too dependent on the men in power.

Several problems worry the public, and are openly discussed in the press. First there are rivalries of both a political and economic nature between provinces, including differences between coastal and interior provinces. Second, there are growing income disparities between rural and urban communities. In 1993 there were many violent incidents involving disgruntled peasants. If the overheating of the economy cannot be curbed, it could lead to more unrest. China's strong inflation adds to the malaise, and all these issues are aggravated by the uncertainty surrounding Deng Xiaoping's succession.

For all these reasons, some foreign experts and some Chinese do not exclude possible serious unrest in the future, while others on both sides think that China will manage to avoid a major crisis.

Other factors must be taken into account. Despite some progress, the legal system remains full of loopholes and may discourage some foreign investors, as has happened recently in a few cases. Moreover, sudden changes, such as the latest financial reforms, may affect FDI. Added to this is the problem of China's administrative system. For centuries, China was more advanced than most countries, with its selection of civil servants through competitive examination. Even now, the ruling elites have not re-created such a system. Recruitment is still too often done without precise, objective rules because, as before, the Communist Party wishes to control the selection of cadres, which leads to much nepotism.

As to the education system, we have seen that it is deteriorating even in a number of advanced research institutes and universities.

On all these points, India appears in a better position. Almost nobody questions the institutions that have proved their resilience over 40 years. India has never experienced, in spite of bloody turbulence, such dramatic crises as China. Even if the Indian system is deteriorating, it is nonetheless rooted in institutions rather than depending on a few key individuals as in China.

India's administration, too, is less influenced by politics than in China. Central services, such as the Indian Administrative Service, remain a factor of relative stability. No less important is the legal system.

With reference to mass education, India stands clearly behind China but in many fields of advanced education it could perhaps be said that India is ahead of China.

It is not easy to draw firm conclusions on basic political issues. Looking at the future, there is a feeling of uncertainty about politics on both sides. Will the Chinese be able to build stable institutions less centred on a few men and one party? Will the Indians continue to muddle through and avoid major crises?

Leaving these questions aside, two factors are clear: China has achieved the maximum possible economic growth in the past 15 years. The same cannot be said of India where, in spite of substantial progress, human and material resources could have been better utilized.

BIBLIOGRAPHY

CHINA

Buck, J.L. (1964) *Land Utilization in China*, New York: Paragon.
Domenach, J.-L. and Richer, P. (1987) *La Chine 1949–1985*, Paris: Imprimerie Nationale.
Etienne, G. (ed.) (1990) *Asian Crucible, the Steel Industry in China and India*, Geneva: Modern Asia Research Center (revised edition 1992, New Delhi: Sage).
La Chine et l'Inde en Transition (population, agriculture, finance) (1992) Paris: CEPII.
Lemoine, F. (1991) *Epargne, Investissement et Systeme Financier en Chine*, Paris: CEPII.
McCormick, B.L. (1990) *Political Reform in post Mao China*, Berkeley: California University Press.
Wang Huijong and Li Boxi (1989) *China Towards the year 2000*, Beijing: New World Press.
World Bank (1989) *China Finance and Investment*, Washington: World Bank.
—— (1990) *China between Plan and Market*, Washington: World Bank.
—— (1992) *Reform and the Role of the Plan in the 1990s*, Washington: World Bank.

INDIA

Alagh, Y.K. (1991) *Indian Development Planning and Policy*, New Delhi: Vikas.
Bhagwati, J.N. (1992) *India in Transition*, Oxford: Clarendon.

Economic Survey, Yearly Report for the Budget, New Delhi: Ministry of Finance.

Etienne, G. and Revel-Mouroz, J. (eds) (1993) *Economies d'Asie et d'Amerique Latine Changements de Cap*, Geneva: Modern Asia Research Center, Olizane.

Gupta, S.P. (ed.) (1993) *Liberalisation, its Impact on the Indian Economy*, New Delhi: Macmillan.

Jalan, B. (ed.) (1992) *The Indian Economy, Problems and Prospects*, New Delhi: Viking.

Srinivas, M.N. (1992) *On Living in a Revolution*, Delhi: Oxford University Press.

Weiner, M. (1991) *The Indian Paradox*, Princeton: Princeton University Press.

12 China's role in world trade and its re-entry to the GATT

A European view

Gian Paolo Casadio

CHINA 2000: A MAJOR PLAYER IN THE WORLD TRADING SYSTEM

China is today an essential, and new, factor in the world trading system. In 1993 China's total merchandise trade (imports plus exports) reached US$196 billion, with US$104 billion-worth of imports (2.6 per cent of overall export merchandise trade) and US$92 billion of exports (2.3 per cent of overall import merchandise trade).[1]

Thus, between 1978 and 1992, China moved from 34th to 11th on the GATT rankings of the world's largest exporters,[2] immediately behind Hong Kong and just above Taiwan. It must, moreover, be noted that, in reality, Hong Kong should rank lower because most of China's exports to Hong Kong are Chinese goods re-exported to third countries.[3] On the other hand, China's lower GATT ranking in world trade in commercial services (22nd among the leading exporters and 24th among the leading importers in 1992) is largely compensated by its spectacular surge as a capital exporter of global reach.[4]

According to the latest data released by MOFTEC at the end of 1992, China had 117 enterprises operating in 120 countries and territories, with a cumulative world-wide investment of about US$ 4 billion. Thus, even excluding those in Hong Kong, the multitude of China's foreign affiliates and their global reach are impressive, especially considering that, as late as 1986, there were only 261 Chinese firms pursuing business in 54 countries. Indeed, China's drive to invest overseas did gain momentum only since the late 1980s and soared during the early 1990s.[5]

In the year 2000 China's role in world trade is bound to strengthen considerably in response to broader trade policy reforms, as the country moves towards a more market-oriented economy. The Chinese government has already announced that it will take the following steps to relax its trade policies:

1 reduce average import tariffs from 45 to 30 per cent;
2 eliminate import licence requirements by two-thirds within three years;
3 abolish the import regulatory tax (a 20–80 per cent surcharge) on high-value goods;
4 abolish any regulations before they are actually implemented.[6]

A further boost to China's foreign trade is expected to originate from the gradual integration of the Chinese Economic Area (CEA)[7] built up around the Chinese territories of southern coastal China, Hong Kong, Macau and Taiwan, with the contribution of the Overseas Chinese network, notably Singapore, the Chinese-dominated economies of east and south-east Asia and the increasing Chinese business interests in Australia, New Zealand, Canada and the United States of America (especially the West Coast). Thus, by the year 2000 – if accelerated growth can be maintained – the CEA (netting out intra-trade) might become the third largest trade entity of the world, well ahead of Japan.[8]

CHINA IS BUILDING A SYSTEM OF GATT-COMPATIBLE TRADE PRACTICE

China has made bold commitments to improve its trade and investment climate. In addition to embracing many international principles, China is now well on the way to establishing a world-class legal structure for copyrighted works and patented products.[9] In particular, China has:

- joined the Berne Convention on copyrights and published regulations that protect existing copyrighted works, including computer software and sound recordings;
- adopted the Geneva Phonograms Convention raising the level of protection for sound recordings;
- amended the Patent Law to extend protection beyond processes to pharmaceutical and agricultural chemical products;
- adopted, most recently, the Anti-Unfair Competition Law, which provides legal protection for unregistered trademarks, trade names, product packaging, and trade dress.

On market access, under the terms of the 'Memorandum of

Understanding' (MOU) – signed in October 1992 between the office of the US Trade Representative (USTR) and MOFERT, now known as MOFTEC – China has offered solutions to many trade barriers (i.e. the combination of non-tariff barriers (NTBs), prohibitively high tariffs and taxes, and the absence of a well-articulated legal system),[10] which make exporting to China a daunting, and sometimes dismal, experience.[11] In particular, China has agreed to phase out

- internal *neibu* trade regulations;
- onerous import licensing requirements such as import 'controls', 'restrictions' and 'quotas';
- restrictive sanitary and phytosanitary standards.

China has, moreover, reassured its trading partners that it does not consider reducing imports to balance its 1993 trade deficit of about US$12 billion – the second-highest deficit on record after a US$14.9 billion deficit in 1985. The increase in imports estimated at about US$200 billion during 1994 and 1995 seems to be becoming a long-term strategy, especially for imports in the sphere of technology relating to energy, transportation, materials[12] and technology renovation. The 1992 market access agreement has, in addition, set the stage for the opening of China's potentially extensive service sector.[13]

As to FDI – which, by all accounts, is booming (doubling in 1993 for the second year in a row) – on 29 December 1993 China passed its first comprehensive company legislation, which, though in need of additional, more concrete rules, covers such areas as legal protection for investors.[14]

To work constructively with Western countries (who fear that Chinese goods might flood their markets during China's transition to a free market economy), the Chinese government – in addition to unification of its dual exchange rate system on 1 January 1994[15] – has reportedly decided to accept, with certain conditions, a special safeguard rule that would cap its exports[16] once they reach a certain level. Last but not least, China has recently changed its method for recording and reporting trade statistics, which will result in more consistency between Western and Chinese trade statistics.[17]

CHINA'S ACCESSION TO THE GATT

China's longstanding application of 10 July 1986 to rejoin the GATT appears today to be making rapid headway[18] – a development that may be linked to the conclusion on 15 December 1993 of the 'Uruguay Round' (a triumph for the multilateral trading system) and to the proposed creation of a new world trade institution (The World Trade Organization or WTO). As a successor to the GATT, the WTO would apparently have clearer and firmer rules (especially on settling trade disputes and overseeing the trade policies of member countries), so as to help establish a more predictable global trading environment.[19] China has a historical link with the GATT. The Chinese Nationalists were one of its founder groups, but having fled to Taiwan, withdrew China from the GATT in 1950. Taiwan, too, was obliged to leave when China replaced it in the UN in 1971.

Thus, today, China – which received observer status in 1982 and officially applied for readmission in 1986 – would prefere to 'resume' membership of the GATT rather than become a new contracting party, so that the 'grandfather' rights of the original GATT parties[20] could be secured. However, while the words 'resume' or 'rejoin' may be used, such terminology does no more than pay lip service to the fact of China's original membership. China is, in fact, willing to negotiate a new 'Protocol of Accession', whereby it is prepared to undertake new commitments to open up its trade regime. Thus, since January 1992, China's MOFERT has produced the following policies, anticipating China's return to GATT:

1 reduction of general tariffs to the prevailing standard for developing countries as defined by GATT, and establishment of import duties on various products in accordance with industrial policy and China's stage of economic development;
2 abolition of the import adjustment tax system (implemented April 1992);
3 establishment as early as possible of foreign trade and antidumping laws, and management of imports based on those laws, plus suitable protection for non-competitive domestic industries based on international practices;
4 reduction of the range of import controls by import licences, by eliminating sixteen of the existing fifty-three items now controlled under such licences and eliminating two-thirds of the items controlled by import licences over two to three years;
5 making the content of import controls transparent, i.e. controlling imports by tariffs, exchange rates, and other economic means instead of administratively;
6 quickly making available public internal documents relating to existing import controls if they are to be continued, and – in

the future – having MOFTEC disclose to the outside world all regulations regarding import control.[21]

The main problem with unblocking China's re-entry into the GATT is the exposure of OECD societies and firms to competition from a country that is culturally different and characterized by much lower wages, standards of labour and environmental protection, as well as by aggressive export practices concentrated in a few sectors (textiles and clothing, toys and games, shoes, sporting articles, electronic consumers goods) which, at times of most severe recession,[22] would be placed at considerable risk.

Western nations, notably the US as the predominant negotiator in the GATT, are therefore pressing for:

- 'fair trade' in goods as well as in services;[23]
- effective implementation of intellectual property rights (IPR);
- improvement of regulations on foreign-invested enterprises (FIEs) to be able to 'balance' foreign exchange;[24]
- amelioration of procedures to obtain approval from various governmental departments before foreign firms can sell their products and services domestically;
- transparency in the cost of domestic and shipping transportations, associated with *de facto* monopolistic power over these transports;
- restraint over continuous devaluation of the renminbi;
- respect of the permitted quotas, instead of using Taiwan, Hong Kong and other ports to hide the origin of Chinese goods;
- more attention to basic workers' rights, as well as to export[25] of armaments to 'dictatorial regimes'.

However, the Western nations' request for special conditions (in part already met by the acceptance of the aforementioned special safeguard rule that would cap Chinese exports under certain conditions, as well as by the significant step towards unification of the exchange rate), has to be viewed in the light of a Protocol of Accession which, in addition to including a wide range of issues, will balance a set of obligations and rights. In particular, China will have to open up its market much further to GATT members, stop providing favourable treatment to a specific GATT member, guarantee that its state trading enterprises will buy and sell in accordance with commercial practice, make available various types of information on trade practices, and, in addition, further reduce tariffs, and cut a host of non-tariff barriers (such as foreign exchange controls, import licensing requirements, bans and quotas, and the use of technical standards and certification requirements to discourage imports).

On the other hand, China will be permitted to control imports in order to protect its balance of payments and foreign exchange reserves, as well as temporarily protect its 'infant industries', provided the process is under multilateral surveillance. China, moreover, is likely to retain high tariffs on cars, refined petroleum products, selected chemicals and fertilizers, rubber, cosmetics, tobacco, cotton and some electronic products.

In such a GATT framework, allegations could be more adequately ascertained,[26] because China, in addition to enjoying stable most-favoured-nation status, would participate in the settlement of trade disputes. Moreover, the Protocol may require periodic reviews of China's membership and may also place restrictions on its privileges[27] (such as the GSP system) while maintaining the imposition of anti-dumping and countervailing duties. China's participation in the GATT system would therefore be good for both China and GATT members because:

1 as a treaty, GATT stipulates a member's obligations and rights;
2 China's role in GATT would provide impetus to the development of a better, more orderly, world trading system and would promote trade reforms (such as transforming GATT's anti-dumping code into an anti-trust code) through the forthcoming WTO;
3 China's accession to the GATT will support Chinese economic reforms, so as to emphasize the importance of the Chinese market, even if the West has a diminishing share of it;
4 Beijing does not object to the possibility of Taiwan being admitted to GATT as a separate customs territory.[28]

EUROPE'S TRADE WITH CHINA

According to the 1993 edition of *China's Customs Statistics*, as well as the data of the 'Comité France–Chine', the EU's share of total Chinese merchandise trade in 1992 appears to have attained around 13–14 per cent, with an 11 per cent share for the EU's exports to China and a 15–16 per cent share for the EU's imports from China.[29] Thus, although the 1993 preliminary data seem to emphasize a new surge of European exports, China's surplus with Europe has increased considerably (US$1.2 billion in 1989, US$3.7 billion in 1991, US$9.3 billion in 1992), causing tensions in specific sectors (textiles and clothing, toys and games, footwear and sports articles, electronic consumers' goods) that also risk dismantling because the 'Uruguay Round' has enforced new substantial tariff cuttings.[30]

In consideration, however, of the declared intention of the Chinese government to cap its exports when they reach a certain level, it would be a mistake for Europe to resort exclusively to strengthened defences against Chinese imports as part of the price of its agreement to the final deal under the GATT. Top priority, instead, should be given to the proper enforcement of the new rules of Europe's single market, which, since the celebratory fireworks of 1 January 1993, has lacked the necessary political impetus to set up a complete common import policy, so as to provide a united front *vis-à-vis* China's view on cooperation with Europe.[31] Furthermore, the EU could provide small and medium-sized European firms with adequate assistance to be able to face the myriad problems of operating with China's trade and investment regimes, notably:

1 country risks (political instability, social instability, changes in economic policies, bureaucracy, insufficiency and negligence of the legal system);
2 contract risks (negotiations for long-term and complicated contracts, difficulties of feasibility studies, demand for a foreign exchange balance, China's shortage of funds/overvaluation of capital in kind, demand for technology transfer, insufficient knowledge of a market economy on the Chinese side);
3 operations risks (complexity and delay in the approval procedures, difficulty with procurement of raw materials and parts, underdeveloped infrastructure, difficulty in labour management, increases in wages and land-use charges, shortage of funds, difficulty in quality control, difficulty in domestic sales/export obligations).

On the other hand, the EU could revamp the 1985 trade and economic cooperation agreement with a Trade Assessment Mechanism (TAM),[32] aimed at:

- identifying sectors in which European and Chinese companies can be more successful in expanding mutually beneficial trade relations, as well as opening markets at reduced prices;
- limiting the risks of serious abuse in the implementation of legitimate instruments of trade policy (defence, quantitative restrictions, subsidies, anti-dumping, tariff classification, rules of origin, standards and certification system);

- facilitating a concerted conscious effort in multilateral economic development projects (such as the Tumen River project in north-east Asia) in the larger economic framework of the CEA and establishing a unique European/Chinese forum that could provide opportunities for leaders to discuss problems directly, as well as a machinery to put into effect political decisions, arbitrations in cases of crisis, exchanges among scholars, students and technical staff (in everything from agricultural science to environmental protection), and
- an anti-harassment clause (to promote the reduction of import barriers, scrap costly governmental regulations, enforce more transparent bidding procedures, and anti-trust laws).

NOTES

1 *International Trade Statistics* (1993), Geneva: GATT: 3
2 'People's Republic of China, Jetro White Paper', *Jetro China Newsletter* 106, September–October 1993: 17.
3 GATT, *op. cit.*: 5.
4 Wu, F. (1994), 'China Capitalises on ASEAN', *Far Eastern Economic Review*, 20 January.
5 *ibid.* (1993), 'Stepping Out The Door', *The China Business Review*, November–December.
6 'China 2000: A Major Player In The Trade Arena', *Agricultural Outlook*, Washington DC: US Department of Agriculture, September 1993: 38.
7 Jones, R., King, R. and Klein, M.(1992) 'The Chinese Economic Area: Economic Integration Without A Free Trade Agreement', Paris: OECD Economics Department, Working Paper 124: 20.
8 *ibid.* (1993) 'Economic Integration between Hong Kong, Taiwan and The Coastal Provinces of China', Paris: OECD Economic Studies 20, spring; Caplen, B. and Levin, M. (1992) 'The New Pacific Capitalism, Chinese Families Are Changing Business On Both Sides of The Ocean', *Asian Business* 1, August; Crane, G.T. (1993) 'China and Taiwan: Not Yet "Greater China"', *International Affairs* 69: 4, 705–23.
9 Simone Jr., J.T. (1993) 'Damming The Counterfeit Tide', *The China Business Review*, November/December 1993; Du Sablon, J.L. (1992), 'Pekin accepte le Jeu du Libre Échange', *Le Figaro*, 23 January.
10 Kaye, L. and Awanohara, S. (1992) 'Trade, Punches Pulled, China/US Forgo a 301 Knockdown', *Far Eastern Economic Review*, 22 October.
11 Sands, L.M. and Lehr, D.M. (1993) 'Expanding Trade and Opening Markets in China', *The China Business Review*, July–August: 10; Lenglet, F. (1993) 'Nos Hommes d'Affaires dans la Jungle Chinoise', *L'Expansion*, 4–24 November.
12 For most of the past decade, imports of consumer goods have been tightly regulated by central authorities, who prioritized hard-currency expenditures for imports, advanced technologies and equipment. Over the last few years, however, the administration of foreign trade has

gradually been transferred from various industrial ministries and specialized import and export companies under MOFERT to the provinces, cities and autonomous regions. Today, most foreign trade is conducted through import/export companies at these local levels.

13 Sands, L.M. and Lehr, D.M. 'Expanding Trade and Opening Markets in China', *The China Business Review*, July–August: 11.

14 Nickerson, D. (1994) 'China's New Company Law, Threat to Overseas Listings', *Far Eastern Economic Review*, 1 January: 3.

15 'China Unifies Exchange Rates', *Far Eastern Economic Review*, 20 January 1994.

16 Katsuhiko Meshino, 'China Accepts Safeguard', *Nikkei Weekly*, 10 January 1994.

17 'China's New Reporting Method Improves Trade Statistics', *Agricultural Outlook*, Washington DC: US Department of Agriculture, September 1993: 42.

18 'China Gives GATT a 1995 Deadline', *International Herald Tribune*, 20 December 1993.

19 Williams, F. (1993) 'Deal Seen as Triumph for Multilateral Rules', *Financial Times*, 15 December; Islam Shada, 'Goodbye GATT, Asia Welcomes Creation of New World Trade Body', *Far Eastern Economic Review*, 6 January 1994; Williams, F. (1993) 'WTO – New Name Heralds New Powers', *Financial Times*, 16 December; Nakamae Hiroshi, 'Japan Shuns Bilateral Style, Unlike US', *Nikkei Weekly*, 10 January 1994.

20 The US can reserve the right to invoke Article 35 of the GATT Charter to deny MFN status to China only if China joins the GATT as a new member.

21 Noriyoshi Ehara, 'China's Foreign Trade in 1991', *Jetro China Newsletter* 99, July–August 1992: 21.

22 Since the advent of the Mejji dynasty in Japan, Western countries have struggled with the idea of Asian competitors: what used to be called the 'yellow peril'. A century later, the Japanese are no longer resented for sucking in capital and technology and spewing out cheap, shoddy consumer goods produced with 'sweated labour'. They are now resented for doing the opposite. But China is now looming on the horizon as a possible second Japan – cubed.

23 Conseil National du Patronat Francais, 'Les Relations Commerciales de la Communauté avec la Chine', Paris, July 1993: 1.

24 Frisbie, J. and Brecher, R. (1993) 'A Tough Balancing Act', *The China Business Review*, November–December: 9.

25 Thus, the United States and other Coordinating Committee for Unilateral Export Control (COCOM) members remain hesitant to ease current restrictions on high-technology shipments to China. Wemple, E.C. (1992) 'An Export Control Clash', *The China Business Review*, May–June: 32.

26 China, for example, claimed victory in a dispute with the United States over allegations that it exported goods made by prisoners, because the US Federal Register stated that US customs officials had found that merchandise made in prison 'is no longer being likely to be imported into the US'. See 'Beijing Claims A Round', *International Herald Tribune*, 6 January 1994.

27 Under the GSP system, developed countries extend non-reciprocal tariff

benefits to qualifying exports from less-developed countries. China is already a beneficiary under GSP in the EU, Australia and Japan. In the USA, instead, the extension of GSP privileges to Communist countries is prohibited.

28 Mainland China and Taiwan would therefore become GATT members simultaneously, thus demonstrating Beijing's flexibility. See Feng Yu-Shu (1991) 'China and GATT', *Far Eastern Economic Review*, 19 December.

29 According to OECD statistics the 12 EU countries ran up a trade deficit of US$12 billion in 1992, while according to Chinese figures it was China that was in deficit. The difference is due to the volume of trade mediated via third countries, particularly Hong Kong. Germany, for instance, conducts more than two-thirds of its indirect trade with China via Hong Kong or other non-EU countries. See 'China: Will Trade Liberalization Promote Change in The People's Republic?', *Economic Bulletin* 2, Deutsches Institut fur Wirtschaftforschung, 1993.

30 De Lipkowski, J. (1993) 'Rapport sur la Proposition de Reglement CEE du Conseil Relative a l'Harmonisation et a la Rationalisation des Procedures Decisionelles des Instruments Communautaires de Defense Commerciale', Assemblée Nationale, Paris, 15 June. See also 'Le GATT dans le Collimateur des Industriels du Jouet', *La Tribune Des Fosses*, 23 November 1993.

31 Hill, A. (1994) 'Balloon Struggles To Get Airborne', *Financial Times*, 5 January; Dale, R. (1994) 'France Can't Kick Protectionist Habit', *International Herald Tribune*, 11 January.

32 A Trade Assessment Mechanism is already in force in the trade negotiations between the EU and Japan.

Index

For Product Safety Concerns and Information please contact our EU representative GPSR@taylorandfrancis.com Taylor & Francis Verlag GmbH, Kaufingerstraße 24, 80331 München, Germany

Printed and bound by CPI Group (UK) Ltd, Croydon, CR0 4YY

08/05/2025

01864441-0002